A Place to Start

Toward and Unapologetic Gay Liberation Theology

j. michael clark

Dallas
MONUMENT PRESS
1989

Published by
MONUMENT PRESS

© 1989, J. Michael Clark

Library of Congress Cataloging-in-Publication Data

Clark, J. Michael (John Michael), 1953-
    Someplace to start : toward an unapologetic gay liberation
theology / J. Michael Clark.
       p.   cm.
    Includes bibliographical references.
    ISBN 0-930383-15-X : $12.00
      1. Homosexuality–Religious aspects. 2. Liberation theology.
3. Homosexuality–Religious aspects–Christianity.
4. Homosexuality–Religious aspects–Judaism. 5. Judaism–
Doctrines.   I. Title. II. Title: Gay liberation theology.
BL65.H64C63   1989   89-38276
261.8'35766–dc20   CIP

For that ever growing list
of the many friends who have died
during the years in which AIDS
has devastated our community--
Ed Acree, Bill Adams, Glenn Breslin,
Jason Byars, Rafael "Ralph" Delgado,
Gus Galvez, Lee Hopper, John Howell,
Ray Kluka, Greg Lewis, Jon Martin,
Max Meltzer, Robbie Moore, Robert Needle,
David O'Shields, Gary Piccola,
Jerry Pyszka, Michael Rasmussen, John Routh,
Dennis Rudd, Fred Seal, Errol Statum, & Mark Wood.
May their energies remain alive with us,
informing our every effort toward liberation.

* * *

Acknowledgements

Work on this text during 1987-1988 was
made possible in part through an
American Academy of Religion Research Assistance Grant.
The author gratefully acknowledges
the Academy's enthusiastic and generous support.

The author also extends a note of appreciation to
Michael Greer and **Mike Feinstein**
for carefully reading and studying
an earlier version of this text;
many of their insightful comments and suggestions
are incorporated herein.

The author also expresses his deep appreciation
and affection to
Bob McNeir
for his moral support & enthusiasm for this project
during the final stages of the manuscript's completion.

*   *   *

Table of Contents

* * *

I. Introduction

Collective grief over Judy Garland's death and collective anger over still more police harassment proved a volatile mixture during the last sweltering weekend of June 1969. The rainbow shattered, angry grieving gay people at last said a defiant "no!" to homophobia and, from the Stonewall Inn on New York's Christopher Street, found the strength and determination to take up the tasks of gay liberation. In the twenty years since Stonewall, many of us who are gay or lesbian have come to realize that being gay is far more than just a matter of sexual behavior; it is rather a whole mode of being-in-the-world, an "existential standpoint" which colors all our perceptions of and interactions with the world and one which also stands over against established cultural and religious standards for gender roles and intimate human relationships. Such an all-encompassing givenness should also nourish and undergird our efforts at spirituality and theology. Surprisingly, however, the gay liberation movement has not as yet produced any body of work truly comparable to that of the other liberation movements of the last several decades. While the civil rights movement has drawn strength from the Black churches, while feminists have shaped their liberation with theological analyses, and while struggling Latin America has created a liberation theology, the gay community has floundered (cf., Clark, 1987a). A discrepancy persists between our spiritual inclinations and even our involvement in institutional religion, and our actual failures until recently to reflectively and systematically participate in theological activity.

In his analysis of homosexuality, for example, Jung (1954) speculated that gay men, in particular, were often "endowed with a wealth of religious feelings . . . and a spiritual receptivity" (p. 21), a speculation which had also informed the early, theoretical anthropology of Carpenter (1910, 1919). More recently, new studies of the native American berdache have consistently demonstrated the historical connection of heightened spirituality and shamanism among gender-variant males in numerous non-Judaeo-Christian cultures (Clark, 1984, 1987a, Roscoe, 1986, 1987, Williams, 1986). Importantly, however, Jung's insight is not only exemplified outside the predominant western religious tradition: Boswell (1980) has shown the extent to which gay men were drawn to pre-Thomist Catholicism, a Catholicism which by the twelfth century had produced at least one gay-sensitive theology, that of "passionate friendship," and at least one gay saint, St. Aelred of Rievaulx (Boswell, 1980, Clark, 1987a, Hallier, 1969, Russell, 1982, Squire, 1981). Gay priests and lesbian nuns, in fact, still constitute a large percentage of Catholic clergy (Curb and Manahan, 1985, DeStefano, 1986) and the ranks of Protestantism are similarly filled. Yet, for gay and lesbian clergy throughout most of Christianity at least, the pulpit is usually also a solitary closet. Self-authenticating coming out as an openly gay person virtually always assures the loss of one's religious orders.

While numerous gay men and lesbians have thus accepted the closet in order to pursue professional religious roles, other gay people within both Christianity and Judaism have also formed official and unofficial support groups within most traditional denominations and have even established their own denomination of churches (the Universal Fellowship of Metropolitan Community Churches, or MCC) and a loose federation of synagogues (the World Congress of Gay and Lesbian Jewish Organizations). Jung's insight and this seeming plethora of gay religious involvement notwithstanding, the vast majority of us who are gay men and lesbians actually find ourselves outside theological discourse and religious institutions; many of us are in fact quite hostile toward a western religious heritage whose official doctrine and tradition, both Jewish and Christian, are unabashedly homophobic.

This ironic discrepancy between a theoretically heightened gay "spiritual receptivity" and the historical involvement of gay people in religious organizations, on the one hand, and the actual dearth of substantial theological activity among gay people, on the other hand, is rooted in the antagonism of orthodox religious doctrine and tradition toward homosexuality generally and toward real, live gay men and lesbians in particular. Daly (1973), for example, speaks for gay people as well as for women when she implies that both groups have been so labelled and marginalized as to have been made "foreigners not only to the fortresses of political power, but also to those citadels in which thought processes have been spent out" (p. 6). Morton (1985) similarly recognizes that rather than speaking a message of liberation to gay men and lesbians, religious institutions more often bespeak alienation and rejection, a message which drives us away from those very institutions. Moreover, as specifically regards theological activity, the fact that the vast majority of both Jewish and Christian denominations blatantly exclude openly gay people from the clergy, the single area in which most graduates of theology schools and graduate programs in religion traditionally find employment, has effectively kept gay people outside serious gay-affirmative theological endeavor.[1]

Responses by contemporary gay people to this exclusion have taken a variety of forms to date, one of which is the apologetic. A great deal of energy has been devoted to scriptural analysis, as if Leviticus and Romans could be compelled to relinquish their homophobic thrust. Similar energies have been expended trying to convince the churches and synagogues that they should accept gay people as co-equal congregants and clergy who are as good in God's eyes as heterosexuals. These struggles have nurtured the numerous denominational support groups which have created gay/ lesbian spaces for traditional rituals and pursued ordinational issues, but which, so preoccupied, have not taken up the task of critical theology as such. Moreover, the single Christian denomination which is uniquely based in the gay community (MCC) has adopted an evangelical Christianity which approaches scripture and the tradition in a nearly literal manner--except those passages and portions which pertain to homosexuality. Consequently, the defensive and assimilationist postures of the apologists (Boswell, 1980, Edwards, 1984, Horner, 1978, Macourt et al., 1977, McNeill, 1976, 1988, Nugent et al., 1983) have done little to nurture assertive gay theological pursuits.

There are, however, at least four exceptions to this summary of the work which has been loyally undertaken within the Judaeo-Christian tradition. Heyward (1979, 1984) increasingly infuses her primarily feminist theology with her standpoint as a lesbian priest, and both Fortunato (1983, 1987) and McNeill (1976, 1988) synthesize theological insights and psychology in their gay-oriented therapeutic work and writing. Also, since his coming out over a decade ago, Boyd (1984, 1987) has interwoven his own gay experience with his poetic, autobiographical, and devotional writing and ministry. Finally, openly gay theological writers are beginning to address the AIDS crisis, not from an apologetic point of view, but from theological and pastoral care perspectives firmly grounded in identification with the gay community (Clark, 1986a, 1987a, 1987d, Fortunato, 1985, 1987, McNeill, 1988, South, 1985). While the work of each of these writers clearly provides very important resources for addressing various needs within the gay/lesbian community, these individuals at best only begin to approach the task of forthrightly doing systematically constructive gay liberation theology.

Given the theological vacuity of much of the apologetic and assimilationist approach to the Judaeo-Christian tradition, and the subsumed or AIDS-specific quality of the unapologetic work to date, a second response to the western theological and spiritual tradition has naturally been utterly antagonistic. While feminist theologian Collins (1974) has written that "many of us [feminists] have become mental or physical drop-outs from institutionalized religion, not because we are irreligious, but because our religious impulses are being killed by [traditional Judaeo-Christianity]" (p. 231), many gay people have simply decided to dispose of both baby and bath-water simultaneously. No small number of gay men, at least, have totally eliminated the spiritual dimensions from their lives and have renounced both gay apologetics and the tradition (Clark, 1987a). Among those most adamantly opposed to the tradition, for example, is an organization of gay and lesbian athiests.[2]

A third approach lies, fortunately, between these extremes and seeks to develop spiritual alternatives both without and within traditional Judaeo-Christianity. The "faerie circle" has produced a number of books and periodicals and continues to rely upon a rather esoteric mixture of Celtic mythology, goddess religion, and other forms of mysticism, metaphysics, and natural ethics, which are neither peculiarly Eastern nor Jewish/Christian (Evans, 1978, Grahn, 1984, 1985, Mitchell and Asta, 1977, Perlinksi, 1984, Thompson, 1987a, 1987c, Thompson et al., 1987, Walker, 1980, Wright and Inesse, 1979). For all its seeming vitality, however, this spiritual movement is itself marginal to the vast majority of gay people and is only now beginning to seek dialogue and unity within itself (Thompson, 1986). A similarly synthetic, or comparative religionist, approach has examined the Jungian archetypal/mythic dimensions of the gay subculture and the spirituality of the native American berdache, while

also elucidating gay-sensitive themes in feminist and
monastic theologies, all as possible resources for gay
spirituality or theology (Clark, 1984, 1987a, 1987b).
Like the other unapologetic efforts cited, however, the
gay spirituality work of both "faerie" and the comparative approach are fragmentary, piece-meal.[3] A thoroughgoing constructive gay liberation theology has yet
to be undertaken and, as such, constitutes the primary
aim and challenge of the present volume.

Morton (1985) implies that her own particular process of theologizing, of doing/speaking/writing liberation theology, is both confessional ("This is how it is
with me") and invitational ("How is it with you?") (p.
xxv). Doing theology requires hearing or listening to
the fragments of individual and communal experience in
order to speak not a final word, but a word which
opens, fosters, and nurtures dialogue. Consequently,
of course, such constructive theology-as-process is always partial, incomplete, and open-ended. The liberation theologian cannot in fact wait until he/she has
shaped a closed, whole system because every thing we do
(who we are and how we are) has a theological dimension
as well as a sociopolitical dimension. Because living
and being are incomplete, fragmentary, and processive,
so must a theology which is infused by our living, by
our engagement in the world, also be always incomplete
and in process. As those of us who are now beginning
to develop gay liberation theology strive to find our
own authentic individual and communal voice(s), we also
must find and/or create someplace from which to listen
and to begin to speak.

Because we are discovering, not unlike Morton
(1985), that forced to the margins of gay/lesbian
stereotypes, of heterosexist norms for assimilation,
and of religious rejection, that our very extremity
shapes our authentic speech to proclaim our gay and
lesbian selves and our lives as good, we are also discovering that our spirituality is "experienced profoundly as . . . political action of the most radical
sort on behalf [of our own oppressed community] and ultimately including all humanity" (p. 98). Spirituality
and being/doing/acting, theology and praxis, fuse; we
cannot wait for completed systems to emerge. Our work
therefore becomes less a culmination of what we or
others have previously done, but rather a prismatic focusing of that work, which in turn radiates outward toward new speech, new dialogue, and ongoing theological
process. A prism of confession and invitation to dialogue shapes our provisional assertions and our frag-

mentary reflections into someplace to start, rather
than to finish, the work of doing unapologetic gay liberation theology. There is no more urgent time or
space for such a beginning than here and now, two
decades after the beginning of contemporary gay liberation at Stonewall and in the very midst of the AIDS
health crisis and the redoubled homophobia which it has
engendered.

Moving then from the mixture of apologetics, biblical exegesis, "faerie," and the other fragmentary
elements of gay/lesbian work in religion to date, toward the tentative development of a gay liberation theology, requires making a fresh start but one not discontinuous with other gay and lesbian efforts to date.
Doing gay theology in fact joins these other activities
in their dynamic, processive dialogue. Our fresh
start, however, will also mean stepping back to examine
methodological concerns and the importance of our experience as a theological source, particularly vis-a-
vis an analysis of patriarchy, homophobia, and AIDS,
insofar as this descriptive/analytical work then pre-
pares us to attempt a provisional and gay liberational
(re)construction of theology. Along the way, our theology will need to wrestle, either implicitly or expli-
citly, with a number of questions. And, while these
questions may be either specifically or only indirectly
and/or partially addressed, their very presence before
us will help us on our way into the process of creat-
ing/doing gay liberation theology.

Among those questions (cf., Plaskow, 1979) is
whether gay theology will be something distinctly different from, or unique to, Judaism and Christianity, or
simply a gay perspective brought to these traditions.
How will gay theology relate to either or both prongs
of the Judaeo-Christian heritage in the west? As loyal
critic? As marginalized reinterpreter? As an equal
partner in liberationist, theological dialogue? Similarly, what will, or should, the relationship of the
gay/lesbian individual, doing theology which is shaped
by his/her particular gay experience, be toward the gay
community and/or toward the often homophobic traditional religious/theological community(ies)? What
critical role should gay theology bear not only toward
the tradition, but toward the gay community itself?
Can gay theology synthesize both the cutting edge of
prophetic criticism with the tenderness of restorative
compassion and the empowerment required for the actual
tasks of liberation?

In addition to these questions related to the nature or place of our theological activity, we will also
need to consider other questions related to the content
and/or presuppositions of our theology. We will need
to explore, for example, whether we can in fact iden-
tify particular instances of God's presence with gay
people, either in our experiences of oppression or in
our efforts toward liberation, or whether a theological
component or interpretation is, at best, only an arti-
ficially contrived afterthought. In other words, has
western religion so thoroughly separated spirituality
from embodiment, bodiliness, and sexuality as to preclude our ever experiencing God as proactive within/for
a sexually marginalized people? Can we successfully
synthesize an understanding of the divine pleasure in
creation, in embodiment, and in sexuality with the historical record of God's championing other marginalized
peoples, however analogically we may do so, in order to
speak both authentically and theologically as a
gay/lesbian liberation-seeking people? All of these
various questions stand before us, not only as we construct someplace to start for ourselves, but as we
actually move into that prismatic focus to develop a
methodology for beginning the process of theologizing,
of doing liberation theology, as gay and lesbian
people.

* * *

* The Descriptive Process *

II. Method, Experience, and Gay Theology

(i) Exploring Methodological Concerns

An implicit element which emerges in gay religious writings which are neither apologetic nor defensive, particularly in that work which is only marginally connected to the Judaeo-Christian tradition (e.g., Clark, 1987a, Evans, 1978, Thompson et al., 1987, Walker, 1980), is an increasing awareness that the seemingly endless and circular arguments to justify gay/lesbian existence with biblical exegesis, to achieve ordination in traditional denominations, and on the part of the Metropolitan Community Church, to receive recognition by and membership in the National Council of Churches, all together have become a futile, Kafkaesque drain upon gay and lesbian energies. The institutional religious system clearly functions so as to defuse our efforts, keeping us waiting and negotiating for a positive response which is unlikely ever to come. Such apologetic efforts, seeking the sanctioned approval of usually white, heterosexual, male religious authorities, are proving a demoralizing dead end, a reminder of the degree to which we are, at best, only marginal to institutionalized religion and its theology. Rather than expending all our energies in such futile pursuits, gay men and lesbians need, instead, to lay an assertive and righteous claim upon the religious traditions and heritage into which we were born--to lay claim upon our rightful place in Judaeo-Christianity, for example, in the west. Gay men and lesbians need henceforth to find in themselves "the courage and audacity to create our own theology" (Boyd, 1987, p. 79), to speak theologically as gay people, rather than continuing to acquiesce, to accept, and therefore passively to endorse our exclusion from religion, spirituality, and theology. Gay people must make a commitment to be a force to be reckoned with in theology, not solely via apologetics, but by claiming and assuming our right to theologize and to speak prophetically (cf., Heyward, 1982).

Gay liberation theology will necessarily be prophetic. Eschewing apologetics and assimilation means
claiming our place at the margins, "embracing our exile" (Fortunato, 1983), and using our position at the
very edge of our religious heritage as our standpoint,
our platform, for interpreting and speaking both to and
from our tradition (cf., Morton, 1985). It entails
standing forthrightly as much in judgment upon our heritage as informed by that heritage. In developing a
feminist theology, for example, Ruether (1983b) has
described a dilemma which gay theology also shares:
"On the one hand, we must confront the fact that scripture and theology have contributed to these very evils
that trouble us. They have functioned as sanctions of
evil. Yet, we discover within [them] essential resources to unmask these very failures of religion" (p.
5). While Judaism and Christianity have unabashedly
sanctioned the evils of homophobia and even gay geno-
cide--in the popular consciousness, at least, no con-
textual exegesis can undo either Leviticus' demand for
death to homosexual men or Romans' vehement homophobia
--that same two-pronged tradition carries also the criterion for self-criticism--the prophetic demand for
justice. The primary exemplary role of women in biblical religion, a role often shared by peculiar or eccen-
tric men on the bare fringes of Israelite society, was
that of prophet (cf., Ruether, 1985). Gay theology
must likewise sanctify and embrace the role of women
and of marginalized men, and speak prophetically to
represent "the power of freedom and newness of life in
which God's word breaks in to speak in judgment on
established modes of life and to open up new possibilities" (Ruether, 1985, p. 175).
    Working prophetically with Edwards (1984), for ex-
ample, gay theology will reject that side of the western religious heritage which worships a judgmental God
"who designates homosexuals as objects of divine
anger," at once realizing the oppression which such
"divine wrath" entails and rejecting the "misdirected
moral condemnation" which is erroneously derived from
this judgmental image of God (pp. 88-89). Gay theology
will prophetically insist that injustice and homophobia, not sexuality, draw divine judgment. Gay theology
recognizes with Ruether (1983b) that "theology must be
done, can only be done, by those who situate themselves
in the reality of oppression, and whose theology is a
reflection of liberating praxis" (p. 27). Gay liberation theology can only be done at the margins, by those
who refuse tokenism and assimilation, by those who par-

ticipate in the sociopolitical tasks and goals of gay liberation, by those who, unashamed, share in the subcultural and frequently ghettoized life of openly gay men and lesbians and, at the same time, by those whose memory of their own closets informs both their theology and praxis with compassion for those who cannot yet embrace their exile. Gay liberation theology must be an assertive and even defiant celebration of life and a reconstruction of theology--at the margins.

Thus, in attempting to participate in the activity of "doing" gay liberation theology, I must retain a certain connection with the Judaeo-Christian tradition as a sort of grounding or context, as the abstract criterion or epistemological framework for my theologizing, not because I currently find myself squarely within either Judaism or Christianity, nor because I have any vested interest in any particular institutional forms within the western tradition, but rather because to adopt or appropriate any other religious framework (Celtic "faerie," eastern religions, etc.) is simply too alien to my existence to be genuinely meaningful for me in my depths, in my perceiving, responding, and being in the world. To do so would clearly require an act of appropriation which in itself would still necessarily be colored by my training and ways of thinking which have been and continue to be shaped by a western or Judaeo-Christian epistemology. I suspect that many other gay people as well can be critical of our religious heritage from the margins or fringes of that tradition, still refusing both apologetics and assimilation, but can also not completely relinquish that tradition.

Both the assumption of a prophetic function for gay theology and the relationship of gay theology (and individual gay and lesbian theologians) to the Judaeo-Christian heritage further entail two other qualifiers for such theological activity. Gay theology must be focused upon the here and now, the particularities of this time and place for gay people, and thus must also be focused phenomenologically, not only in the subjective experience of gay people both communally and individually, but also in the subjectivity of each gay/lesbian theologian's perceptions of, participation in, and interpretation of gay life. Indeed, theology for us must be focused not upon heaven, but upon earth, always pointing toward the horizontality of God in our midst, a God dependent upon human justice-seeking and -making to be manifest. As Heyward (1982) has said, theology is not "about God as God is in Godself, but rather about us as we experience God in this world at this time among ourselves" (p. 20). Our activity, our theology and praxis, is grounded in our subjectivity, our phenomenological experience, and is, consequently, heavily "anthropological" or humanity-oriented, as Rubenstein (1966) has described:

> The ultimate relevance of theology is anthropological. Though theology purports to make statements about God, its significance rests on what it reveals about the theologian and his [sic.] culture. All theologies are inherently subjective. They are statements about the way in which the theologian experiences his [sic.] world.
>   . . . The theologian . . . is in reality communicating an inner world he [sic.] suspects others may share.
>   . . . From a technical point of view, theological statements would seem to be most precise when they are enunciated in a phenomenological context. (p. 246)

It is not coincidental, then, that all specific liberation theologies have in fact emerged as post-death-of-God theologies. Only once the secular and anthropological grounding for theology had been established and legitimated, as in and by death-of-God theologies, could subsequent theologians reclaim God, his/her limits notwithstanding after Auschwitz or in the midst of AIDS-suffering and AIDS-death, and focus theology upon human experience and human needs in the here and now.[4] Moreover, given gay theology's particularly tenuous or marginalized and critical relationship to religious givens, gay theology is continuous with, and yet at some distance from, primary and often homophobic sources such as scripture and church documents). Consequently, gay theology is a legitimate responding to, a reinterpreting of and building upon/from the secondary sources, upon/from those writers who have already begun to recast primary sources into liberational forms. Gay theology thus becomes another, "tertiary" layer, a further extension of theological activity in the service both of liberation and of a God who is always with those people who seek liberation and full humanity. Says Neusner (1979),

> . . . We must grant to theologians . . . the freedom as constructive religious thinkers to propose fresh perspectives on, and even alterations

in, the world view and ethos of [faith]. . . . The
tasks of theology today begin in the exegesis of
exegesis done. But they lead to the doing of the
exegesis of this time, the interpretation of our
world and of its days. (pp. 84-85)

This methodological standpoint means gay theology
depends heavily upon the individual theologian; it de-
rives from what I come to believe, based upon and informed by my sources and my experience and interpretation of gay life, for which I alone, and not those
sources, am ultimately responsible (cf., Heyward,
1984). Doing and writing gay theology becomes a dialogue of and about personal understandings, in order
for us to discover commonalities and to celebrate differences. Our theologizing is thus provisional, tentative, dynamic, partial, and never authoritatively complete or "once-and-for-all," except as any of us appro-
priates parts of this activity for our personal and
shared lives as gay men and lesbians. Our theology, as
an ongoing activity, must exist in the "morally ongoing
openness" of mutuality, reciprocity, and dialogue (Heyward, 1984, p. 225). It indeed aspires to be the communication of an "inner world," or perspective upon the
world, which the theologian "suspects others may share"
(Rubenstein, 1966, p. 246). Heyward (1984) elaborates:

The more theology reflects the specific and particular experience of those who shape it, the more
credible theology is to others. . . . Good constructive theology is done in the praxis of concrete situations, in which the doers of theology
speak for and about themselves, rather than for
and about others or humanity in general by attempting to universalize their experiences of what
is true or good.
. . . What this means, methodologically, is
that theology must be done modestly, in recognition that all theological images and patterns are
limited--in terms of truth and intelligibility--by
the boundaries of the life experiences of those
who construct them. (pp. 223-224)

Our modest particularity and our provisional sharing of
gay theology as an activity ("doing theology" or "theologizing") can ideally help us, therefore, to avoid
projecting any of our work upon another as "univer-
sally" true. The dialogical or dynamic quality of our
work stands over against pseudo-objective, "fixed" the-

ologies which are not really objective at all, because they are actually couched in/colored by a "heterosexist epistemology" of white, male, upper class, heterosexist bias (cf., Clark, 1986b, pp. 11-14, Heyward, 1984).

If indeed, "the vision of the theologian is affected by the particularities of his or her experience" (Christ and Plaskow, 1979, p. 20), then I must acknowledge here, up front, all the particularities of my past, my upbringing, my training, my gender, my economic standing, and my race. For if my theological activity and reflection have any broader, dialogical value for us as gay people, it will come through my acknowledging, and sometimes transcending, my particularity, and not from my failing to confront my "presuppositions." In so exploring and elucidating each individual's subjectivity, gay liberation theology also acquires a confessional quality which must necessarily undergird the modesty of our provisional assertions. The confessional quality of this work for me, for example, is shaped by a life of paradox, of seeming contradictions, many of which are actually resolved by the fact of my own, openly gay identity: I am an ordained United Methodist minister who was never allowed to serve a church after I completed seminary; I am, subsequently, a trained scholar who has yet to find an academic appointment; I am a white-collar professional whose income is that of a devalued, pink-collar clerk; I am a secretary who writes books and articles on literary criticism and theology; I am a white southerner whose native region and whose own siblings, steeped in southern Protestant fundamentalism, cannot welcome me; I am a male who refuses to play the accepted masculine role; and, I am an enculturated Christian who has co-founded a gay and lesbian synagogue.

The unifying theme, however, which cuts across these paradoxes is my gayness. My gay being is not just a matter of what I do in bed with a lover, but my way of perceiving, interpreting, interacting, and being in the world. It is my standpoint for resolving contradictions, for defiantly creating wholeness or integretous personal unity out of paradox and conflict, and for doing theology. These seeming contradictions, and through them my own experience of gay life and gay oppression, are the particular web or nexus of being, of personal subjectivity, from which this gay theologian must convey to those who would share in this dialogue, that my modest assertions, my understandings of God, of people, of the divine/human relationship, however provisional and partial, are grounded in personal integrity (cf., Heyward, 1984).

This emphasis on subjectivity must not, however, emerge without a context, without qualification. Ruether (1983a) reminds both feminist and gay theologians that we cannot rely on mere subjectivity; we require grounding in an "historical community and tradition" for our prophecy to be authentic criticism: "One cannot wield the lever of criticism without a place to stand" (p. 18). We are brought back to our rootedness at the margins, on the fringes. We are called to synthesize our gay/lesbian being with an often homophobic and yet equally justice-seeking tradition, and in the process of effecting that synthesis, to derive the critical principles for gay theology. Among those criteria will be an insistence upon the right of gay people to full humanity--spiritually, socially, politically, and medically. Boyd (1987), for example, has insisted that "our spiritual needs cry out to be met, honestly and fully, [and to be] integrated with our sexual and other needs" (p. 84). Our theology will thus seek to nurture full humanity or wholeness, for gay people and ultimately for all people, by reintegrating sexuality and spirituality with full, unhindered participation in social existence, while nevertheless remaining critical of the sociocultural status quo. It will in turn also affirm and celebrate the particularity and difference of genuine pluralism (cf., Boyd, 1987) and reject exclusivity, seeking instead an inclusivity of all genders, classes, and races, and sharing with Ruether (1983a) the belief that "any principle of religion or society that marginalizes one group of persons as less than fully human diminishes us all" (p. 20).

Furthermore, this drive toward wholism and inclusivity also means our gay theology will not individualize or spiritualize either failure (sin) or redemption, but will examine the corporate and systemic/structural character of human injustice and reformation, thus adopting Ruether's (1983a) principle of the "dynamic unity of creation and redemption": "We cannot split a spiritual, antisocial redemption from the human self as a social being, embedded in sociopolitical and ecological systems" (p. 215). As Rubenstein (1966) further reminds us, we need not only to exhort our tradition toward social justice, but also to incorporate some means for acknowledging corporate failures to fully accomplish such humanitarian concerns and thus to develop compassion toward ourselves and toward others for our shared failures which sustain oppression. Our theology will thus remain "anthropological," connected with the actual life of our people and other people, accounting for and not dismissing the negatives of historical, biological existence, while simultaneously affirming the intrinsic value of life in itself, apart from any supernatural validation. We will accept the limits of God, whereby God is not a deus ex machina, and thereby take seriously our human responsibility for creating justice. Our realistic "tragic vision" (Rubenstein, 1966, p. xi), however, will lead us not into despair, to waiting for rescue, but rather to an empowered ability to fuse our ideas with participation in the tasks and processes of change, toward a synthesis of theology and praxis, or, as Heyward (1984) has described it, toward a "theology and ministry of radical participation" (p. 68).

Taking seriously our historical and biological life and its limitations, as well as taking seriously both the limits of divine power to rescue us and thus our responsibility for action, for fusing theology with "radical participation," also means our gay theology will not ignore AIDS, tragedy, or death. No gay theology will hold our attention, much less our respect, unless it confronts both homophobic violence and AIDS. Moreover, we may actually discover in our very experiences of both human injustice and the absence of divine rescue, a strange empowerment and therein God's compassionate companionship on behalf of the victims of oppression and tragedy. God's intimacy with us enables us to forgive divine limitations, to develop compassion for one another (and even for the oppressor), and to claim in our depths the spiritual resources for appropriate responsibility for shaping our own lives, for seeking social change, and for caring for those who are suffering from AIDS. Our refusal to succumb to despair and our facing the future, in spite of homophobia and even AIDS, in "radical participation," becomes the corporate gay/lesbian embodiment of our synthesis of theology and praxis.

Our methodological considerations of the provisional nature of gay theology thus far include a rejection of apologetics and of requiring outside spiritual authority or religious validation, in exchange for an assertive, prophetic role at the margins of Judaeo-Christianity. Gay theology thus shifts the focus from the vertical to the horizontal, to the here and now particularities of gay people and of God's presence on our behalf. It fuses subjectivity with a grounding in both gay/lesbian life and in the justice-seeking side

of our heritage. It moves toward a wholism of humanity, and of gay and lesbian humanity, and does not
flinch from the realities of either human injustice or
divine limitations in our present experience; it ex-
horts us to assume responsibility for active participation in our community and in the world. Consistent
across this range of considerations is an absence of
reliance upon scriptural or ecclesiastical authorities
and, instead, an assumption about the value of gay/les-
bian experience as the grounding for our dialogical
theologizing. As we move, then, from methodology and
the beginnings of theology fully into that activity, we
must in fact begin by revaluing and understanding our
experience, by indeed affirming our experience as gay
people as the appropriate locus of gay liberation theology.

(ii) Revaluing Experience and Story

Our experience as gay and lesbian people in a pre-
dominantly homophobic western culture and ethos is the
present locus of, and ultimately the primary source
for, our particular liberational theologizing. Importantly, as early as 1968, Fackenheim insisted that "the
analysis of the human condition constitutes the necessary prolegomenon of all modern Jewish and, indeed, all
modern theology" (p. 101). This return to the pheno-
menology of human experience in post-death-of-God theologies has perhaps found its fullest elucidation as the
very grounding for theology in the work of various feminist theologians. Indeed, feminists' high valuation
of retrospect (minority history) and story (communicated and shared minority experience) for informing
theology and the tasks of liberation can be understood
as equally paradigmatic for gay theology. Feminist
theology has essentially recovered and revalued human
experience, and particularly the experience of oppressed and marginalized minority peoples, as a legitimate norm for appraising and evaluating theology and as
an acceptable standpoint or source for critically (re)-
constructing theology. Says Collins (1981), "Feminist
theology shares with all other forms of liberation theology a rootage in the historical experience of oppressed and obscured subcultures that have existed
within and over against white western male culture" (p.
343). Consequently, religious tradition mediated by
scripture and church doctrine or dogma can now take a
"back seat," informing theological work as a valuable
resource, but as one no longer holding any oppressively

binding authority over us. Theologizing now becomes grounded in "a realization of our experience [and] the capacity to be aware of, and to reflect upon, the experience of being human" (Heyward, 1984, p. 7). Specifically, minority experience and story becomes the norm for doing prophetic liberation theology; theology and praxis are inseparably fused (cf., Heyward, 1984, Morton, 1985).

The reasons for this combined anthropological and phenomenological focus for any liberation theology are manifold (cf., Clark, 1987c). For example, as any oppressed group comes to self-awareness and begins to raise its collective voice for liberation, it immediately assumes the task of self-identification, of defining itself as a people or subculture. A part of that process is claiming personal and communal history, as well as reclaiming that history from the oppressors who, in writing majority history, necessarily usurp and distort the history of oppressed peoples (cf., Morton, 1985). (Re)claiming both personal, individual experience of the recent past and the present, as well as the history of like persons over time, are vital activities for creating personal and group identity (cf., Christ, 1980). Stories are the vehicle for both experience and history, as each shapes and informs the other. Writes Christ (1979a), "There is dialectic between story and experience. Stories shape experience; experience shapes stories. . . . In a sense, without stories there is no experience" (p. 229, cf., Christ, 1980). In other words, a shared past--both a history and traditions which shape and are shaped by contemporary experience--is vitally important for any oppressed or marginalized people, both as a source of identity and as a ground of empowerment. But, as Collins (1979) has further insisted, "It must be their own tradition, their consciously claimed heritage, not a tradition [a history or identity] imposed" by their oppressors (p. 158).

(Re)claiming particular minority experience and story therefore yields not only a sense of identity/ reality/validation; it also nurtures the very empowerment needed for the tasks of liberation. As Satloff (1983) has indicated, (re)claiming experience and telling stories act to name the demons of oppression and in naming them to rob them of their power: "The act of telling a story or naming an event ritually (i.e., psychologically] deprives a violation of its power" (p. 198). The "self-conscious journey through personal and communal history" enables an oppressed

group to wrest its identity and history from the oppressor, as well as to gain control over its own history and thus over its own destiny; in so doing, marginalized people cease to be merely passive victims of
history and begin to (re)create their own reality in
both the past (history) and the present (Satloff, 1983,
p. 197). Collins (1979) elaborates:

> In the process of telling our stories as a con-
> scious, political act, we begin to define our-
> selves and our reality. . . .
> As we collect our stories, they begin to
> shape themselves into a body of experience . . .
> that can no longer be denied. They become the
> collective self-expression that feeds and streng-
> thens those who are able to hear. . . .
> Through the telling and retelling of our
> stories, the inessentials are gradually sloughed
> off, until only the veins, the life-bearing ves-
> sels, remain. [Then] we begin to see the patterns
> of triumph, steadfastness, of salvation and liber-
> ation inherent in them. . . . We discover the se-
> cret that keeps hope more alive in the oppressed
> who are conscious of their oppression than in
> those who do the oppressing. (pp. 153, 155)

Recognizing the "patterns of triumph, steadfastness, of
salvation and liberation," and hence of the divine co-
presence on behalf of the oppressed, all of which were
hidden from us before we (re)claimed our experience,
empowers and strengthens us as gay and marginalized
people. There is a theologically cutting edge to our
experience which indeed informs present and future
praxis.
    This fusion of experience (praxis) with theoreti-
cal reflections upon God's presence with, or advocacy
on behalf of, the oppressed utterly recasts theology.
Collins (1979) goes so far as to say that "nothing that
is of us can be alien to our theology" (p. 152, emphasis added). Further elaborating on the thoroughness
with which experience should inform theology, she says,

> . . . Theology begins with our stories: What
> we do with our time; how we feel about our fami-
> lies, our friends, our coworkers, our bosses; how
> we feel about money and who gets it; what we do
> when we get up in the morning; how we make it
> through the day; what pains us, enrages us, sad-
> dens and humiliates us; what makes us laugh; what

enlightens and empowers us; what keeps us holding
on in moments of despair; where we find separation
and alienation; where we find true community and
trust. (p. 152)

Heyward (1984) is following this same line of thought
when she subsequently suggests both that theology is
"the capacity to discern God's presence here and now
and to reflect on what that means" (p. 7) and that the
effectiveness of our theological reflections "rests on
the extent to which we understand and trust our experience and our visions" (p. 158); however, "we can do
neither as long as we internalize the perceptions of
reality that have been shaped historically for us by
those whose interests fly in our faces" (p. 158). Increasingly, then, the efforts both to reclaim minority
history and experience from their shaping by the oppressors and to develop a theology based upon that reclaimed and revalued experience place liberation theology at odds with the "a priori presuppositions of tradition" (Collins, 1981, p. 343). The "elitist mode" of
pseudo-objective theologies, shaped as they so often
have been by a white, male, heterosexist epistemology,
have in fact merely been ways to preserve the power of
those who have monopolized theological and religious
structures, over against those peoples designated by
the elite as Other (Collins, 1981, cf., Clark, 1986b).
Developing a theology based upon minority experience
thus leads the liberation theologian into a tension between personal experience and traditional theological
sources and norms (cf., Umansky, 1984).
    Ruether (1983a) has realized the irony that scrip-
ture and tradition, including religious rituals and
symbols, are themselves "codified collective human experience" (p. 12). Our Judaeo-Christian heritage began
in experience, and yet, because that experience was
primarily codified by heterosexual men, it subsequently
came to be used to restrict all later human experience.
The scriptures, for example, "have been shaped in their
formation, their transmission, and, finally, their can-
onization to sacralize patriarchy" (Ruether, 1985, p.
ix). A "closed canon" of scripture and a narrow, male-
restricted ecclesiastical authority over doctrine and
tradition have forced feminist theologians to reject
even attempting to "read themselves into" accumulated,
canonized (and hence closed) religious experience. Gay
theology must do likewise. Indeed, feminist theologians have realized that "the exclusion of our experience from the funding of sacred stories may point to a

basic defect in the perception of ultimate power and
reality by the traditional stories" (Christ, 1979a, p.
230). Our very exclusion, whether as women or as gay
people, becomes a criticism of scripture and tradition.
Revaluing minority experience, therefore, means pene-
trating/resolving the conflict of experience and tradition by forcibly reopening the canon. Says Ruether
(1985),

> . . . Every new upsurge of the liberating
> spirit must challenge the efforts of fossilized
> religious authority to "close the canon," to de-
> clare that God has spoken once and for all in a
> past time.
> . . . We are not only free to reclaim re-
> jected texts of the past . . . in light of which
> canonized texts may be criticized; but we are also
> free to generate new stories from our own experi-
> ence. (p. 247)

The demand upon gay theology, then, from feminist theology's own reclamation of experience and critical encounter with "closed" tradition, is to search out, to
discover and recover, and to further develop our own
experience and our own paradigmatic stories, within
certain limitations.

Heyward (1984) has begun this process for gay theology when she insists that it is time for gay men and
lesbians to "tell our stories, to listen carefully, to
begin to experience our experience, to risk realizing
and sharing our own senses of confusion, fear, frustra-
tion, anger, even rage, about what is done to us, and
what we do to ourselves and others" (p. 85). At one
level, that of story in its written, literary form, gay
people have long been in the process of capturing and
transmitting our particular experience. We do not need
to attempt to fit ourselves into, or read ourselves
into, heterosexualized experience, history, or tradition, because in the years since the Stonewall Inn
riots (1969), gay people have in fact rediscovered a
fortuitous wealth of stories which reflect the particularities of gay history and experience and which depict
that experience, not from the oppressor's viewpoint,
but from a gay point of view (Clark, 1987c). Within a
half-decade of gay liberation's birth at Stonewall, for
example, gay scholars had already begun to articulate a
uniquely gay-sensitive approach to the interpretation
and evaluation of past and present gay literature (Crew
and Norton, 1974). And, although writers such as White

(qtd., Young, 1981, p. 7) have disagreed over the issue
of "gay sensibility" and critics such as Adams (1980)
have questioned the pragmatic value of identifying gay
fiction as a specialized genre, other writer/scholars
have built their work upon these very concepts. Bronski (1984), for example, has persuasively argued for
the reality of a particularly gay way of perceiving the
world, a gay sensibility which necessarily affects gay
artistic expression. And, while Bronski's supportive
historical survey of gay expression in various media
lacks a certain depth, Austen (1977) has provided a detailed gay (male) literary history until the early
1970s and Clark (1986b, cf., 1987c) has examined and
elucidated both the gay critical work of the decade
after Stonewall and, upon that foundation, has continued to characterize gay male literary history in fiction through the outbreak of AIDS in the early 1980s.
In broad overview, this literary history of gay experience or gay sensibility, at least with fictional
stories, emerges as an alternating pattern of "hostility and begrudged acceptance" in the years before liberation, as a bursting-forth during the 1970s of a
proud fiction which openly and unabashedly advocates
gay life, and as a maturing fiction at the turn of the
subsequent decade which includes self-criticism,
straight-gay transitions (from within marriages), gay
relationships, and finally, an awareness of the impact
of AIDS on gay male experience (Clark, 1986b, pp. 11-
12, 24, 30, cf., pp. 1-32, 120-123).

This process of elucidating and articulating gay
and lesbian experience immediately encounters certain
limitations, however. As gay people begin to get clear
as to what our experience is and is not, we are brought
back to the issue of particularity, to the absence of
any single, monolithic experience of gay being, given
the great diversity among gay men and lesbians. We
must avoid both universalizing our experience, or so
particularizing our experience, in ways which exclude
anyone. We must realize the partial, fragmented, and
incomplete quality of what we do, both acknowledging
our diversity of gender, race, economic class, and life
style, while continuing to struggle with concepts which
remain unclear for us, such as "gay community"--who do
we mean and who might we inadvertently be excluding
(cf., Collins, 1981, Christ, 1979a). Fortunately for
us, even starting with the fragments, certain themes
and certain historical events emerge from our diversity
to provide us with a provisional core of theologizable
experience.

In terms of gay history, Rubenstein's (1966) discussion of theologically meaningful kairos-time helps
us to look for inbreaking realities whose impact on gay
life and gay being radically changed how gay people
have lived and experienced their lives. Chief among
these was the shift from Hellenistic, pre-Christian attitudes toward sexuality and homosexuality to an increasingly homophobic religious and cultural view, a
view which achieved normative status with the rise of
Thomist Catholicism (Boswell, 1980). While earliest
Christianity wavered between overlooking homosexuality,
particularly in its own professional ranks, after
Thomas Aquinas the church increasingly endorsed and
sanctioned open hostility toward and even capital punishment for gay people (Crompton, 1978). Religiously
and culturally motivated gay genocide proceeded apace--
capital punishment for gay men and lesbians in the west
did not abate until the nineteenth century (Crompton,
1978)[5]--until it achieved its fullest expression under
Nazism. Hitler's adamant opposition toward anything
unmasculine which might undermine the "German spirit"
required the incarceration and eventual deaths of thousands of gay people, primarily gay men: Steakley
(1975) cites the estimate of the Protestant Church of
Austria that approximately 220,000 gay men were killed
during the Third Reich; Crompton (1978) uses the
rougher, traditional estimate of 100,000-400,000; and,
Plant (1986), himself a gay Jewish survivor of the era
who fled Germany in 1933, provides data from his
archival research of extant Nazi records, yielding
29,323-43,495 gay deaths, including 4,000 juveniles and
six lesbians, although lesbian acts per se were never
outlawed by Nazism (pp. 149, 230-232, 235, cf., Clark,
1987c). Whatever the actual numbers, whether under
Nazism specifically or during the history of Christianity more generally, the first and primary fragment of
gay historical experience is that of oppression, and
even of legalized genocide, on the part of both church
and state.

In a dialectical tension with gay oppression in
modern times, gay people have also glimpsed liberation
and discovered the beginnings of empowerment, those
"patterns of triumph, steadfastness, of salvation and
liberation" which Collins (1979) described. For example, in Germany from 1897 until the rise of Nazism,
Magnus Hirschfeld's Scientific Humanitarian Committee
of the Institute of Sexual Science in Berlin advocated
gay rights and the decriminalization of homosexuality
(Crompton, 1978, Mehler, 1979, Steakley, 1975, cf.,

Clark, 1987c). After World War II, American gay men
and lesbians experienced a gradual subcultural and political awakening which culminated in the Stonewall
Inn/Christopher Street riots, during June 1969 in New
York. This moment of kairos-time exchanged gay passivity before homophobic harassment for pride-filled gay
assertiveness and inaugurated a decade of sociocultural
openness, of political protest, and of promiscuous,
celebratory sexual freedom utterly new to gay experience. The renaissance of gay literary critical activity was itself among the first fruits of this new
openness, as was an overall hunger for gay/lesbian history. The works of Katz (1978) in American history, of
Boswell (1980) in church history, and of Williams
(1986) in native American ethnology all testify to a
wide-spread need among gay people not only to discover
and to articulate anti-gay persecutions over time, but
also to elucidate positive gay historical moments as
part of that process of developing gay/lesbian identity
and empowerment.

     Unfortunately, however, Anita Bryant's anti-gay
campaign of 1977, the Everard Baths fire in New York in
1978, and the assassination of openly gay, San Francisco city supervisor Harvey Milk in late 1978, all together soon functioned to disillusion gay people as to
both the wisdom of easy sexual freedom and the real
difficulties involved in seeking sociopolitical change
(cf., Clark, 1986b). Finally, the outbreak of AIDS in
the U.S., first and foremost in the gay male community,
and the increase in homophobia and anti-gay violence
which has resulted, have meant a further shifting in
gay self-understandings, gay sexual behavior and life-
styles, and gay sociopolitical goals. The theologizable fragments of gay and lesbian experience have thus
come to include, historically, the various persecutions
and the gay genocide of Nazism; personally, the experience of marginalization and homophobia; and, communally, the experiences of confronting, responding,
mourning, and healing the tragedy of AIDS, of discovering both the limits of our mortality, our ability to
grieve, and our vast capacity to care for one another
in the face of suffering and death.

     In addition to the fragments of gay/lesbian exper-
ience which emerge from the long view, from the sweep
of history and contemporary events, other fragments
emerge at the developmental or individual, (auto)bio-
graphical level of gay experience (cf., Clark, 1987c).
Gay theology may also reflect upon the personal experience of self-recognition; the individual struggle to

exchange social and familial rejection and sex-negativity for self-affirmation; the risk-taking yet celebratory process of coming out; and, the retrospective
reclamation of our personal histories as we infuse our
pasts, our childhoods and youths, with gay identity,
gay being, and gay meaning (Cotton, 1987). A further
extension of this process is our individual appropriation of gay/lesbian history--with all its negatives--as
well as our search within history for more positive
kairos-events and our recognition of the gayness of
various artists and writers, saints and martyrs and
leaders--all as we celebrate those times and cultures
wherein homosexuality was traditionally honored.[6]

As we gather together all these fragments and the
diversity of gay/lesbian experience as the resources
for even provisional theological assertions, we may
also realize the degree to which the gay/lesbian sub-
culture(s), sexuality, and sensibility have all been
shaped by, in reaction to, heterosexism and homophobia.
As we seek to theologize in a manner continuous with
the Judaeo-Christian tradition, we are compelled to
sift out the "prophetic-liberating" themes of steadfast
love, of justice, of love for neighbor, of a God who
favors the outcast (cf., Ruether, 1983a), from the
heterosexist and patriarchal ideology of a religious
heritage which has more often sanctioned homophobia and
gay genocide. We discover with Fortunato (1983) that
the only way for us to draw upon our fragmentary and
diverse experience as gay people is to go deeper, to
penetrate gay oppression and to elucidate the systemic
structures of patriarchy, of dualism, and of homophobia
(cf., Morton, 1985). As we thus move beneath the sur-
face of our experience into an analysis of the oppression text of our lives as gay men and lesbians, we will
have further pursued the revaluation and reclamation of
our particular minority experience, which feminist theology has advocated and which gay theology must also
undertake, to that point at which our vision becomes
clear and we discover therein the empowerment in gay/
lesbian experience and being for (re)constructing a gay
liberation theology.

*   *   *

III. Patriarchy and Gay Oppression

(i) Patriarchy and Dualism

From the earliest days of the post-war women's movement in the U.S., first lesbians, and later gay men as well, have come to realize that the very same systemic structures which are interwoven throughout the entire history of western consciousness, culture, and religion undergird both sexism and heterosexism. Patriarchy and the hierarchy of dualisms which it entails sustain both forms of oppression. Goodman et al. (1983), for example, have said that,

> . . . gay oppression is part of the system of patriarchy and cannot be overthrown without the destruction of patriarchy as a whole. The relationship between patriarchy and heterosexism is important . . ., for the liberation of gay men is bound up with the liberation not only of lesbians but of all women (p. 107, cf., Siegel, 1979).

Gay oppression is part of the very fabric of our society, reinforcing both male socialization to fear homosexuality and female socialization to remain passively attached to a traditional, dominant male. This combination of homophobia and sexism is the very core of heterosexism: "A complex, self-contained system of oppression, heterosexism is also a form of sexism, a part of patriarchy. It maintains the subservience of women to men by punishing homosexuality and any deviance from the currently accepted range of masculine and feminine heterosexual roles" (Goodman et al., 1983, p. 29). Furthermore, because heterosexism punishes male nurturance, gentleness, non-aggressiveness, and any male aversion to power and domination, heterosexism also promotes (male) violence (Goodman et al., 1983). Importantly, however, especially for any gay theology which hopes to bridge the gender gaps among gay people, heterosexism is systemic, structural, absolutely interwoven with western society. Neither indi-

vidual gay men, nor individual heterosexual men, should
be blamed or held responsible for the historical development and current existence of patriarchy and heterosexism.   If gay theology is to reconcile gay men and
lesbians, it must nurture a praxis of forgiveness; we
must each forgive the other for our unwitting entrapment in the very structures which oppress us.   At the
same time, we can also insist that both individual men
and women, gay men and lesbians, are responsible for
whenever they fail to be aware of, and thus act in ways
which sustain, heterosexism: "Women's enemy is the
system of patriarchy, not individual men. . . . Men did
not choose to be sexist [or] their socialization as
males. . . . Men [should, however,] take responsibility
for stepping out of sexism" (Goodman et al., 1983, p.
94).
     The structures against which we together struggle
are deeply embedded in our society and culture, as well
as in our western religious heritage.   In fact, heterosexism, the inordinate valuing of heterosexual men and
their procreative sexuality, entered western consciousness simultaneously with the earliest beginnings of
Judaeo-Christianity.   Bauman (1983) sardonically re-
marks, "Attributing sanctity to male gender and phallus
initiates the whole saga of the Jewish people with
Abraham's everlasting covenant with his god through a
mark on his penis" (p. 91).   What began with Abraham
and the patriarchs of Judaism influenced Christianity,
which in turn influenced all subsequent western consciousness.   Morton (1985) in fact concludes that "com-
pulsory heterosexuality or homophobia" not only "permeates the patriarchal religious system [but actually]
appears to find in patriarchal religion its foremost
stronghold" (p. xxx).   Human history in the west has
thus been the history of the simultaneous development
of an all-encompassing patriarchy in both religion and
society:

     The story of human history in the West has been
     [one] of increasing patriarchal power . . . in the
     Bronze Age, then . . . in the triumph of Christi-
     anity, and finally overwhelmingly with . . . In-
     dustrialism.   Corresponding to this rise has been
     a fall, first in the status of women, then of
     rural people, then of gay people, then of non-
     white people. (Evans, 1978, p. 49)

As a result of this historical progression, gay people
share with women and all other marginalized people a

heritage of increasing restriction, as the social and
religious structures of patriarchy became established.

The human quest for social and psychological
structures has been motivated throughout the historical
development of patriarchy by the need of sentient beings for "ontological security," by the need for meaning, controlled change, and guidance for the life journey (Walker, 1980, p. 16). The social "myths" which
have resulted, however, only provide general identity
structures; they cannot account for unique, individual
human needs and potentials. Moreover, anyone who cannot or will not conform to the general pattern must be
punished, according to the myth system. Patriarchy has
indeed developed a vast and detailed system of "living
myths" which presume to define and delimit people and
their "sex roles, work roles, sexual behavior roles,
collective standards of moral belief, politics [and]
religion," all of which are based on a hierarchy of
strong men/weak women (Walker, 1980, p. 17). Similarly, "love and sex patterns are closely regulated by
the social myth system. Who you can love and/or have
sex with, how and when you can, are controlled by
myths" (Walker, 1980, p. 22). Patriarchy, then, has
clearly developed beyond the simple male/female dichotomy; it has become an all-encompassing structure over
time, a structure of "aristocracy over serfs, masters
over slaves, kings over subjects, racial overlords over
colonized people" (Ruether, 1983a, p. 61), people over
the earth's limited and exhaustible resources--and
heterosexuals and homophobia over gay men and lesbians.
The fundamental/original dualism, based upon the dichotomy of masculinity and femininity, has in fact spawned
an entire hierarchy of dualisms which has fostered and
sustained oppression, including gay oppression (cf.,
Clark, 1987a).

Feminist theologians were among the first to describe the ways in which the fundamental dualism of male
and female provided a scheme for all subsequent dualisms and, by means of that scheme, to create a system
of hierarchical values which has always stood oppressively over against both women and gay people (cf.,
Collins, 1974, Daly, 1973, Ruether, 1972, 1975).[7] Over
time patriarchal dualism gradually entailed not only
the polarization of feminine and masculine, but also
the opposition of body and soul, body and mind/intel-
lect, world and self, passion and reason. The subjuga-
tion of the former term in each of these pairs to the
latter term became the model for all subsequent polari-
zations, discriminations, and oppressions. Dualism

thus extended patriarchy's control over anything and anyone designated as Other, whether over resources and their distribution (classism), over countries and peoples (imperialism), over non-Christians and, hence, Jews (antisemitism), over non-whites (racism), over women (sexism), and over all non-heterosexual forms of sexuality (homophobia) (Goodman et al., 1983, cf., Plaskow, 1983b). The combined force of the last two, of sexism and homophobia, has kept sex roles in place, precluding real intimacy between men and women, and especially between men and other men: "Homophobia . . . helps keep the masculine/feminine dichotomy in place, which deprives individuals of wholeness and maintains men's power over women"; moreover, heterosexism "trains us to believe that safe, caring, supportive relationships between men are impossible" (Goodman et al., 1983, pp. 3, 35). Bauman (1983) reiterates the powerful implications of the developing interconnectedness of sexism and homophobia when she insightfully adds, "Fear of being treated like a woman--losing one's manliness--is the source of homophobic feelings and behavior in heterosexual men [who] will cease being homophobic [only] when they are ready to accept the absolute and unequivocal equality of women" (p. 91).

Ultimately this drive to control, especially to control sexuality and human interrelationships, developed within Christianity as an ascetic spirituality utterly opposed to the body-affirming doctrine of creation (Collins, 1974, Ruether, 1972, cf., Fortunato, 1987). This persistent mind/body or spirit/body dualism in Christianity was not a novel conception, however. Christianity infused already dualistic Greek ideas with a parallel set of concepts already implicit in first century Judaism between ruhniut (the sacred or spiritual realm) and gashmiut (the profane world of the physical, of bodiliness); this dualism which cut across the Judaeo-Christian heritage and colored their combined influence upon western culture and thought both reflected and shaped a need to regulate and control unruly sexuality "because of its threat to the sexuality of men" (Plaskow, 1983b, p. 225). Satloff (1983) has even gone so far as to speculate that (heterosexual) men are constitutionally unable to synthesize secularity with spirituality, that for men there is an "irreconcilable split" between things physical, such as sexuality and bodiliness, and things spiritual (p. 200). Finding its fullest expression, then, in Christianity, this "irreconcilable split," this patriarchal need to polarize the "self" or the spirit from the world and the body, quickly led to categorization, to the polarization of the "self" from other persons. The accompanying hierarchical values clearly placed hetero-sexual, ascetic (hence sexless) men over against both women and homosexuals, who were more associated with sexuality (in childbirth or in promiscuity) and with the passions and the irrational (the uncontrolled). Indeed, private, individual sexuality became the heart of religious doctrines of sin and salvation, while so-cial injustice and social reformation were ignored by the patriarchally ensconced and ecclesiastically sanc-tioned status quo (Ruether, 1972).

In a religiously imbued culture increasingly based on sex-negative values, to refuse to accept the so-called structures of reality as normative for one's life, to celebrate sexuality or any of those aspects of life similarly disvalued, particularly in non-hetero-sexual (and non-procreative) ways, was/is to court dis-aster. Says Collins (1974), "To go against the order of society as legitimated by religion (to deny its cos-mic reality) is to make a compact with the primeval forces of darkness--and those who go against it are then seen as either evil or mad" (p. 56), or both. And Christianity at its worst has burned the evil, mad non-conformists both in full blaze at the stake (women, particularly witches) and slowly upon the embers and faggots (homosexuals, particularly gay men). Overall, patriarchy's disproportionate devaluation of human sex-uality not only led it to externalize, objectivize, and empty sexuality of spiritual meaning; it also led west-ern culture, and particularly Christianity, to be ob-sessed with the very sexuality it sought to stifle with asceticism and witch hunts. Moreover, Evans (1978) persuasively argues that systemic, structurally em-bedded patriarchy continues to,

> . . . teach that humans are superior to ani-
> mals [nature] and that "civilization" consists in
> getting as far away as possible from our animal
> nature. . . . When alienated from their animal na-
> ture [and hence, bodiliness and sexuality], people
> come to view it as evil, and then look for an out-
> side authority figure [or male god] to keep it re-
> pressed. . . . [Ultimately, this] objectification
> of nature . . . has resulted in the deadening of
> our feelings" (pp. 127-128);

it has undercut our very capacity for human(e) life.

It becomes increasingly clear that the narrow categorization of people and behaviors which has resulted from patriarchy and dualism, the restrictions and either/ors particularly of hetero- versus homosexuality, have diminished all human sexuality and undermined the fecund energies which nurture human relationships and which motivate human love and justice, the very stuff of humane existence (cf., Heyward, 1984). The sex-roles further devised by patriarchy, dualism, and homophobia interfere with the creation of genuine human relationships and justice in society. Heyward (1984) has insightfully described the resultant dilemma for women and gay people:

> The labels we use do not express, but rather distort, the most important things we can know and say about . . . human sexuality. . . .
> As a social structure, the heterosexual box intends to permit no androgyny . . . nor does it encourage us to cast off the burden of sex roles [since it] is built entirely out of sex roles. [Moreover, it does not allow for] real, mutual love between the sexes [or for any] support at all for mutual love between women or between men. (pp. 75, 79)

By making sexuality sinful, and by further confining sexuality to rigid gender roles and reducing its appropriate place solely to that of procreation, patriarchy has also severed sexuality from intimate human loving: "Our society has not cultivated in us the capacity to link sexuality and love, to relate caring for another to physical attraction to that person" (Doustourian, 1978, p. 335). Moreover, on its instrumentalist side, patriarchally procreative sexuality anachronistically ignores the problems of an overcrowded and nearly resource-exhausted world. More importantly still, it ignores the relationally enhancing power of sexuality as the expression of love and mutuality in relationships. It fails to acknowledge the possibility that human sexuality, as loving, pleasuring, humanizing, and empowering, is intrinsically valuable (cf., Doustourian, 1978, Heyward, 1984).

Overall, then, patriarchy has been a progressively dehumanizing force in the west, diversely branching into increasingly specific and restrictive dualisms which, like the tangled branches of a tenacious and deadly vine, have nearly choked the life from the original, created good of human existence. The progres-

sive development of sexism, heterosexism, and homophobia has occurred simultaneously with the delineation of
structures and categories which either include or exclude human types, but which utterly fail to account
for or to allow for, let alone foster and encourage,
the richness of human uniqueness and diversity. Moreover, as permissible relational styles, sexual behaviors, and gender roles have become more clearly and
rigidly defined, people have become increasingly alienated from other people, from themselves, from their
bodies, and from their sexuality: Sexuality has tragically become separated from human loving. The sexual
liberation of recent decades has not undone this fundamental alienation, and humankind remains particularly
conflicted as to the rightness, wrongness, or even sinfulness of human sexuality. We are so obsessed with
sexuality that we are blinded to larger issues of oppression and social justice (cf., Heyward, 1984). Fortunato (1987) has articulately described our dilemma,
our continuing alienation from the reality of our embodiment as human beings:

> At a subliminal level . . . many of us still feel
> . . . that it is somehow holier (purer) to be non-
> sexual; holier (more selfless) to pass up worldly
> pleasures than to enjoy them; holier (humbler) to
> deny oneself and submit to someone else--anyone
> else--than to exercise one's free will. . . . We
> remain a schizophrenic culture, constantly bat-
> tling some deep-seated sense of shame about what
> our bodies are and what they do. (p. 58)

In such a "schizophrenic" and life-denying culture, for which the inbreaking of AIDS seems only to
confirm the devaluation of human bodiliness and human
sexuality, it is not surprising that the challenge
which homosexuality represents--toward sex roles, toward dominance/submission, toward narrowly defined and
life-denying/love-denying sexual behaviors--is "profoundly subversive" (Goodman et al., 1983, p. 36). It
is also not surprising that a culture so restricted and
so defended would feel compelled to bring its fullest
energies to bear upon the tasks of opposing and op-
pressing "profoundly subversive" gay men and lesbians.
Indeed, the structures and dynamics of patriarchy and
dualism, of sexism, heterosexism, and homophobia, together shape the context in which we experience gay oppression as the grounding for theological reconstruction and social reformation.

(ii) Homophobia and Gay Oppression

The Hebrew term galut describes a community of
people in exile, and exile is the very concept which
encapsulates, for Fortunato (1983), the "gestalt" of
gay oppression, the "constant, chronic feeling of not
belonging, of being threatened and rejected," which
permeates our experiences as gay men and lesbians (p.
86). What is especially striking about our oppression
as gay people, virtually unlike that of any other group
in America today, is that the oppression of gay people
is not only firmly grounded in the structures of patriarchy which are intertwined in American consciousness;
gay oppression is also religiously sanctioned and le-
gally encouraged. Some 26 states still consider homosexuals as criminals, an opinion upheld by the 1986
Supreme Court ruling in Bowers v. Hardwick. Patriarchy's hold over us is truly "tyrannical":

> The withdrawal of full public legitimacy from a
> human being on the basis of minority status con-
> stitutes tyranny. The will of the majority, when
> it denies legitimacy and human rights to the mi-
> nority, is tyranny. What a tragedy it is when
> Holy Scripture is exploited callously and blasphe-
> mously to support tyranny and deny human worth in
> the sight of God. (Boyd, 1984, p. 147)

Legalized gay oppression, the legal tyranny over
the lives of gay men and lesbians, stems from and is
upheld by a blurring of the separation of church and
state, by the efforts of patriarchal legislators and
justices to enforce majority morality, a morality itself based upon some very poorly conceived theology.
Fox (1983), for example, writes that gay people have
been "a special victim of the fall/redemption spiritual
tradition. Indeed, all oppressed groups have been.
. . . This tradition begins its theology with [priva-
tized, usually sexually related] sin and personal
guilt. It has proven an invaluable tool for maintain-
ing the status quo," particularly regarding acceptable
sexual morality and behavior (pp. 191-192). Heyward
(1984) is even less constrained when she interprets the
peculiar synthesis of religion, morality, and social
values which patriarchy brings to bear upon gay people:

> It is not hard to know or imagine why homosexual-
> ity has been considered such an anathema. It is
> sexual. It is not in marriage ([the virtually

-36-

only, legally] legitimating parameter for sexuality). It is for pleasure in companionship rather than for the duty of procreation (sexuality's theological justification). Moreover, homosexuality is seen [as] orgasmic, wild, uncontrollable, hedonistic. It is viewed by men as men's attempts to be "like women" (read: sexual, physical, non-spiritual) and as women's attempt to reject men (read: that which is good). (p. 17)

Institutionalized religion, in collusion with popular morality and governmental sanction, has encouraged "hiddenness, shame, guilt, and broken lives" among gay people, while fostering a "false respectability," a double-standard as to what is sexually tolerable outside legal marriage as long as it is heterosexual (Boyd, 1984, pp. 81, 92, 120, cf., Morton, 1985).

The clear result of these combined forces is that long ago gay people, their lives, and their particular talents went underground. A community in exile, galut, shaped a subculture whose temples and town halls and social clubs became the gay bars and the mythic realm of the night, where/when gay people could dare to gather together for fellowship, mutual support, and yes, loving sexuality (cf., Clark, 1987a). Two brief decades of above-ground, daylit gay liberation have not displaced this particular center of our communal being. While we are increasingly open and visible throughout society and in the struggles both for gay rights and for an adequate public (governmental, social, and medical) response to AIDS, we still carry with us not only the memories but also the present realities of oppression. Many gay people are still ghettoized in urban neighborhoods and our subculture is still very much shaped by and consigned to spaces and times which are nonthreatening to our heterosexist oppressors. As a result, Altman (1987) cautions the gay community, and gay theology, that our lives and our thinking must avoid being too "inward-looking," too defensively ghettoized or gay-centered; he fears that our ghettoization, both literally and metaphorically at the margins, makes gay people, "too ready to accept unnecessarily limited ambitions" (p. 19). Boyd (1984) further explains this dynamic:

One can never speak adequately of homosexuality in American society without also considering the social atmosphere that encases and represses it. Many of the feelings and actions that appear to be

characteristic of homosexuality are in fact responses and reactions created and shaped by that
atmosphere. (p. 89)

Homophobia in church and state has shaped not only
the gay subculture, but gay self-understandings, behaviors, and styles/mannerisms as well. The swishing
sissy or the ultra-butch dyke pose no threat to a
heterosexual populace safely ensconced in their gender
roles; that the so-called "average" boy or girl next
door, or son, daughter, cousin, parent, might be gay is
truly discomforting. Of far greater concern for gay
theology is the impact of homophobia and ghettoization
upon gay interrelationships. While a consistent theme
in the writings of Carpenter (1910, 1919) and Hay
(1987) or throughout the poetry of Walt Whitman (cf.,
Moritz, 1987) suggests that by lying between the hierarchically opposed (heterosexual) opposites, gay people
can be more relational, mutual, democratic, and both
androgynous and non-classist, real ghettoized gay life
often remains hierarchical and exclusive. Mirroring
the patriarchy which circumscribes it, the gay subculture, among gay men at least, has frequently created
its own hierarchies of economic status, race, age, sexual style, and appearance. Rather than actually embodying the ideal possibilities of a "non-possessive
love" free of jealousy and/or a non-objectifying, mutually subjective relating (Hay, 1987, pp. 282, 286), the
sexually focused gay bar subculture, shaped as it has
been by heterosexual values and the heterosexual need
to control and bracket gay people, has often actually
undercut gay mutuality. Gay men, at least, have too
often sustained the love/sex dichotomy, treating both
self and others solely as sexual objects . . . until
AIDS. Hay (1987) elaborates:

The catalyst of spiritual crisis within the gay
movement has brought many gay men face-to-face
with the appalling dichotomy between, on the one
hand, the nurturing sensitivity and concern for
each other in a mutuality of sexual intimacy that
we all profess to be seeking and, on the other
[hand], the desolation and alienation from self
and from each other that more often takes place as
we make sexual objects of ourselves and each other
in pursuit of . . . expected behavior in bars and
baths. (p. 288)

Gay self-criticism, however, must be grounded not in self-blaming but in compassionate reflection and action. Our community's response to AIDS, for example, has taught us that we can transform gay baths into health centers and gay bars into gathering places which are more socially and communally mutual and less sexually objectifying. We can realize with Boyd (1984) and Clark (1987a) our need for gay spaces on the margins of heterosexual acceptability as the physical location both of our celebrations of gay life and of our launching our liberation struggles, as from the Stonewall Inn in 1969. Moreover, we can reflectively penetrate the patriarchal structures which maintain our ghettoization and (re)learn to nurture non-competitive and non-self-loathing gay mutuality (cf., Altman, 1987, Heyward, 1984). Before his death, Goodstein (1985), for example, ventured to suggest that many of the problems which gay people have with being gay emerge in the spiritual struggle with the essentially religious roots of popular morality and legal restrictions, a struggle dominated by a sense of sexual shame which results because we assume that we are breaking biblical and traditional commandments, which we still imbue with authority, and not just secular laws. This shame maintains our closets and paralyzes our capacity for action. In collusion with our gay ghettoization, the biblical authority/shame/closet structure, when still accepted at any level by us, perpetuates itself and enables both religious and civil oppressors to retain their power over us.

Blaming the victim, holding gay men and lesbians responsible for homophobia and/or gay ghettoization (or, conversely, for "flaunting" our gayness), is another tool of heterosexism which is just as powerful as religious and legal restrictions, just as dehumanizing as our confinement to marginalization or exile safely at bay in the ghetto and in the night, just as demoralizing as our socialization into shame, guilt, and powerlessness before oppression. Moreover, it "lifts the legitimate burden of guilt and responsibility from the backs of those with the social and political power to cease the victimization" (Heyward, 1984, p. 207). Earlier in her text, Heyward (1984) again addresses victim-blaming, speaking prophetically both to and on behalf of gay men and lesbians:

I do not say that we choose whether or not we are loved. We do not choose to be loved, and this is a critical moral distinction. For we are not re-

-39-

sponsible for the un-love that comes our way. We
are not responsible for the injustice that is done
to us. We are not responsible for others' failures to love us, themselves, or others. In other
words, the victim of injustice is not to be
blamed, and please hear this well. For this blaming of the victim is a moral outrage. (p. 187,
last emphases added)

A mandate comes through the social, legal, and religious restrictions upon our being and our lives,
through the analyses of Altman (1987), Boyd (1984,
1987), Goodstein (1985), and Hay (1987), and through
the prophecy of Heyward (1984), which demands both that
we analyze and understand our oppression as gay people
(cf., Clark, 1987d), and that we must move from that
understanding to speak prophetically, to theologize.
    Fortunato (1983) asserts that oppression is simply
"what gay people face when they are authentic," when
they are honest with themselves and, certainly, when
they are honest with others (p. 87). Early in the process of gay self-awareness, oppression includes self-
denial (the denial of one's homosexuality), religious
doubt (the seeming irreconcilability of gay identity,
homosexual behavior, and one's spirituality), and the
consequent guilt and senses of unworthiness, loneliness, and fear of disclosure (the closet) (Fortunato,
1983). Once an individual is identifiable as gay, oppression broadens to include a wide range of experiences, first among which is the potential loss of a job
or the denial of one's right to practice his/her pro-
fession, including any consequent financial frustra-
tions. Job security and the hope for advancement dissolve as one is ignored, passed over, or worse, never
even allowed admittance to the professional system
(such as with the church or academia) (Fortunato, 1983,
Goodman et al., 1983). Goodman et al. (1983), for example, have argued that "jobs that are available to
lesbians and gays are primarily blue collar or service-
oriented. Middle- and upper-class jobs are not easily
available to openly gay people (p. 43, emphasis added).
Similarly, Fortunato (1983) goes so far as to speculate
that openly gay people "fall into the lowest national
income categories" (p. 81). The combination of sexism
and homophobia clearly consigns a large percentage of
gay men at least to jobs which have traditionally been
reserved for women; the gay men in such jobs are, accordingly, devalued and paid as women and not as "real"
competitive and productive males. The myth of "gay

disposable income" is just that, the privilege of a
minority of (usually closeted) gay men.

In addition to impaired economic survival, and unlike other minorities, openly gay people often experience rejection and avoidance by their natural familial
support systems, which in turn encourages gay ghettoization (cf., Fortunato, 1983, Dunkel and Hatfield,
1986). Even in the relative "safety in numbers" of an
urban gay ghetto, however, gay oppression still includes incidents of verbal and physical abuse (anti-gay
violence) and the absence of (secular or ecclesiastical) legal protections. Gay people enjoy no legal protections: Gay sex is still criminal in 26 states, making any public display of affection acceptable for
heterosexuals utterly taboo for gay people; gay aliens
may be denied entry into the U.S.; gay parents may lose
not only custody of, but even visitation rights to,
their children; and, all gay people are subject to police harassment and, when anti-gay crimes are reported,
often find themselves punished (blaming the victim) and
their attacker(s) set free: "Gays are assaulted, confined to jail, forced into psychiatric 'treatment,' and
even murdered--all for simply being gay. 'Queer-bash-
ing' is a popular sport" (Goodman et al., 1983, p. 13,
cf., Fortunato, 1983). Moreover, gay and lesbian couplings enjoy no legal or financial benefits, no social
support, no tax breaks, no spousal insurance benefits,
no public ceremonies to hallow our relationships. Gay
partners cannot "marry," "divorce," or bequeath with
any assurances. Same sex couples may even experience
difficulties in finding housing or tolerant landlords.
In a society which so stresses the value of (heterosexual) nuclear families and which consequently eschews
gay promiscuity, this lack of support for and sometimes
outright hostility toward gay couples, gay "surrogate
families" (cf., Clark, 1987d), is especially reprehensible. Goodman et al. (1983), for example, explain
that "the need for secrecy makes it difficult to build
and maintain good loving relationships. Secrecy vastly
increases the complications and problems of being intimate. . . . It adds insult to injury, then, when
[heterosexuals criticize] the frequency with which our
relationships may be broken" (p. 13).

Thusly marginalized or "exiled" (Fortunato, 1983),
gay people are forced into the frustrating position of
trying to nurture and sustain self-worth and self-
esteem while confronted with both religious exclusion/
condemnation and the absence of legal protections and
social structures. We must learn to love ourselves and

others "in the face of utter rejection" by a society steeped in heterosexual (usually white, male) values (Fortunato, 1983, p. 18). Simply by virtue of being gay or lesbian, gay people must not only give up attachment to what might have been but wasn't; we must also let go of what the present and the future might have held but now will not (Fortunato, 1983). This constant state of embattlement by a surrounding, homophobic society feeds self-denigration and internalized oppression. The constant losses and constant fear are "wearing, draining, and demoralizing" (Goodman et al., 1983, p.13). Moreover, "that gay people must expend greater energy to accomplish traditional goals [in the face of so many obstacles] is a constant drain upon energies which could be directed toward the achievement of other goals badly needed by our society, our communities, and ourselves" (Uhrig, 1984, p. 101). The constant drain of homophobic rejection, of shame and self-hatred, coupled with the seemingly endless obstacles against full actualization of our human potential, deflects gay/lesbian energy from efforts at genuine social change. Gay theology must, therefore, be an active participant in the processes of re-valuing gay and lesbian selves, of affirming gay and lesbian self-images and gay and lesbian couplings, and of freeing gay men and lesbians from "the cracks" of ghettoization, in order to free and to nourish the energies needed for liberation (Goodman et al., 1983, pp. 56, 100).

(iii) Oppression and Gay Spirituality

Fortunato (1983) further indicates that by penetrating or going through our senses of oppression, grief, and anger as gay people--by going deeper--we can ultimately discover and touch our spiritual grounding, our wellspring of compassion, empathy, and empowerment (cf., Morton, 1985). Because gay people are all too painfully aware that "justice does not always triumph and evil is not always punished" and that "life is seldom fair and even less frequently rational" (Fortunato, 1983, p. 55), gay men and lesbians must work through denial and bargaining (the closet), and through anger and depression, to achieve genuine self-acceptance. We must grieve both the trivial and the not so trivial losses, all those situations and opportunities in the past, present, and the future which have been and are and will be denied to us, simply because we are gay or

lesbian in a homophobic, patriarchal society (Fortunato, 1983, cf., Clark, 1987d). Says Topper (1986),

> . . . Gay and lesbian persons need to look
> into themselves and grieve the fact that life is
> not fair to them. . . . This grieving, if it has
> been done properly, facilitates and encourages the
> gay person to a deeper level of life, a deeper
> meaning system, a deeper set of values, indeed, a
> deeper spiritual existence. (p. 57)

Once we are able to push past our suffering, to touch
and express our anger, to grieve our losses, and to realize that, as gay people, we have no secured future,
we may then discover with Fortunato (1983) that God's
presence is revealed not in heterosexual acceptability,
but in the depths of grieving gay/lesbian losses and of
transcending oppression here and now, and that we can
thus embrace our outcast status, our marginality, our
exile.
    By "taking life as it comes," by confronting and
not denying the "pain that life includes," and by doing
our grief work as gay people, we are freed to move on
(Fortunato, 1983, pp. 56, 107). We can discover God's
presence in both our anger and our grief; we can use
our very experience of oppression to heighten our
"spiritual receptivity" (Jung, 1954); and through this
process, we can discover both the spiritual and communal empowerment for moving on, for living in "radical
participation" (Heyward, 1984) in the present processes
of liberation. Working through our sense of oppression
enables us not only to revalue and to accept our good
gay and lesbian selves and our sexuality in the present; it also enables us to reclaim our personal (and
our corporate) past, retrospectively accepting the
givens of our lives and choosing to relinquish those
things from which we were/are/will be excluded. According to Fortunato (1983), moving from passive victimization to an assertive, self-emptying place on the
margins can open us to both the inner peace and the empowerment of having (re)discovered our wholeness as gay
people and the rightfulness of our place in the cosmos
and with God:

> In order for gay people to get to a place where
> they can love in a world that rejects both their
> loving and giving, they first have to embrace a
> consciousness that transcends the society that re-
> jects them as misfits, a cosmic wisdom that com-

prehends the oneness of the universe in which the
gay person inexplicably "belongs." . . . Once you
know, at the core of your being, that you have a
rightful place in God's creation, that nothing can
separate you from the love of God, then it doesn't
matter what people say or do to you. Then you are
free to give and love--anyway. (p. 40)

Gay men and lesbians can transcend oppression by confronting and not denying our losses; we can be empowered by the energies of grief and anger to claim
God's presence in our midst, to celebrate our gay-
selves, to struggle together for justice, and therein
to assume our prophetic and reforming roles (Fortunato,
1983).

From our deeper and broader self-acceptance and
our deepened spirituality, gained through confronting
gay oppression, we learn indeed that "the God of the
bible . . . is biased in favor of the anawim [the op-
pressed]. . . . It is . . . in the space of oppression
where God is to be heard" (Fox, 1983, p. 195). We
learn that all of creation, with all its great diversity including homosexuality, is good (Topper, 1986).
We also learn to be aware of and to assume appropriate
responsibility for the "masks," the roles, which we assume under heterosexism and homophobia; and, in "naming
the demons," we are able to set aside those roles, to
be freed from them (Boyd, 1984). So freed, and empowered by God's companionship with us and advocacy for
us at the margins, we are also able to develop a more
inclusive compassion not only for ourselves and for one
another, but for other marginalized and struggling
people as well (and ultimately even for our oppressors). Says Boyd (1987), for example, gay people are a
"broken people who understand the brokenness of others"
(p. 79). Shurin (1987) similarly elaborates:

This is our spiritual occasion: That we are a
people who define our identities by the fact of
love. In calling ourselves gay we say that love
is central, and after the shame and guilt, and yes
after the anger, love remains a word we can speak
unabashed while others cringe at its too-telling
power. (p. 259)

We can, furthermore, exercise our creativity and our
greater willingness to risk experimenting with life options otherwise precluded by patriarchy and heterosexism. We can nurture our deepened spirituality and

meaning systems and insist upon celebrating life and
human sexuality in the very midst of rejection, suffering, and oppression (Topper, 1986, cf., Fox, 1983, Morton, 1985).   We can create our own defiant wholeness
and, from our grounding in cosmic self-acceptance, tap
the energies needed to fuel our quest(s) for justice.
    However, there is yet another wrinkle in the
fabric of our experiences of gay life and gay oppression. For gay men in particular, there is yet another
challenge to our efforts to analyze our oppression and
to develop psychological and spiritual wholeness.   The
cosmos has thrown a monkey wrench into the machinations
of our survival as gay people in an already heterosexist, homophobic, sex-negative, and life-denying culture: AIDS.   Acquired Immune Deficiency Syndrome.   A
virus which is blind to right or wrong, to goodness or
badness, and to gender and/or sexual orientation, the
fact that some 70% of cases to date have been gay men
notwithstanding.   And our homophobic and heterosexist
culture has responded to AIDS by coming down harder
still upon the gay/lesbian community.   The inbreaking
of AIDS has redoubled gay oppression.   Consequently,
while the slow processes of coming to understand gay
oppression, to nurture gay spirituality, and to articulate a gay theology might have proceeded in ways little
different from feminist analysis or liberation theology, the reality of AIDS suffering, death, and grief
in our community, coupled with renewed homophobia and
anti-gay violence--as if these and not safer sexual
practices or a speedier medical resolution could protect self-righteous, AIDS-fearing heterosexuals--places
everything we do in a different perspective.   It adds
another layer to our oppression text and it will shape
our theology in ways which will differ from feminist
and other liberation theologies.   Our particular minority experience of human injustice is further complicated by the random cruelty of the cosmos and our realization of God's limitations in tragedy.

(iv) AIDS and Redoubled Oppression

    Morton (1979) has remarked that "modern religious
structures function . . . to evade death" (p. 162).
Indeed the dichotomizing force of the western "fall/
redemption spiritual tradition" (Fox, 1983, p. 191)
separated spirituality from all things bodily, at once
blaming our human embodiedness for sin and mortality
and consigning only our spiritual essence any hope of
immortality.   The ensuing development of eschatological

hope was thus shaped by a negation of all things physical, including human sexuality, which was sublimated to a sexless, disembodied, male spirituality. The eschatological concept of salvation became increasingly individualized, displacing historical and social visions and imperatives, and the idea of a personal, spiritual, and hence disembodied existence for eternity came increasingly to displace the realities of human mortality (Ruether, 1983a, 1985, cf., Fortunato, 1987). Rejecting and devaluing the mortal body in favor of the eternal, immortal spirit further led Christianity at least to associate the life-giving sexuality of women (and ultimately all sexuality) not with life, but with death. Devaluing sexuality (and thereby all unabashedly sexual people) became a means for avoiding human embodiment and mortality:

> Eschatological hope has been related to an alienation from and disappointment with bodily life and its processes [e.g., sexuality]. . . . In seeking [immortality], eschatology has also tended to despise . . . merely finite processes [sex, birth] . . . not as symbols of life [and renewal] but as symbols of death. Sexuality [has] become despised as [an indicator] of a sinful life whence comes death. (Ruether, 1985, p. 224, cf., p. 162)

Ruether (1983a) thus writes that the "rejection of sexuality . . . or, rather, antisexual asceticism is itself based on the fantasy that, by escaping . . . sexuality . . . one can also free oneself from finitude and mortality. The escape from sex . . . is ultimately an attempt to escape from death" (p. 144). The additional link in western religious thought between sexuality as the heart of sinfulness and sinfulness as the cause of/the reason for human mortality, as a divine punishment for sexual "sin," has widened the gulf between sexuality and spirituality and thus further damned those people who insist upon being sexual. To be sexual, according to this tradition, particularly in non-heterosexual and non-procreative ways, is to choose bodiliness, sinfulness, mortality, and death over the hierarchically "higher" values of eternal, spiritual life. Ruether (1983a) thus responds, "We must question the [heterosexual] male theology of . . . sexuality as the cause of sin, and mortality as the consequence of sin. This very effort to sunder us from our mortal bodies and to scapegoat women [historically, and all gay people, particularly gay men today] as the cause of

mortality and sin is the real sin" (p. 152). Patriarchy's "real sin" is further manifest in a viscious
circle whereby the social and religious condemnation of
gay people, particularly of gay men, has historically
so undermined gay self-esteem and self-worth as to com-
pel many gay men to seek personal confirmation in ex-
cessive or compulsive sexual gratification, which in
turn placed them increasingly at risk for AIDS and
hence at risk for further social and religious condemnation (Shelp, Sunderland, and Mansell, 1986).

By being sexual, sexually different, and even sexually promiscuous (unmonogamously and unrigidly and un-
regimentedly sexual), lesbians, and gay men in particular, are naturally seen by this tradition as the most
arrogant rejectors of "higher spirituality" and thus
already as corrupt death-bringers, a view strongly re-
inforced by AIDS devastation in this particular community. In the present tragedy of AIDS, this tradition
of dualism and hierarchical values, of eternal spirituality and disdain for sexuality and bodiliness, blames
those who are suffering and dying of AIDS for their
dilemma. AIDS appears to justify blaming the victim,
albeit "this blaming of the victim is [really] a moral
outrage" (Heyward, 1984, p. 187). Shelp, Sunderland,
and Mansell (1986), for example, have realized that
"the faceless threat of AIDS to people is personified
in gay men. As a result, fear and anger about AIDS
[gets] translated into fear and anger toward gay men"
(p. 7). Moreover,

. . . because of the stigmas attached to the
disease and the primary at-risk populations
. . . there have been few expressions of sympathy
or compassion by people who claim moral and political leadership in the United States. Instead,
people with AIDS are said to deserve their diseases. Public support is undermined and the work
of people who provide care is disparaged as a consequence. The situation is unconscionable . . .
and lamentable. (Shelp, Sunderland, and Mansell,
1986, p. 179)

Fortunato (1987) further elaborates on the ways in
which non-procreative, pleasured sexuality, death, and
AIDS have been linked in the popular, religiously based
consciousness to justify the increased oppression and
scapegoating (blaming) of gay people, particularly gay
men and gay people-with-AIDS (PWAs):

-47-

> Living embodied . . . means that you must always
> deal with death lurking in the shadows. . . .
>   There is a sense in which gay people have al-
> ways represented mortality to the world: deeply,
> darkly, archetypally.   Since in our sexuality we
> are patently non-procreational, we intimate death
> to people. . . .
>   And now we who are gay [gay men at least]
> . . . have been linked in the public's mind with a
> frightening, mostly fatal disease. . . . It has
> made us expedient scapegoats, because we and AIDS,
> and especially the synergistic combination, remind
> a society bulwarked against death of their inevi-
> table ends. (pp. 80, 81)

Gay liberation theology, as a result of the combined
force of AIDS and anti-gay AIDS-phobia, must confront
not only the imposed suffering and human injustice of
heterosexism, homophobic persecution and anti-gay
scapegoating and violence; it must also wrestle with
physical, natural suffering and dying (tragedy) and
reach some understanding about death and about God's
limitations in tragedy and death (theodicy).   It will
have to account for and bless our grief (cf., Clark,
1986a) and our own constant confrontation with mortality and death.   It will have to examine not only the
experience of gay oppression, but the ways in which
AIDS functions to redouble that oppression.
     Fortunato (1985) emphasizes the numerous fears
which AIDS adds to our experience of gay oppression,
particularly for gay men for the immediate future--our
fear of already having AIDS as we await symptoms to appear or a diagnosis to be pronounced; our fears regarding the limbo uncertainty of AIDS-related complex
(ARC); our fears about the physical process of AIDS itself; our constant grief and fear and guilt as survivors, and as survivors who might have passed the virus
to our friends, lovers, and partners in the early years
before we understood safe-sex practices; and, finally,
our fear of AIDS-phobic, homophobic hatred and anti-gay
violence (cf., Shelp, Sunderland, and Mansell, 1986).
Of the latter fear, Fortunato (1985) says,

>   . . . AIDS is terrible to live with also be-
> cause it makes us painfully aware that there are
> tens of thousands of people "out there" who hate
> us, who are overjoyed about AIDS, who are chuck-
> ling as we are dying; tens of thousands of fine,
> upstanding American citizens who are rooting for

> the virus that is killing us. Even worse . . . we
> are being blamed by many for every case of AIDS
> that develops in the "straight" community. One
> result of this scapegoating is that "fagbashing"
> has increased at an alarming rate. . . . In the
> long run, the unleashing of such blatant homopho-
> bia may be the most damaging effect of this insid-
> ious disease. (p. 6)

The admixture, then, of AIDS-phobia and homophobia in
the popular consciousness not only confronts gay men
with the very real prospect of having to adjust to a
terminal condition at some not too distant point; it
also revives all the pain of the processes of self-dis-
covery, self-acceptance, and self-disclosure (Stiles,
1986). Because AIDS reconfronts gay men with the entire spectrum of gay oppression, whatever equanimity
with himself and the world a gay man may have achieved
regarding his gayness is severely threatened by AIDS
and AIDS-phobic homophobia.

The practical ramifications of combined AIDS-phobia and homophobia are such that "many of those with
AIDS lose their jobs, their friends, their lovers,
their living quarters, their insurance, and, in a number of cases, medical care and preparation of their
bodies for burial" (Howell, 1985, p. 483, cf., Shelp,
Sunderland, and Mansell, 1986). They may also experience further isolation from or utter rejection by their
families, as they are abandoned to die among strangers,
or conversely, they may discover that their well-mean-
ing families have excluded their gay friends and lovers
from access to the processes of caring and grieving for
them (Shelp, Sunderland, and Mansell, 1986). Gay PWAs
are confronted both by this irrational, victim-blaming
behavior toward them and by their own self-blaming,
whenever they accept the sometimes subliminal and sometimes blatantly explicit social and religious condemna-
tions of their sexuality and of their very lives, their
very value as human beings, while they are simultaneously confronted by the pain and physical wasting of
each new symptom, each new opportunistic infection, by
the pain and discomfort of medical treatments, and by
the sheer hopelessness and terminality of AIDS, which
now carries a 96% mortality rate for cases diagnosed by
1981 (Fortunato, 1987). So burdened, gay PWAs need to
die with dignity and not grotesquely, to die surrounded
by friends and loved ones and not alone, to die assured
of the value of their lives both here and now, as well
as after their deaths (Fortunato, 1987, Shelp, Sunder-

land, and Mansell, 1986, cf., Clark, 1987d). They need to pursue the whole dying process and its various stages as gay men and as gay PWAs for whom the doubling of oppression in a homophobic society makes them different from any other non-gay, non-AIDS terminal patient (Clark, 1987d).

For those of us who are as yet survivors, our fears and uncertainties, our grief and guilt, are further complicated. To our fears regarding our own exposure is the added pain of hearing, often weekly, of another friend who has been diagnosed or who has died. In our twenties, thirties, and forties we are constantly confronted with the ongoing loss of our peers, an experience more developmentally appropriate for adults seventy and older, or for men in combat. We are surely battle-fatigued. And, when we lose friends or even a lover, our grief itself is often frustrated. Because our sexuality is outlawed and our relationships unprotected by law, we often have no forum for our grief. We are frequently excluded from the funerals of our loved ones by families and parents who are themselves struggling, perhaps for the very first time, with both a son's homosexuality and a son's AIDS. Because in the popular consciousness an AIDS diagnosis is virtually a declaration of homosexuality, families and newspapers hide the cause of death with euphemisms; we cannot even claim our dead in order to mourn them. And, finally, an alarming number of Americans favor quarantine or internment for PWAs, for persons-with-ARC (PWARCs), for HIV carriers (the HIV virus is the putative cause of AIDS), and even for persons merely suspect (read: all gay men), an isolation which would be life-long insofar as HIV infection or "mere suspicion" remains incurable (Rowland, 1986). Like Jews in Nazi Germany or Japanese-Americans here in the 1940s, our redoubled oppression as gay people, because of both AIDS-phobia and homophobia in society and in government, may find its ultimate expression in our total and utter dispossession as human beings. History should remind us all that but a short distance lies between the concentration camps of "protective custody" and the machinations of extermination, of (gay) genocide.

Writers such as Fortunato (1985) insist that even in the dismal gloom of AIDS-redoubled gay oppression, the possibility of spiritual deepening nevertheless remains alive. AIDS has shaped the gay community, and gay men in particular, into a people of increasing compassion, of response and caring. The gay communities, both gay men and lesbians, were the first to form

agencies to minister to the sick, the first to lobby
for increased funding for AIDS research and care, the
first to teach pastors and churches how to care, how to
minister to PWAs and PWARCs (Clark, 1986a, 1987d, Fortunato, 1987). AIDS is focusing for us a theologizing
which is our praxis, strengthening our "thirst for justice" and sharpening our rage at the heartless ones who
claim AIDS is God's punishment and who are happy at gay
deaths. Says Fortunato (1985),

> . . . I have come to know in my guts that the
> anawim [the oppresssed] deserve justice. It is
> our God-given right. And the onus of moral re-
> sponsibility for its provision is on everyone's
> shoulders except the oppressed.
> . . . The bottom line is this: God favors
> the outcast. The anawim nestle especially close
> to God's bosom. (p. 9)

AIDS has, for example, clarified our need and our demand to bless and sanctify gay couplings as redemptive,
nurturant, intrinsically good relationships and not
merely as convenient, monogamous forms of disease control (Fortunato, 1985). AIDS has also underscored the
need to nurture gay spirituality, apart from apologetics, and to develop a gay liberation theology which
affirms and celebrates the plurality and variety of
God's creation, including the full spectrum of human
sexuality, as good (cf., Fortunato, 1985): "Gay people
have much to teach organized religion about uncondi-
tional love in openness and vulnerability, the truth of
human diversity and reality, and the nature of God as
the Creater of diversity, the Lover who created life"
(Boyd, 1987, p. 83).
    AIDS has, clearly, forced us to raise significant
questions for the activity of theology. Heyward
(1984), for example, stresses the empowerment of loving
relationships, wherein sexuality is active, in her own
gay-sensitive feminist theology. How, then, can we
stay in touch with our sexual power-in-relationships,
or in community, in the face of AIDS? Has AIDS, or increased monogamous coupling, or "safe sex" changed or
diminished our sexual power? Can we celebrate sexuality, can we love apart from a rigid, AIDS-phobic mono-
gamy (albeit prudently and safely), and still (re)claim
the bonding power, the prophetically motivating power,
of our sexuality amidst AIDS, AIDS-phobia, and homophobia? Can we still, can we again, insist upon the unqualified, intrinsic goodness of non-procreative sexu-

ality as the expression and source of love, pleasure, empowerment, and God's co-delight, over against the hatred and judgment which AIDS has evoked? It is especially crucial, now more than ever, that we do so. Moreover, our very raising of these and other questions, as we with open eyes penetrate our experiences of gay oppression and reactionary AIDS-phobic redoubled oppression, and our beginning, however partially, to respond theologically to these questions and to care for our suffering friends, indeed constitute the birth of that activity which can become a gay liberational reconstruction of Judaeo-Christian theology.

*   *   *

* A Theological Reconstruction *

IV. Reconceptualizing God

(i) God and Gender Duality

Both women and gay people experience oppression
under patriarchy because its hierarchy of dualisms de-
lineates gender roles which narrowly prescribe certain
activities and sexual behaviors and which rigidly pro-
scribe others. As "not-men," both women and all gay
people are thereby devalued. This systemic structure
both shapes and is shaped by and sanctioned by western
religion. The very images and symbols of both Judaism
and Christianity reflect and sustain dualism, particularly the male/female dichotomy. Because Judaism focuses upon liturgy and prayer and not, traditionally,
upon the development of systematic theology, as has
Christianity (Janowitz and Wenig, 1979, cf., Christ and
Plaskow, 1979), Jewish feminists in particular have become increasingly concerned about this relationship of
gender to our images of and language about God.[8] While
realizing that God in godself clearly transcends sexuality and gender, these women are aware of both the selective and partial nature of language and the significant and powerful impact of religious symbols upon human existence (Plaskow, 1983b). Geller (1983), for example, asserts that how we think about and image God
affects both our self-reflection and our ways of responding to others. Because language "controls reality," shaping how we "conceive and perceive" the world
(Satloff, 1983, p. 191), masculine images of God and
masculine language in liturgy combine not only to describe God's nature, but also to justify "a human community which reserves power and authority to men" (Plaskow, 1983b, p. 228). Elsewhere, Plaskow (1983a) elaborates:

> Male language has effects, both political and psy-
> chological: socially and personally, it accustoms
> us to male power in society and makes this power
> seem inevitable and right. . . .
> If the image of God as male provides religious
> support for male dominance in society, then the

image of God as Supreme Other would seem to undergird dominance of any kind. God as Other can become the Holy Warrior who . . . sanctions destruction of peoples perceived as Other. . . . God
. . . easily becomes the head of a vast hierarchy.
(pp. 4, 6-7)

Jewish feminists have thus perceived the ways in which
patriarchy with its attendant hierarchy of dualisms has
shaped language itself to sustain those very dualisms
and values by which women (and gay people) are devalued
and excluded: "The maleness of God is not arbitrary.
. . . It leads us to the central question . . . of the
Otherness of women" and of anyone not heterosexually
male (Plaskow, 1983b, p. 227).

Christian feminists have similarly realized that
religious symbols have "both psychological and political effects, because they create the inner conditions
(. . . attitudes and feelings) that lead people to
. . . accept social and political arrangements that
correspond to the symbol system" (Christ, 1979b, p.
274). The worship of a male god, or of God through exclusively masculine symbols, legitimates the "political
and social authority of fathers and sons in the institutions of society" (Christ, 1979b, p. 275), thus sustaining patriarchal hierarchies which oppress those not
at the top, those people designated as Other, as not
heterosexually masculine (cf., Morton, 1985). Morton
(1985) even contends that such "images function powerfully long after they have been repudiated intellectu-
ally" (p. 46). Consequently, even with very abstract
conceptualizations of God, images can survive which enable people to function on two different and even con-
tradictory levels simultaneously. Abstractions may
still inadvertently be linked to God as "he" or "him"
(Daly, 1979a). Gay theology must take this whole ana-
lytical process one step further: Masculine images for
God not only reinforce male superiority in society and
religion; they also reinforce heterosexism. Traditional understandings of masculinity polarize gender
and sexuality and thus exclude "unmanly" gay men and
"unladylike" lesbians. Clearly, gay people and gay
theology must join both Jewish and Christian feminists
in the tasks of wresting "linquistic control from men"
and thereby of reconceptualizing God (and reality) in
inclusive ways (Satloff, 19

Changing the ways in   but this flattens the   od and
conceptualize our religious   experience of gay men   rn the
ways in which liturgical l   ⟍   shapes
                               women/lesbians
                                               see 57.

our thinking, can be a first theological step toward a prophetic corrective. Changing language and images about God and faith may better enable us to seek justice, to reevaluate roles, and to transform patriarchy (cf., Geller, 1983). Plaskow (1983a), for example, has acknowledged that "while changing imagery may not catalyze structural change, structural change may be impossible without a change in imagery" (p. 6); moreover, "when we cannot imagine tampering with the symbols that have come down to us, our image of God has become idolatrous" (p. 13). Changing our imagery and language, however, must not entail a simplistic rejection of our heritage without our first having some alternatives: "Symbol systems cannot simply be rejected, they must be replaced. Where there is not any replacement, the mind will revert to familiar [oppressive] structures at times of crisis, bafflement, or defeat" (Christ, 1979b, p. 275). Our efforts toward change must be firmly grounded, therefore, in our theologizing from the experiences both of our oppression and of God's presence therein. We must articulate a "concept or image of God that we can affirm and that makes sense of our experience" both individually and as a people, a community (Plaskow, 1983a, p. 9, cf., Umansky, 1982).

We will need to develop, therefore, a greater sensitivity to qualitative differences between those inherited concepts of God and the divine/human relationship which are oppressive and those "which encourage self-actualization and social commitment" (Daly, 1979a, p. 57). We will want to employ as a criterion of selectivity an understanding of God which encompasses the "relation between personal empowerment and participation in an inclusive cosmic power and the social locus and reference of this sense of energy" (Plaskow, 1983a, p. 11). We will want to recognize and nurture our capacity and responsibility for acting in and transforming the ongoing social order, aware that "we experience that power as rooted in participation in God" (Plaskow, 1983a, p. 11). Reimaging or reconceptualizing God thus becomes "not just politically important but spiritually essential . . . to a recognition of the importance of language in conveying the [religious] conviction that men and women are made in the image of God" (Umansky, 1985, p. 439).

Both men and women, both masculinity and femininity therefore, must be included in our new understandings of God. However, to transcend the dichotomy by eliminating human gender (or even human sexuality) from our concept of God, would simplify our task at the cost of depersonalizing God. We must therefore struggle both with moving beyond identifying God as male and with retaining a theistic or personal understanding of God. In fact, our western or Judaeo-Christian religious heritage would make little or no sense to us without the "metaphor of a divine person in a covenant relationship of mutual responsibility and love with human persons" (Gross, 1983, p. 236). We are caught between our anthropomorphic (and gender-polarized) understandings and images of God as living, relating, and personal, and our realization that "the metaphor of a gender-free person is impossible" (Gross, 1983, p. 236, cf., Fackenheim, 1968, Christ and Plaskow, 1979). Gross (1979) encapsulates our dilemma:

> I am convinced that [Judaeo-Christianity] is theistic through and through and that theism--the view that the absolute can be imaged as a person entering into relationships of love and responsibility with humans--requires anthropomorphism. But I am equally convinced that images of a male person without complementing images of God as a female person are both a mirror and a legitimation of the oppression of women" (p. 168),

. . . and of gay men and lesbians. The inherent problem with our need for anthropomorphisms, in other words, is our humanly entropic tendency to slip back into comfortable, patriarchal, and oppressive forms (Christ, 1979b). Says Geller (1983), for example,

> . . . Jewish tradition recognizes that God is not male. To limit God . . . is idolatrous; God is understood by tradition to encompass [and to transcend] both masculinity and femininity.
> . . . But given the constant [male] references to God in . . . prayer . . . and given our childhood memories of imaging God as an old man . . ., it is no surprise that to the extent [we] do conceptualize God in human terms, [we] often think of God as male or masculine. (p. 212)

Consequently, because we must think of God in personal and hence anthropomorphic terms, in spite of the partial and incomplete nature of such language and images, we need very self-consciously to balance masculine and feminine terms, images, and attributes, to assert the feminine whenever we assert the masculine (Gross, 1983). We must also remind ourselves, however,

that images and metaphors for God do not capture, contain, or limit the reality of who God is and what God
does. When the metaphorical power of images is lost
and the images are reduced to literalisms, the focus
upon the metaphor itself instead of upon what it signifies becomes idolatrous, as in patriarchal, literal
fundamentalisms in both Judaism and Christianity. We
must remember that ultimately all our religious expressions, images, and metaphors say more about the people
using them, than about God. To unreflectively assume
or revert to the latter is always idolatrous (Gross,
1979). Thus, as Gross (1979) continues, to retain a
theistic concept of God as a personal, relational energy, as a co-suffering and intimate companion, "the
best we can do is to attempt to keep our anthropomorphisms from being idolatrous and oppressive. The only
way we can simultaneously retain [personal God lan-
guage] and overcome the problems of exclusive male God
language is by adopting female forms . . . in addition
to male forms" (p. 172). Our discourse about God becomes a balancing act, holding human gender in tension,
and our understanding of God becomes increasingly androgynous.

To avoid reinforcing male dominance and heterosexist superiority with our religious language--to approach a truly balanced or androgynous discourse--we
ultimately need to move beyond all simplistic either/
ors. Merely displacing a male god with a goddess will
not do (cf., Morton, 1985). Goddess language, for example, still "reckons the holy in sexist terms" (Morton, 1985, p. 151) and thus only underscores the idolatrous nature of assigning gender to the divine, whereas
an androgynous god who unites in godself all genders,
gender attributes, and sexualities avoids/transcends
idolatrous linguistic limitations (Umansky, 1982). Be-
sides its tendency toward idolatry, absolutizing female, matriarchal God language is also not liberating
because it only serves to reverse, and not dissolve,
(hetero)sexism. Morton (1985), for example, has com-
plained that,

. . . too many women in the Goddess movement
[still] see the Goddess as "out there" or "up
there"--all powerful and all loving. In other
words they perceive with a patriarchal mentality
which does nothing but make a matriarchy the opposite of a patriarchy structurally and function-
ally. The authoritarian ruler has only changed

sex but the authoritarianism has yet to be exor-
cised from one's consciousness. (p. 217)

To avoid such a simplistic and equally oppressive reversal, Fiorenza (1979) has insisted that "language
about God has to transcend patriarchal as well as matriarchal language and symbols, while at the same time
employing a variety of human expressions to reflect a
pluriformity of human experiences" (p. 139).
 The process of restoring a balance of masculinity
and femininity to our conceptualizations of God ultimately requires not displacing one with the other, but
complementing each with the other (Umansky, 1984, cf.,
Gross, 1979, 1983). It requires a "sexually dimorphic"
language and image system which acknowledges both the
limits of language and the fullness of God, and which
does not threaten monotheism, but which rather enhances
our concept of God (Plaskow, 1983b, p. 229). Our understanding of God will no longer be narrowly and idolatrously heterosexually (or sexlessly) male, but will
include/embrace a spectrum of gender and sexuality and
not just a polarization of these (cf., Plaskow, 1983b).
McLaughlin (1979) has even discovered a limited historical precedent for such a "sexually dimorphic" or bisexual understanding of God. The writings of both
Christina of Markyate (twelfth century CE) and Julian
of Norwich (fourteenth century CE) describe God as nurturant mother as well as father/king and disclose the
"androgynous character of the transcendent" (p. 105):

 A result of this grounding of God language in the
 life of women as well as men was an opening up of
 metaphor and naming that broke through the andro-
 centric and patriarchal tradition to a vision of
 God as mother, nurse, nurturer, and midwife as
 well as father, king, and lord. . . . The realm of
 the transcendent included . . . a Mother/Father
 God, at least in certain corners of the tradition.
 (p. 104)

 Like Morton (1985), however, Ruether (1983a) also
warns against using this historical precedent to develop only a simplistic fusion or grafting of female
imagery to male imagery. Balance is not achieved if
our images only vascilate between stereotypes: "God/
ess language cannot validate roles of men or women in
stereotypic ways that justify male dominance and female
subordination. Adding an image of God/ess as loving,
nurturing mother, mediating the power of the strong,

sovereign father, is insufficient" (p. 69). Like
Fiorenza (1979) and Morton (1985), she is concerned
that female language alone is no more liberating that
male language alone, and, furthermore, she rejects any
image, male or female, which makes God a parent and
thus prolongs "spiritual infantilism as virtue" and
makes autonomous self-assertion a sin (Ruether, 1983a,
p. 69). The wedding of feminine and masculine imagery,
therefore, must move beyond mere balancing, beyond the
precedent of Christina and Julian, toward a synthesis
which eschews both paternalism or maternalism for ma-
ture human liberation.[9] Consequently, in reclaiming
feminine aspects and language for God and in uniting
these images with masculine images, both feminist theology and gay theology must (re)create a genuinely androgynous or bisexual language for theology, religion,
and spirituality which facilitates a genuine synthesis
rather than a simplistic balancing of gender, and which
thus moves theology beyond gender duality. We must,
for example, conflate our senses of God as transcendent
and God as personal--to avoid projecting God as Other--
realizing in the synthesis that the "androgynously
transcendent" God is intimately, bisexually/multisexu-
ally/pansexually personal in our horizontal relationships. We are invited to a "participation in being"
(Daly, 1979b) which embraces all gender and all sexuality as well.
    To reconceptualize God as including both genders,
as androgynous or bisexual, points beyond the importance of mere gender for God language to the importance
of sexuality itself for theology. Gender role dualism
developed not only to delimit male and female behaviors, but to control human sexual interaction and interrelationships as well (cf., Morton, 1985). Gay liberation theology must insist not only that an all-encompassing inclusivity of genders is important for our
understanding of God, but also that loving, caring, orgasmic sexuality should be held together in psyche and
mythos, in theology and spirituality, with wholeness,
nurturance, independence, and creativity. To restore
sexuality to conceptions of God further extends the
process of affirming people, especially those people
marginalized for their gender (women) or for their sexuality (gay people) (cf., Clark, 1987a). In seeking
just such an inclusivity of both sexuality and gender
in our discourse about God, Green (1983), for example,
contends that men need the feminine and that women need
the masculine elements in religion. He insists that
our human search for intimacy, tenderness, and warmth

in religious experience, "our capacity for love, surrender, or passion" vis-a-vis religion (p. 251), cannot
be adequately described in male or in sexless terms:
"There is no way, without turning to images of the feminine, or without thinking of [sexually intimate] relationships . . . that most men can express the degree of
love, passion, and warmth that the spiritual life may
arouse in them" (p. 250).

Gross (1983), however, is also astute to the ways
in which sex-negative values--the patriarchal divorce
of (mortal) human embodiment and (immortal) spiritual-
ity--make us reluctant to sexualize God: "The rejection of sexuality as an acceptable religious symbol is
. . . connected with fear and rejection of our embodied
condition. . . . Because we are embarrassed by our own
sexuality, we reject it as a suitable symbol for deity"
(p. 245). Because sexuality entails our physicality
and our mortality, a reunion or coincidence of opposites in our reconceptualization of God--one which sees
male/female, spirituality/sexuality, and life/death as
one and which accepts human (and even divine) limits--
restores sexual/spiritual wholism and frees sexual imagery to be used for God. New images of reconciliation
"with ourselves, our bodies, our limits" frees both God
and people from the confines of patriarchy (Gross,
1983, p. 246). Reuniting and transcending both genders
in an androgynous, pangendered, or pansexual conceptualization of God thus leads to a reunion of sexual, be-
havioral polarities, which in turn begins a process of
dissolving/reconciling all the dualisms which oppress.
We discover that our understanding of God is no longer
narrowly and dualistically idolatrous, but that it continues to open, to broaden, and to include the fullness
of God's limitless being.

Indeed, the ongoing struggle, particularly in feminist theology, to reunite masculine and feminine linquistic and conceptual opposites still reflects/sus-
tains a basic polarity whose terms (male/female), even
if equalized, remain a tension of and not a unity of
opposites. The effort is still grounded in heterosexist distinctions of gender and sexuality (cf., Morton,
1985). Reconceptualizing an androgynous God who truly
embraces, blesses, expresses, and is embodied in all
possible forms of sexuality, gender, and gender-role
mixing more thoroughly answers the dilemma. Green
(1983), for example, insists that God is utterly beyond
all duality and polarization and suggests that we can
exchange our notions of a static male god, or even of a
bi-polar god, for a "dynamic, multifaceted, ever-flow-

ing, separating and uniting, new kind of ten-in-one monotheistic deity" (p. 255). The tension, then, is clearly not within godself, but between a pluriformity in deity and our human dualistic anthropomorphisms: "Must we not rather say that we are at once male and female in relating to God, who is him/herself at once male and female, both of them inadequate metaphors to describe the mysterious self beyond all gender, . . . all distinctions, but lacking none of the passion" (p. 259). As "mysterious self," God remains personal, and, as pangendered and pansexual, God is not genderless or sexless. Daly (1979a) similarly advocates relinquishing all dualisms which posit God as Other and moving in our reconceptualization toward a God of empathy will all oppressed peoples.

Gay men and lesbians, in particular, as those people defined as intermediate, as third gender, as between and therefore as threatening to rigid polarization, need to insist in our theologizing that neither God, nor people, nor genders and gender roles, nor sexuality need be dichotomized at all. Both/and is possible. Gay embodiment in fact reflects and embodies/incarnates the divine coincidence or confusion of opposites. Our theological language can then move to reflect mutuality, fulfillment, and human potential across and including all separations of gender, class, culture, race, and religion (Fiorenza, 1979). Our spirituality and theology would then,

> . . . enable all kinds of people to affirm themselves as whole human persons, chosen and loved by God, and partaking in the divine reality. Moreover, such . . . spirituality would empower all of us to take on responsibilities for eliminating discrimination, oppression and . . . sexism and for building a new community of mutuality and pluriformity which would [reflect and participate in God's presence, energy, life, and love]. (Fiorenza, 1979, p. 140)

With Ruether (1983a), we can reject mother/father, female/male, matter/spirit dualisms for a language of God as redeemer, as liberator, as the "source of being" who "fosters full personhood" for gay men and lesbians and for all oppressed peoples (p. 70). God becomes the grounding for our embracing both our physical, material existence, as bodies, and our creative potential, as spirits. God becomes revealed, manifest, not in opposition, but in healed and harmonious relationships with

our bodies, with other people, and with the earth itself (Ruether, 1983a). Images of God which contain and
confuse all opposition can help us to balance not only
masculinity and femininity, but life and death as well,
defusing the dualistic hope in otherworldliness and divine rescue and enabling us to accept both our human
limits and finitude as well as our human responsibility
(Gross, 1983). They can displace male/female duality
in God by combining God's transcendence with God's relational covenant with us, with God's intimate and liberating justice and mercy on our behalf (Christ and
Plaskow, 1979, Gross, 1983). Gross (1983) in fact suggests a number of images which blend and cut across
gender polarities: God can be at once strong and
trustworthy, exerting every effort on our behalf, while
also being a nurturant creator and caretaker. God can
be sexually fecund and orgasmically creative. And, God
can be teacher and mediator, a "giver of wisdom and pa-
tron of scholarship and learning" (p. 245).

As gay and lesbian people bringing our particular
experience(s) of oppression into dialogue with feminist
thinkers in the shared tasks of liberation and theology, we realize that the relationship of gender dualism to our conceptions of God extends far beyond the
limitations of English pronouns to affect all the other
names, titles, attributes and images for God which also
need balancing and/or reconstruction. Thus, we will
want to reinforce and sustain the value of certain images developed and/or rediscovered and resanctified by
feminist theology, while also working to contribute
further to the process of developing new images for God
which move liberation theology farther beyond the confines of gender duality. We can insist that God is not
only androgynous, but that God is androgynous in the
broadest possible, pangendered sense; that God is not
only bisexual, but that God is pansexual. God embraces
in godself the entire spectrum of gender and gender expression, of sexuality and sexual expression. God is
inherently sexual and fecund (orgasmic, creative, aesthetic), and gay men and lesbians represent valuable
and divinely loved embodiments of the pluriformity of
the divine nature (cf., Boyd, 1987). Thus neither genderless nor sexless, our God is intimately personal, a
co-suffering advocate of the marginalized and a co-suffering companion with limited powers to rescue us from
tragedy, but with an infinite capacity to empower us as
we assume responsibility for responding to tragedy and
for creating justice. God is a limited and yet empowering companion whose own sexual and creative urge is

toward human responsibility and healthy, mutual relationships between godself and people, between people
themselves, and between people and the earth (cf., Heyward, 1982, 1984). God is a nurturant companion with
us in oppression and tragedy who, through us, stands in
strong judgment upon hatred and oppression (Clark,
1986a).

God's role as both a personal companion and a
ground of empowerment, both of which transcend gender
polarities and embrace all human sexuality, has become
most clear for us who are gay men and lesbians in the
present tragedy of the health crisis of AIDS within the
gay male community. While AIDS is not exclusively a
gay men's disease syndrome and while our compassion
must include all who are suffering, dying, and grieving, AIDS has struck our community the hardest. It has
in many cases been the catalyst for our praxis of response and caring as well as for our theologizing. By
confronting AIDS head-on, by wrestling with tragedy as
well as with human injustice, gay theology assumes the
responsibility and the opportunity for synthesizing
theodicy with gender concerns, in the hope of achieving
not just an appropriate "tragic vision" (Rubenstein,
1966), but a deeper, broader reconceptualization of the
God of all human liberation.

(ii) God and Human Tragedy

Among Jewish feminist theologians Umansky (1982)
has suggested that one way of moving theological language beyond gender duality and the patriarchal hierarchy of polarized values which it entails is to speak of
God as both/and, as both strong and weak, as both good
and bad: While God is not responsible for specific
evils, God is somehow ultimately responsible for the
fact, the reality, that evil exists at all. She consequently encourages us both to relinquish our customary
notions of God's absolute goodness and unlimited power
and to reconcile our revised beliefs about divine goodness and power with the reality of evil. Whether a god
who is responsible for evil in any sense is still a
worshipworthy god remains unclear, however. The reality of evil and the problem it thus poses for theology
(theodicy) is a major concern for other contemporary
Jewish thinkers as well. Both Rubenstein (1966) and
Fackenheim (1970), for example, wrestle with the con-
tradiction inherent in a heritage which bespeaks God's
proactive powerfulness in history, particularly within
Jewish history, and a contemporary memory of six mil-

lion senselessly murdered under Nazism. An all-powerful and all-loving God who nevertheless allows the mur-
derous tyranny of a Hitler to reach such proportions
makes no sense: "How can one believe in a providential
history and still take seriously the vast evil which
occurs in it?" (Fackenheim, 1970, p. 5). Although
Judaeo-Christianity has traditionally acknowledged the
realities of human injustice (e.g., in Jeremiah) and
even of disease and death (e.g., in Job), Auschwitz and
Hiroshima are so overwhelming in their evil, human suffering, and death as to pose a serious threat to the
notion of a god powerfully and mercifully acting in
history (Fackenheim, 1970).

     Neither Fackenheim (1970) nor Rubenstein (1966),
consequently, is willing to hold God responsible, in
any sense, for such overwhelming evil in history.
Rubenstein (1966), for example, develops a "tragic
vision" or "tragic wisdom" which asserts both "the in-
evitability of pain and evil, along with real moments
of joy and fulfillment, as long as life continues" (p.
220). Eschewing otherworldly, escapist eschatology, he
goes on to say that "we have nothing to hope for beyond
what we are capable of creating in the time we have al-
lotted to us. Of course, this leaves room for much doing and much creating" (p. 221). He has clearly
shifted the onus of responsibility for both evil and
good from God to people. His "tragic vision" entails a
god who is a compassionately involved, justice-seeking
and -demanding energy, and yet a god who is also
limited in power and who therefore suffers his/her
limits by sharing human suffering both in tragedy and
in the painfulness caused by failed human responsibility. What might be read as despair or cynicism in
Rubenstein's (1966) work, therefore, is not a denial of
God, but an utter denial of God as primarily judge or
rescuer. It is a loud assertion of the importance of
human responsibility to seek and to create justice and
quality of life. Mourning the "death of God" becomes,
for him, a metaphor for our experience of the anxiety
involved in both the loss of our human innocence and
the assumption of human responsibility which Auschwitz
and Hiroshima have forced us to confront and to accept.
Hitler is responsible for the six million. Those individuals who failed to intervene responsibly and those
persons who forfeited integrity for safety as accom-
plices are responsible. Meanwhile, God died with those
who died in the camps, God suffered with those who were
tortured, and God grieved with those who suffered the

loss of loved ones because of failed human responsibility.

The fact of AIDS, however, the reality of the deadly HIV virus attacking the immune systems of thousands of people, the majority of whom in America have been gay men to date, is not in itself a matter of human responsibility. No individual is responsible for the existence of the virus or for the way it wreaks its havoc within the body. If the notion of a god all-powerful in history is destroyed by Auschwitz, Hiroshima, and human hatred (whether antisemitism or homophobia), then the notion of a god benevolent in nature is also meaningless in the face of AIDS, human suffering, and death. God must not be limited just by the extent of human responsibility or its particular failure. And yet, as Fackenheim (1970) cautions us, resolving theodicy--whether in the face of human injustice (Auschwitz) or in the face of nature's cruel imperfections (AIDS) or in view of the simple reality of suffering and tragedy as a common factor in all human experience --must keep God active and present in human experience, even if this means reconceptualizing God once again, not only to allow for human responsibility, but also to acknowledge additional divine limitations and co-suffering. All else threatens to make God as meaningless as suffering is tragic. Indeed, the present reality of AIDS confronts gay theology with the challenge to go beyond the work of Rubenstein (1966), Fackenheim (1970), and Umansky (1982) and to articulate a co-suffering God who is not only intimately bound up in human decisions, but who also suffers both human injustice and natural evil, with us in the here and now of our experience.

The outbreak of AIDS and its devastation, particularly within the gay male community, has long been a theological issue as well as a medical dilemma. While the Religious Right has repeatedly pronounced AIDS as God's judgment upon both homosexuality and a gay-permissive society, we have watched our vital and heretofore healthy lovers, friends, and acquaintances suffer and die. As we continue to wait impatiently for the medical, political, and social systems to resolve the dilemma, we are forced to confront our pain, our mourning, and our human need for meaningfulness, as well as our fears and our own mortality. We reconsider our notions of life beyond death (cf., Fortunato, 1987), aching because eternal life or reincarnation cannot undo the premature shortening of this life for our dying loved ones. We wonder as to God's involvement,

God's position, in this crisis. We seek both to understand the AIDS crisis theologically and to learn how to respond appropriately to it on all its various levels (Clark, 1986a, 1987d). A number of writers from both Judaism and Christianity, in addition to Rubenstein (1966) and Fackenheim (1970), have addressed the dilemma of affirming God's radical goodness in the face of very real suffering or evil. Hartshorne (1948), Cobb (1965, 1969), and Sherburne (1966) have worked with the "process philosophy" of Whitehead (1926) to develop a philosophically precise resolution compatible with Christian teaching, while Kushner (1981) has synthesized personal insight and Jewish thought to confront a real human tragedy, the death of his fourteen-year-old son.[10] A synthesis of process philosophy and Kushner's (1981) insights can enable us to develop a theological perspective on AIDS and all human tragedy, a perspective which also broadens and deepens our efforts to reconceptualize or reimage God for gay liberation theology.

Kushner (1981) begins his reflections on theodicy by examining four unsatisfactory responses to the question of why essentially good people suffer. All of these assume that God is the source or ultimate cause of evil as well as of good, while attempting to salvage a traditional understanding of God as simultaneously all-loving, all-powerful, and totally in control of the cosmos. All four of these responses are equally unsatisfactory responses for either the AIDS crisis or gay liberation theology. The first response is the assumption that we deserve whatever we get, that God is primarily a cosmic judge who confers divine rewards and punishments in perfect correspondence to individual sin (Kushner, 1981). The Religious Right has best exploited this particular belief. Since the Right assumes that homosexuality is grossly sinful, they virtually applaud the AIDS crisis as a form of divine retribution upon gay people (cf., Fortunato, 1985). Because the threat is so grave (30% of persons-with-AIDS are not gay) and because evil must be controlled or circumscribed lest the presumed righteous also fall victim, the Right must rationalize such tragedy to exclude themselves from its effects.

There are clearly a number of problems with this view. It encourages the kind of self-blame and self-hatred with which gay men and lesbians have been contending for decades. It undoes gay liberation's efforts to enable gay people to accept and celebrate themselves. Coming from outside the gay community,

such assertions also function to "blame the victim,"
adding condemnation to the pain of AIDS-suffering and
AIDS-death (cf., Kushner, 1981, Heyward, 1984). Unable
to accept the burden of guilt, yet endorsing this role
of God as a cosmic judge, a sufferer may find himself
or herself hating God for the unfairness of such "punishment," thus alienating himself or herself from spiritual sources of compassion and only increasing one's
sense of guilt (Kushner, 1981). Similarly, a person-
with-AIDS who endorses such a theological view might
choose to shift the blame to sexual partners, also
alienating himself or herself from human sources of
compassion. A final problem with this response to suffering is that is simply does not fit reality. Our
common sense experience demonstrates that good is not
always rewarded nor evil punished. Innocent children
die, and a god who could make a child suffer to punish
a parent is exploitative and morally reprehensible
(Kushner, 1981). It is simply a reality that justice,
cosmic or earthly, does not always prevail, especially
for those who are marginalized and socially outcast, as
gay people are (cf., Fortunato, 1983).
    The second response assumes that there is some
"big picture," a divine purpose, scheme, or aesthetic
by which suffering makes sense to God even if it is beyond human understanding. A merely aesthetic god who
could exploit the pain of innocent individuals (as with
AIDS) or groups (as with the Holocaust) for some scheme
to which the human contributors are never privy is more
reprehensible than a judging god. Less even than some
notion of cosmic justice, the divine aesthetic or a
cosmic plan can never justify an AIDS-death (cf., Kushner, 1981). The third response, that suffering is a
divine teaching device, is no more satisfying and
equally exploitative. No lesson can justify the extent
of human suffering and tragedy; many people fail such
testing or are broken by tragedy. The dead certainly
cannot learn (Kushner, 1981)! Although gay men may be
learning about safer sex and deepened relationships, we
would gladly forego our newly gained insights to have
spared thousands of lives. Moreover, whatever wisdom
we gain is meaning and interpretation applied after the
fact. It is a response to, neither an explanation of
nor a justification of, the AIDS crisis. Finally, the
wishful thinking involved in the hope/promise of divine
justice and restitution beyond death, whether in eternal life or in a future reincarnation, cannot compen-
sate for the pain and death we experience in the only
reality we actually know (cf., Fortunato, 1987). Life

after death cannot undo the foreshortening, whether by AIDS or any other tragedy, of young lives. That potential is forever lost. Moreover, such otherworldly belief too often only serves as an excuse for ignoring present pain and for evading present responsibilities (Kushner, 1981, Heyward, 1984).

Human nature seeks understanding here and now, not hereafter. If AIDS is not divine judgment nor part of some cosmic scheme, if the tragedy is too grave to justify testing or to await eternal clarification, then the haunting "why" lingers. God's power and God's goodness (as mercy, love, justice) and the essential value of creation (the worth of every life, including that of gay people and persons-with-AIDS) remain in apparently unresolvable tension. Kushner (1981) has wisely discerned a resolution nevertheless, couched in the literary art of the anonymous editor/writer who took a legend about God's and Satan's wager, an innocent suffering man (Job), and three would-be comforting friends, and then added to that his own interpretation, the voice of God in the whirlwind.

The book of Job is a metaphorical description of the conflict involved in trying to affirm simultaneously three incompatible theological propositions, one of which must eventually be rejected (Kushner, 1981): (a) God is totally absolute and all-powerful. (b) God is all-good (-loving, -merciful, -just). (c) Creation, and hence people, are essentially good, as affirmed in the Genesis narratives of creation. The text affirms both Job's innocence, faithfulness, and righteousness, as well as the reality of the complete devastation and physical pain which he suffers. The tradition queries if indeed he is innocent, why such tragedy? In their efforts both to keep evil non-threatening and controlled and to defend God's absolute power, Job's would-be comforters reject the third proposition, Job's goodness and worth. In terms of the four responses, they assert that Job must have sinned, and/or that if he is being tested, his anger at God indicates failure (hence, another sin!). Their own condemnation is added to Job's losses and pain. Job is a blamed victim. Job, on the other hand, knows he is innocent and upright and also assumes God's all-powerfulness. He therefore rejects the second proposition, God's goodness. After all, God has been initially portrayed as a gambling compatriot of Satan. God is the all-powerful, divine schemer whose cosmic plan is unrevealed to Job or to anyone. Such a god is whimsical and irrespons-

ible, a tyrant who is outside the "limitations of justice and righteousness" (Kushner, 1981, pp. 40-41).

The Job-writer could not accept either of these
solutions and ultimately rejected the first proposition, God's absolute power. He subsequently added the
portrayal of God's coming to Job in the whirlwind to
the materials of the original legend. God does not di-
rectly address Job's questions here, but the blustery,
boastful demands as to Job's presence at creation
thinly veil a divine vulnerability. God essentially
inquires of Job, could he do any better? God is doing
everything possible for goodness and justice in the
cosmos; could any person in God's place do any better?
The Job-writer thus affirmed both divine goodness and
human worth, while challenging traditional understandings of divine power. If God is all-good and suffering
is real, God's power must be limited (Kushner, 1981,
cf., Ewing, 1976).

This conflict between concepts of divine goodness
and power and the realities of suffering is primarily
the result of a (patriarchal) theological dualism which
has alienated God from creation. Consistently, the insistence that God is an all-powerful and all-good creator, who brings forth an essentially good creation from
nothingness, has required a doctrine of fallenness to
account for evil. "The fall," however, makes mere humanity (or worse, one woman) responsible for the en-
trance of all evil (human and natural) into the entire
cosmos. Moreover, a serpent-Satan and a mysterious
tree have been necessary, additional props to explain
how an originally good humanity went bad. Another,
negative ingredient (evil) has continued surrepti-
tiously to insert itself into the good ingredients
(God, cosmos, humanity) of creation. This unavoidable
element which shatters the purity of our creation
mythology (and which we currently experience as the
pain, suffering, and grief of AIDS-death) points toward
a fundamental problem with the initial dualism upon
which the entire structure has been built.

Perhaps instead, both creator (God) and creation
(creative material) are together from eternity. Since
creation is actually portrayed in Genesis as the verbal
ordering of chaos rather than as an activity ex nihilo,
we may even biblically understand that God and chaos
are co-eternal. God and creation are one, a yin/yang,
two sides of a unitary cosmic coin. Just as creative
energy and malleable chaos are one, so the energies for
wholeness, beauty, variety, and harmony, and the entropic forces of resistance, fragmentation, and death, are

-71-

united in a singular, dynamic tension. God and evil are also co-eternal, yin and yang. The cosmic system itself simply exists and is, therefore, morally neutral. Such an understanding enables us to see that while God may be independent of the particular results of creation, he/she is not able to be not creating. Since God must create, he/she needs creation. From this divine need also springs God's loving, healing relationship with that creation with which he/she is co-eternally bound. Creation and humanity can thus no more divorce themselves from God than God can separate godself from creation.

Furthermore, a genuine relationship cannot exist where one partner has absolute, coercive power. The divine/human relationship, therefore, also entails limitations upon divine power, creaturely or human freedom to relate, to love, or to respond, and a divine capacity to be intimately affected by the other partner(s) in relationship (cf., Heyward, 1982). Divine power is thus not tyrannically coercive, but persuasive and nurturing, limited to allow creation's response. While God's basic ethical purpose is absolute (an urge for cosmic good, for the best creative possibilities to be realized in every instance), God is also capable of appropriate response; we do affect the divine nature. God can experience an increase in joy or be a co-compassionate presence in suffering. He/she is present in pain, seeking good, although he/she cannot eliminate the cause of that suffering.

This portrait of a limited god is not one with which we are at first satisfied. This is not what we think we want God to be like. We want God to be all-good and all-powerful, to reward, punish, and rescue us from pain. We want God to be a deus ex machina who swoops in to save us. And, somehow, we expect divine judgment as to when and where rewards, punishment, or rescue are appropriate to correspond with our personal values and judgments. In actuality, however, the variety of human values and the narrowness of human judgments and prejudices make this both impossible and undesirable. More importantly, if God were absolutely powerful, then wise, caring, or prudent choices, or acts and feelings of love, would all be a sham, because they all require freedom. If God were an all-powerful rescuer, we would be mere automatons offering empty emotions and actions to a tyrant who allowed no other choices; we would have forfeited responsibility for moral choices and compassionate actions in exchange for unquestionable judgments and security. Seen in this light, an all-powerful god is no more desirable to us than it was for the Job-writer.

As we are able to relinquish our dubious demand for a deus ex machina and begin to accept God's intimate interrelationship with creation instead (his/her capacity to be affected by creation and to respond appropriately), we realize how much more worshipworthy is a limited god who shares our joys and pains than would be (or could be) any tyrannical cosmic rescuer. As Hartshorne (1948) has said, "A wholly absolute God is totally beyond tragedy" (pp. 149-150). Such a reconceptualized understanding of the divine nature, therefore, not only has the potential to change much of our thinking about pain and suffering, but it also "defends God" much more adequately than Job's friends, because it relieves God of the burden of being the source or cause of tragedy. Nevertheless, when we are faced with tragedy, with the suffering and senselessness of an AIDS-death, for example, we still ask "why?" If neither God nor the limits of human responsibility is the answer, we may turn to the cosmic system itself to demand response, "why is there evil at all?"

As our explorations shift from considerations of the divine nature to an examination of the cosmic tension of good and evil, we want to seek ways of understanding evil's reality without forsaking God's continuing importance for us in our present experience (cf., Fackenheim, 1970). Kushner (1981) thus compassionately asserts that, as hard as it often is to accept, some things just happen for no reason. There is randomness in the cosmos. The cosmos is a balance, an interplay of good and evil which is simply reality, and we cannot (any more than Job could) reorder the cosmos. The harshness of such reality is qualified, however, when we realize that this randomness also affects God (cf., Kushner, 1981). If the divine energies are always directed toward the maximum good for every creature in every instance, in spite of the risks of evil, then randomness affects the extent to which the divine will is effective. Moreover, as an influenceable and responsible intermediary between opportunities (good) and risk (evil), God also experiences every outcome and seeks, as appropriate response, to meet every influence or occasion of evil with counter-influences for good.

If creation is in fact the evolutionary and never completed ordering of chaos (not creatio ex nihilo), and if God and chaos are co-eternal and united, then "pockets of chaos remain," according to Kushner (1981, pp. 52, 66). "Randomness" is thus another name for "chaos," for the entropic stuff of creation which is free not to respond to the divine creative urge. It is the opposing inertia in the unitary (monotheistic) tension with divine energy from which cosmic dynamism springs. "Randomness" or "chaos" is evil for humankind because of our awareness of pain, our capacity for suffering, and the ways in which these combine to alienate us from God's goodness, co-suffering, and empowering presence. The inbreaking of random chaos, humanly experienced as tragedy, simply happens. It is that "aspect of reality which stands independent of [divine] will, and which angers and saddens God even as it angers and saddens us" (Kushner, 1981, p. 55).

If creation and cosmos are so far from perfect completion, we may further wonder why sentient creatures who could be aware of pain and who could so suffer emerged when we did. Cobb (1969) has argued that cosmic movement or process (God and the chaotic, creative material together) entailed a necessary progression toward biological life and death, human existence and sentience, experiences of greater intensity and harmony, and spirituality and moral values. If God had failed to elicit human life on earth when he/she did, the opportunity and its potential for good might have been lost forever. From the divine perspective more freedom and less control (persuasion rather than coercion) has allowed a richer spectrum of valuable, good experience to occur. More freedom and the absence of coercive control means that the risk of evil, the risk of inbreaking chaos, is also proportionately greater. The reality is that freedom, possibility, responsibility, and all the positive values and experiences of human history on this planet have been possible because of this non-coercive process and at the risk of evil or inbreaking chaos (cf., Cobb, 1969). This is the best cosmos possible, given the balance of possibility (good) and risk (evil); nevertheless, randomness/chaos still exists while God does all he/she can do on behalf of good (and all he/she ought to do short of becoming a tyrant) in every instance. Moreover, while God may have "a hard time keeping chaos in check and limiting the damage that evil can do" (Kushner, 1981, p. 43), he/she also shares not only the risk(s) of evil, but also both the good and the bad of human experience. God is also a co-victim of chaos and of tragedy.

With specific regard to the AIDS crisis, we need to realize that our bodies are also subject to randomness. Like the larger cosmos, our bodies are equally a mixed blessing, a mixture of possibility and risk. As physical, sentient beings, we can enjoy creative thought, compassionate love, and the wonder of sexuality. Bodiliness, gay/lesbian being, and sexuality are wonderful gifts, even if physical existence is constantly at risk of things without and things within. In our sexual behavior, as in all other things, we take the risks (of sexually transmitted diseases and of AIDS) because of the potentially greater goods of sexual fulfillment and of loving and being loved. Limiting our risks with safe-sex practices, or even losing the gamble of risks, does not invalidate the worth of the sexual love and human compassion that a person has experienced. The harsh reality of AIDS does not invalidate the basic worth of gay or lesbian being as one of the various forms of human life which God elicited, sanctified, and celebrated from chaotic sexual possibilities.

Having a friend's or one's own life cut short is tragic in terms both of the pain of dying and of the loss of future possibilities in human interaction. But a life's premature ending does not undo the value of the life that has been lived. We must remember and hold onto the good of all these lives; this is also a part of what God is and does. The past with all its joys and sorrows is retained in the divine nature and affects God's continued creative interrelationship with us. Stimulating AIDS research (and its ultimate benefits beyond AIDS) and motivating us to reappraise our sexual and relational styles of behavior are a part of the divine appropriate response. Safer, more caring, and more responsible sexual behavior, deepened and more committed relational patterns, and any resultant medical discoveries are not, however, reasons which justify AIDS; AIDS simply happened. These are, however, all parts of the divine/cosmic process of transmuting present evil into future good.

Kushner (1981) again qualifies reality's harshness. Nature, he reminds us, "is morally blind, without values" (p. 59). Viruses have no consciences and natural or biological laws cannot discriminate between good and bad people; nor, given divine fairness, can God choose whom to favor with immunity to those laws or whom to rescue. More, rather than less, chaos would result if either of these were the case. The mixture of randomness and the AIDS virus, of risk factors and natural laws, simply makes some of us susceptible and some of us not; it simply leads some of us to exposure and precludes the exposure of others. We can lessen our risks, but neither sickness nor health are matters of divine judgment on what we deserve or some part of a divine scheme; again, AIDS simply happened.

If cosmic randomness and not God is the source of the AIDS crisis, persons confronted with this tragedy may nevertheless turn to God as one source of help. Unfortunately, the realization that God is not a rescuing deus ex machina may initially lead the suffering individual not to an awareness of divine compassion, but to an awareness of God's limitations. Our human consciousness of tragedy and AIDS-death, coupled with our awareness of the absence of a rescuing god, leaves us empty. Added to our suffering is our grief over the loss of a parent-god or a rescuer-god. In our pain we cry for refuge and feel ourselves answered by silence, by seeming divine impotence (cf., Kushner, 1981). Fortunately, however, our Judaeo-Christian heritage does not leave us in this painful vacuum. Fackenheim (1970), for example, agrees with Kushner (1981) and with our own experience of tragedy when he reiterates that neither the concept of human sin/responsibility nor notions of God's mystery, hiddenness, or limitations are alone sufficient in the face of catastrophe and tragedy. He goes on to remind us that our tradition also asserts that, in the supreme crises wherein people experience God's absence or god-forsakenness, God is actually lamenting with those who are suffering. Our heritage remains open to God's presence "even in times when the actuality is only a memory and a hope" (p. 43). Moreover, if God is neither judge nor rescuer in the midst of tragedy, then God is also not responsible for either our suffering or our rescue. Our grief at divine absence can be slowly transformed into a sense of relief that, having freed our conception of God of those notions which alienated us from divine companionship (omnipotence, judgment), we can now turn to God for comfort, compassion, and the empowerment for appropriate response (cf., Kushner, 1981).

Although we may want to relinquish personal control to seek rescuing security in divine intervention, we are confronted with reality. Our friends have suffered and died. We fear our own AIDS-related suffering and death. We may not like reality, but we are not given an alternative. The difficult task is not to allow randomness, evil, or death to destroy our faith in God's intentions, presence, and compassion. Suffering in this sense does test faith and may transform our religious understandings, but God is not the cause of, nor is he/she responsible for, the testing situation. If we can relinquish our theological misconceptions, we are thereby freed to realize that God's love is borne from his/her need for creation, his/her interrelationship with creation, and his/her desire for the good. God is not indifferent to our pain, but shares our frailties, weaknesses, and suffering. Because he/she is a co-victim, God's love is compassion, understanding, empathy, and ultimately, the energy for transforming and transcending tragedy. God is a supportive, strengthening companion who is in fact most present in our deepest experiences of god-forsakenness--at Auschwitz, in AIDS-death, and in silence. Unable to be a vertical deus ex machina, God is a horizontal presence of empowerment for victims of tragedy and for victims of exclusion and marginalization. God's own anger at tragedy and injustice, and his/her compassion, are clearly on the side of the victim (cf., Kushner, 1981, Heyward, 1984).

God's own anger and grief at tragedy and injustice, God's compassion for the sufferer and the victim, become increasingly important for those of us struggling with AIDS in our community and in our theology. Heyward (1984), for example, reminds us that liberation theology is "thoroughly a theology . . . in which God's goodness, love, and justice can be experienced in the context of God's powerlessness" (p. 110); moreover, "God does not bless, sanctify, and glory in suffering. . . . God empowers us toward our release from suffering" (p. 194). God is not absent in tragedy; God is actually the grounding of our empowerment to assume responsibility both for providing care for those who suffer and for seeking justice on their behalf. God undergirds our capacity to bear each other up with empathy and compassion, enabling us "to realize and claim our power to effect good, our capacity to make a positive difference, our co-creative ability" (Heyward, 1982, p. 159). Struggling to resolve theodicy, to understand where God is in natural tragedy, ultimately brings us back to the reflections of those who have struggled with God in the tragedy of failed human responsibility. God is as limited by "random chaos" as he/she is by human freedom and responsibility. And yet, God is not absent, either; human action and human response-ability are the location or locus of God's activity in history (Fackenheim, 1970). God's present empowerment, in addition to divine co-suffering companionship, lies in the hope for redemptive change which is embodied in responsible actions which stand in judgment upon those present structures of injustice which blame the victim of tragedy or injustice: "God's power is ours--to the extent that we choose to make this tender power in-carnate in history" (Heyward, 1984, p. 117).

Realizing that God is not a rescuer, then, further enables us to realize that we are the ones whose responsibility it is to help the sufferer (Kushner, 1981). When we take responsibility in the absence of god-the-rescuer, genuine divinity is revealed as the empowerment and sustenance which can enable us to transcend self-pity and the fear of our own deaths. Once so unencumbered we can provide support for persons with AIDS, reappraise our relational styles and sexual behavior, and create meaning out of tragedy. We can also discover divine empowerment as we realize the righteousness of our anger at injustice and the need for prophetic, corrective activity in the face of both oppression and suffering (cf., Kushner, 1981). Our new understanding of God as a pangendered and pansexual personal energy, as well as a co-suffering, compassionate presence in suffering and victimization, thus moves our theological activity, as a dynamic process, through the issues of gender duality and theodicy to other concerns. Confronting tragedy, like confronting our oppression as gay people under dualistic and homophobic patriarchy, forces us back to anthropology. Our efforts to reconceptualize God and to penetrate theodicy consistently prevent our idolatrously capturing God within our limited images of the divine and continually force us to reexamine human ways of being and acting in the world. As Kushner (1981) himself reminds us, penetrating theodicy to reconceptualize God as present, horizontal, and limited, both by randomness in nature and by human responsibility, shifts the question from "why?" to "what do I do now, and who is there to help me do it?" (pp. 60-61). With Rubenstein (1966) and all post-death-of-God, liberation theology, the focus for gay liberation theology becomes less about God and shifts instead to that of human responsibility.

✱   ✱   ✱

V. Reclaiming Human
Responsibility

(i) Rediscovering our Jewish Sources:
Fackenheim, Rubenstein, and Others

Consistently, death-of-God theologies, liberation theologies, and theological reconceptions of God's limitations and co-suffering intimacy have all rejected the escapist otherworldliness and apocalypticism of first century Judaism and subsequent, gnostically informed Christianity. Gay liberation theology and gay spirituality must similarly move beyond just an awareness of oppression and the development of a "tragic vision" (Rubenstein, 1966) to a theological standpoint which is our praxis. Says Morton (1985), for example, "all theologizing, philosophizing, and politicizing take place within the context of a social and political situation that both conditions the way we act and think and, in turn, is affected by our thinking and acting. No longer can we separate theory and practice [or] action and reflection" (pp. 181-182). Consequently, our gay theology must be done in the very activity of bearing up one another to make and to enable God-with-us as the empowerment both for responding to and overcoming tragedy, and for tirelessly demanding, seeking, and creating justice for gay people, for all persons-with-AIDS, and for anyone else marginalized by patriarchy and heterosexism (cf., Heyward, 1984). Our theologizing, as an activity or praxis, must help to shift the historical emphasis in theology from that of God acting and directing and manipulating, wherein humanity bears little responsibility (a vertical divine/human relationship), to that of people bearing the responsibility both for actualizing God's intentions and for creating understanding, images, and actions of the divine in the world (a horizontal divine/human relationship).

Rubenstein (1966), for example, has argued that otherworldly hopes and an idolatrous, blind obedience to some putatively omnipotent and omniscient Will is merely a way of relinquishing responsibility, which in turn allows evil--as failed human responsibility--to gain its sway (cf., Heyward, 1984). To value this life here and now, whether after Auschwitz or in the face of homophobia and AIDS, requires no other cosmic or other-worldly meaning, value, or validation; while we may have "absolutely no grounds for eschatological hope," we do have hope in this world (Rubenstein, 1966, p. 258). Our realistic hope lies in the human capacity for responsible actions of compassion and justice.

Unfortunately, however, the major thrust of our western religious heritage, shaped as it has been by a body-denying and hence world-denying dualism, has muted this demand for this-worldly human responsibility. Both fundamentalist and mainstream Christianity still emphasize the salvation of the "immortal soul" by means of a narrow focus upon right belief and moral purity. Christianity has consequently either ignored or been hostile out-right toward those groups which it has excluded because of their perceived immersion in this world. For those of us determined to construct and to develop liberation theology within the western religious tradition, however, this life-denying strand of our tradition need not be our only resource. We may find among the alternatives that the Judaic sources of our tradition and the development over time of the Jewish strand of our western heritage can serve together as a significant prophetic corrective for irresponsible otherworldliness and thus as a valuable resource for our efforts in gay liberation theology.

Both Rubenstein (1966) and Neusner (1979), for example, contend that Judaism has traditionally focused not upon eschatological hope, but upon the ethical realities of human relationships, that it expresses its theology not through systematics or dogmatics, but "through the pattern of deeds performed by the practitioner of Judaism" (Neusner, 1979, p. 78, cf., Christ and Plaskow, 1979, Ozick, 1983). As a result, Judaism is "intensely practical . . . about this world and about the human being"; moreover, "in the pain and the suffering, in the living in the face of the dying, is the sacred" (Neusner, 1979, p. 85). The radical presentness of Jewish ethical concern and the insistent here and now quality of the divine in Jewish religious belief have led Greenberg (1981) to interpret Jewish history as a processive realization of human equality and justice.

From slavery to the abolition of slavery, to the institution of the periodic (Jubilee year) forgiveness of debts (to prevent an unjust concentration of wealth), to the development of a covenantal society, the history of Judaism discloses a trend from hierarchy to covenant, from a vertical god of judgment and command to a horizontal God intimately present in suffering and with the oppressed (Greenberg, 1981). The Jubilee year, for example, was historically the concrete enactment of the belief that peace and justice were the meaning of redemption in prophetic Judaism. Forgiving debts and freeing slaves, resting from the accumulation of material gain and the exploitation of the earth's resources, were cyclical efforts to restore society to an ideal norm (Waskow, 1983, Ruether, 1985). Informed by the belief that redemption is "a continuous process that needs to be done over and over again within history," the recurring Jubilee and the prophetic tradition helped nurture and sustain a deep, ongoing concern within Judaism for the radical transformation of society toward justice, in this world (Ruether, 1985, p. 196). This veritable obsession with justice has even led Waskow (1983) to exclaim that Judaism is "the oldest, longest-lived resistance movement against oppression that is known in human history" (p. 269).

Importantly, a number of Christian writers have realized in their own theological work the reason(s) for Judaism's particular emphasis on social justice: Body/soul dualism was and is foreign to Judaism. Consequently, the concept of immortality, a dualism of this world and the next, is simply not a traditional Jewish idea or teaching. Says Fortunato (1987) of traditional Jewish belief, "God's blessing was to be known now, in this life in all its worldliness" (p. 45). Pushing even deeper, Ruether (1985) acknowledges that neither were the Sumerian, Babylonian, or earliest Hebrew sources of Judaism focused in any way upon a "human escape from mortality" (p. 217). Despite a certain growing apocalypticism in some first century Judaism, Judaism was instead "focused originally [i.e., fundamentally] on this-worldly hopes, emphasizing the winning of justice and righteousness" as the cornerstone of the covenant with God as delineated in the commandments (p. 219). Ultimately, of course, Christianity and not Judaism pursued and developed first century apocalypticism and its accompanying dualisms. If Christian theological writers such as Ruether (1985) and Fortunato (1987) have nonetheless recognized that the radically monotheistic nature of Judaism precludes a dualistic rejection of this world and hence of social justice, and if Jewish writers such as Neusner (1979), Waskow (1983), Greenberg (1983), and others are un-

abashedly adamant about Judaism's historical pursuit of
social justice, then we may safely assume that an understanding of Judaism's this-worldly and non-dualistic
emphases upon human responsibility and upon just human
interrelationships can both inform gay liberation theology and serve as a prophetic corrective against the
world-denying and frequently justice-avoiding forces in
contemporary western religion and culture.

Among the various Jewish thinkers herein considered, Fackenheim (1968, 1970) provides the most thor-
ough articulation of the themes of justice and responsibility in Jewish thought, for our efforts at an anthropological theology of liberation.   He insists,
first of all, that "if there is a single religious affirmation which . . . has remained basic to Jewish belief until today, it is . . . a sense of responsibility
in the social realm" (1968, p. 189), a sense of seriously confronting the realities of evil and--instead of
seeking escapist solutions (divine rescue) or merely
passively waiting (otherworldly hope)--"rolling up the
sleeves" to assume responsibility, jointly with God, to
redeem evil in the here and now (1968, pp. 166, 168).
Importantly, however, along with the expectation of or
commandment for human action in Judaism, goes the pro-
mise of God's action as well: "Because divine action
makes itself contingent upon human action, a relationship of mutuality is established"; this mutual relation
is the basis of covenant, by which God "becomes a partner" with people who take responsible and responsive
action (1968, p. 248).   As with both process thought
and the work of Kushner (1981), we are brought back
again to an understanding or conceptualization of God
as one intimately personal and relational, a co-partner
for our lives in the world.   This mutuality and reciprocity in the divine/human relationship ultimately
means that our encounter with God's presence is ful-
filled only by and in human action(s).   Moreover, our
capacities to respond and to act, or our failures to do
so, also affect or limit God's power: We create/en-
able/empower God's presence in the world when we act
responsibly, and we curtail or undermine God's power
when we fail to act or when we choose evil actions
(Fackenheim, 1968, 1970).   The ultimate responsibility
for meaningful, compassionate, and justice-seeking
action is thus squarely upon human shoulders.   God is
primarily neither judge nor rescuer, but rather one who
joins right actions as a responsive, sanctifying, empowering, and strengthening co-partner.   We are called
not to wait passively for divine action, but rather to

assume responsibility for decisive actions which consequently make God's presence effective in the world
(Fackenheim, 1968, cf., Bonhoeffer, 1953).

For Judaism, this divine/human mutuality and in-
terdependence becomes manifest in history: "Salvation
. . . occurs within history, not in an eternity beyond
it, nor for a soul divorced from it, nor as an apocalyptic or Messianic event which consummates history.
It therefore points necessarily to human action" (Fackenheim, 1970, p. 14). Because human actions and failures to act are, respectively, either a sharing with or
a turning from our covenantal partnership with God, human action assumes "decisive historical meaning" (Fackenheim, 1968, p. 252, cf., p. 262). Mutuality entails
response and God responds to both human action and human failure; this dialogical process over time constitutes the meaningful (or redemptive) quality of history. Moreover, because, "a meaning at once manifest
in history and yet indifferent to poverty, war, and
tyranny is unthinkable to the Jewish mind" (Fackenheim,
1968, p. 255), the ethical force of the mutual God/hu-
man relationship, of the demand for human responsibility, is toward the persistent pursuit of social justice.

This emphasis on human responsibility and social
justice, within history, means that sin and repentance,
judgment and salvation/redemption, are also public and
collective for Judaism. Sin cannot be reduced to pri-
vatized sexual issues; nor is salvation a matter of individual purity and immortality divorced from the world
(Ruether, 1985). Consequently, Rubenstein (1966) rejects an understanding of guilt constructed upon a concept of original sin. We are not fundamentally sinful
because of who we are (as people or, specifically, as
gay people, for example); sinfulness is not a fundamental quality of our very being. Such "cosmic guilt" is
simply too big, too compelling (necessitating scapegoating), and too paralyzing (precluding corrective
action). Rubenstein (1966) recommends, instead, that
we reconstruct a more realistically proportioned, humanly scaled understanding of sin and guilt only in direct correspondence with our failures of responsibility. Our guilt should be realistic in relation to our
capacities to seek forgiveness, to effect restitution
and reconciliation, and to experience atonement at the
horizontal level of human relationships. Vertical,
cosmic acts of scapegoating and sacrifice (whether in
racist, antisemitic, or homophobic genocide) are no
longer required, because God has immediately or a pri-

ori accepted all people, confirming the value and meaning of all human life (Fackenheim, 1968, cf., Tillich, 1948).

Moreover, the divine acceptance and blessing of human existence make self-acceptance "mandatory" (Fackenheim, 1968, p. 247); self-denigrating pity and powerless eschatological passivity, ritually/symbolically groveling in self-debasement for the crumbs beneath the Eucharist table, for example, are not only unnecessary but are actually offensive. We are accepted; as gay and lesbian people, we are accepted and blessed by God a priori. We need no longer apologize to ourselves or to other people for being who we are. God's acceptance and intimate mutuality, of course, further entail God's making people responsible for their actions, for fulfilling divine purposes in history and here and now (cf., Fackenheim, 1968). If anything is original or fundamental, it is not human sinfulness but rather that, along with divine/human mutuality and the command for interpersonal/social justice, we are accepted and loved by God and we are thereby endowed with the capacities for self-acceptance and the energies for assuming responsibility. The eternal and immutable command of justice and responsibility in Judaism (cf., Ozick, 1983) is thus not an unreasonable expectation or a goal vertically beyond our experience(s) in history; it is realistically within our grasp, horizontally here and now in our relationships, in our sociopolitical and cultural situation.

Various Jewish feminists have, of course, recognized the ironic discrepancy between this ideal of a Judaism progressively disclosing human equality and justice, and the reality of Judaism's historical patriarchy. The Torah and the tradition resound a loud "no" to the victimization or dehumanization of any group-- except women (Ozick, 1983). Similarly, contemporary Judaism remains conflicted about gay people, endorsing gay civil rights but not gay being (homosexuality) as such. Says Saslow (1987),

. . . [This] ambivalence, ironically, comes from the conflict between the moral traditions of an ancient people--the very founders of the Judaeo-Christian proscriptions that justify Western homophobia--and that same people's tragic first hand knowledge of the effect of repressive bigotry on any small, "deviant" minority. (pp. 38-39)

Ozick (1983) goes on to say, however, that while the silence of Torah on a particular oppression makes the tradition an accessory to that oppression, the overall demand for justice requires that both Torah and tradition be self-correcting, open to its own prophetically critical force. Specifically, then, for gay people, the hostility of Torah toward idolatrous homosexual acts, historically used to oppress constitutionally gay individuals, also stands under the prophetic judgment of Judaism's own demand for justice. A dialectic thus emerges between the historical, human interpretations of the Law regarding women and gay people, and the prophetical ethical force undergirding that tradition. Ultimately, for the sake of the integrity of the tradition itself, the absolute value of justice for Judaism requires making justice explicit for both women and gay people (cf., Ozick, 1983).

Because Judaism has traditionally valued right action over right belief, treating others well rather than requiring absolute ritual or dogmatic purity, its historical "activism in the cause of freedom and justice" must now also apply to both women and gay people (Bauman, 1983, p. 94, cf., Bloch, 1983). In fact, a number of concepts related to the absolute value of justice not only support Ozick's (1983) contention regarding the self-correcting power of prophetic Judaism, but further enhance the work of Fackenheim (1968, 1970) and Rubenstein (1966) as resources for a gay liberation theology informed, at least in part, by Judaism. The concept of "mitzvah" or good deeds in fulfillment of the Law, for example, is "best understood as responsibility expressed in daily action," according to Alpert (1984, p. 14). Similarly, "tikun olam" means "taking concrete actions to make the world a better place" and ultimately entails reconciling and healing "all the world" (Alpert, 1984, p. 14, Saslow, 1987, p. 111).

Gay and feminist writers have also elucidated less specific understandings equally important to Judaism and equally valuable to our efforts at gay liberation theology. Judaism's "generally sex-positive" tradition of sexuality as a vehicle for religious experience and friendship, as a means for expressing loving and humanizing mutuality, for example, upholds the value of non-procreative sexual pleasure in relationship (Saslow, 1987, p. 111). Love-making on the Sabbath is traditionally a double blessing! Judaism has also traditionally valued and protected the privacy of its own community and thus respected the privacy of other groups, the privacy of home and relationship, and the

privacy of sexual intimacy between consenting adults in
relationship (cf., Bloch, 1983). Most of all, Judaism's historical experience of oppression and even genocide engenders in contemporary Judaism a deep appreciation of the plight of other marginalized groups. The
clear condemnation of homosexual acts in the Mosaic
code notwithstanding, the majority of contemporary
American Judaism is committed not only to supporting
gay "civil liberties," but also to wrestling with the
"thornier moral and theological issues" with which both
the feminist and gay movements confront it (Saslow,
1987, p. 38). The absolute principle of justice and
not the letter of the Law is the bottom line in non-
Orthodox Judaism today.

The dialectic between the patriarchal silence of
Torah toward women and its homophobic fear of idolatry,
on the one hand, and Judaism's monotheistic rejection
of a dualism which devalues human life and its insistence instead upon justice in this world, on the other
hand, is clearly resolved in favor of justice, in an
understanding of God's intimate, horizontal participation in history, and in the demand for responsible human action. Rejecting dualism and otherworldliness
(eschatology), the Jewish sources of our western religious heritage have upheld and celebrated the value of
this world, of human action in the world, and even of
human sexuality, all within the context of God's horizontal covenant or co-partnership with us (cf., Fortunato, 1987). Because God-with-us is primarily neither
judge nor rescuer, we are enjoined to reclaim human responsibility and to act decisively and justly, as if
indeed a vertical god does not exist (cf., Rubenstein,
1966, Bonhoeffer, 1953). And yet, the tradition also
makes clear that this demand is not unreasonable. Not
only are we endowed with the capacity for responsible
actions of compassion and justice, but when we so act,
we effect God's horizontal presence in the world and
are in turn empowered by the divine. Reclaiming our
responsibility for embodying forth the absolute value
of justice--as people and as gay people--enables and
sustains our mutual relation with God. God is intimately present and proactive with and for the oppressed
who decisively take responsible actions in pursuit of
justice, here and now. Herein lies Judaism's corrective and informative force for a prophetic gay liberation theology. Moreover, while the value of this-
worldly justice has often been overlooked by Christianity's concern with a next-worldly salvation of the individual (cf., Fortunato, 1987), Christian feminists

such as Heyward (1982, 1984), Ruether (1983a, 1983b, 1985), and Collins (1981) have been able to recover the fundamental Jewishness of Christianity and the this-worldly ethical concern of Jesus and his work, in order to develop a post-Christian view of justice and mutual relation at once continuous with Judaism and equally important for the development of a gay liberation theology.

(ii) Pursuing our Post-Christian Possibilities: Heyward and Ruether

Christian feminist theology has astutely reappreciated and reappropriated a number of the liberational themes of prophetic Judaism in ways which can also inform our efforts in gay liberation theology. Heyward (1982), for example, is adamant that theological activity should be biased toward making love and justice in this world and thus should shun any eschatological focus. She recognizes that eschatological otherworldliness too often leads to injustice and irresponsibility manifest as a hatred of those people whose lives differ from an eschatological norm of Christian purity. Moreover, eschatology attributes "penultimate value to ourselves and to what we experience as real in the present world" (p. 131). Shifting the theological focus from creeds to action, she argues instead that spirituality should be this-worldly, grounded in our human interrelationships and experience. Theology can be constructed from our experiences of justice and injustice in both the religious and sociopolitical realms. Theology is thus subjective, experiential, and "fundamentally relational" here and now (Heyward, 1984, p. 228). Ruether (1983a) shares this disdain for any eschatological obsession which denies human limitations and which, in seeking immortality for individual souls, consequently neglects both the earth and humanity, both ecological and social justice. Believing that orthodox Christianity's "preoccupation with death and the survival of the soul after death comes from a religiosity rooted in male experiences of killing and death, while a female-based religiosity would focus on this-worldly nurturance of the person within society" (Ruether, 1985, p. 223), she urges people to a reconciliation with their proper limits, within the natural cycles of creation (Ruether, 1983a). Her theology revalues not only this life and this "world," but this very earth in its fundamental created goodness:

To be human is to be in a state of process, to change and to die. Both change and death are good. They belong to the natural limits of life. We need to seek the life intended by God/ess for us within these limits [by a] return to harmony within the covenant of creation.

. . . Conversion to the earth and to each other . . . is a model of change more in keeping with the realities of temporal existence. To subject ourselves to the tyranny of impossible expectations of final perfection means to neglect to do what can and must be done for our times.

. . . Our responsibility is to use our temporal life span to create a just and good community. (Ruether, 1983a, pp. 255, 256, 258)

As with the logic of Judaism, then, the rejection of eschatological dualism and the revaluation of this life focus theology anthropologically upon human responsibility and human action. Heyward (1982) thus seizes the offensive when she insists not only that "God . . . depends upon humanity for making good/making justice/making love/making God . . . in the world" (p. 159), but, more importantly, that "there can be . . . nothing in heaven or earth--not even a deity--that is more valuable, any more important, any better, than human love for humanity" (p. 181). Loving humanity, our "voluntary participation in making right-relation [justice] among ourselves, constitutes our love of God. To love humanity is to befriend God. The human act of love, befriending, making justice is our act of making God incarnate in the world" (p. 9). We discover again that God and humanity are mutually relational, bound in a cooperative partnership (covenant) whereby God also needs us, needs our right and just relating in the world. If God is indeed a limited, horizontally present, and deeply intimate co-suffering and co-creating partner in creation, then we help to "create" God. We bear the responsibility for "creating" or making God effective in the world. The extent of God's reality, as real effectiveness, depends upon human actions and interactions with others to make justice. The responsibility is again squarely upon our shoulders.

Because God's power is limited, in fact dependent upon humanity, we must act responsibly; our acting creates and empowers God, who in turn nurtures and strengthens our empowerment to seek justice. Or, again as Heyward (1984) says, our responsibility is to "make God in-carnate in the world . . . by choice, commitment,

and action in the world, which becomes the most pro-
found of prayers (p. 99). Conversely, of course, rejecting God's intimate but limited horizontal nearness
and expecting God to be an all-powerful agent and vertical rescuer, like rejecting this world in favor of
some other spiritual realm, abdicates human responsibility. With Rubenstein (1966), Heyward (1982) thus
insists that "we can never again abdicate our responsibility to an omninpotent deity" (p. 183). Indeed, to
cry the death of God (cf., Rubenstein, 1966) is not
really an indictment of God's limits or vertical absence; it is instead an indictment of utterly failed
human responsibility.

A vertical, all-powerful, rescuing god is not just
dead; he (!) never existed. The horizontal, co-partner
God, however, who shaped the Jewish covenant through
lived experience, also informs the revaluation of this
life and the reclamation of human responsibility which
are equally important concerns for feminist theology.
The understanding of the divine/human relationship
which these concerns entail in turn shapes the conceptualizations of sin (human evil), justice, and redemption further disclosed by that theology. Feminist theology, for example, agrees with Judaism that both sin
and salvation or redemption are collective and this
worldly (cf., Collins, 1981). Sin, specifically, is
not a cosmic fall into individualized bodily and sexual
existence; sinfulness lies instead in the social structures of injustice and oppression as well as in our human passivity before, and thus complicity in, those
systems of injustice (Ruether, 1983a, Heyward, 1984).
Ruether (1983a, 1985) argues that the preconditions for
these structures of (social/human) evil or sinfulness
are the dichotomizing forces, the dualisms, of patriarchy. Constructing polarities always creates categories which objectify and dehumanize the "other,"
which in turn creates at least the possibility for directing "radical evil" toward those groups designated
as "other" (Heyward, 1982, p. 89): "Evil comes about
precisely by the distortion of the self-other relationship into the good-evil, superior-inferior dualism," a
dualism frequently used to justify the exploitation,
condemnation, and even genocide of the impure "other"
(Ruether, 1983a, p. 163). The eschatological dualism
which posits a cosmic fall into this worldly sinfulness
further sustains an oppressive, objectified view of the
"other": "Fall stories function to conceal the real
evils of society by 'blaming the victim,' by making
victims of social evil, such as women [or gay people],

appear to be causes of evil. . . . Fall stories function to . . . justify oppressive social arrangements" (Ruether, 1985, p. 88). The passivity of waiting for rescue, change, or return to an otherworldly, pre-fall condition also impairs human choice. A patriarchically dualistic understanding of sin thus not only sustains oppressive categories; it actually undercuts our capacity for corrective action (cf., Ruether, 1985).

Rejecting individualized (sexual) and dualistic (eschatological) understandings of sin, while revaluing human responsibility, indeed changes the meaning of sin and evil for feminist theologians. Neither "original" nor "a condition of being" (Collins, 1981, p. 346), sin must be understood instead in a social or relational (anthropological) framework: "Sin . . . is never just 'individual'; there is no [human] evil that is not relational. Sin exists precisely in the distortion of relationality, including relation to oneself" (Ruether, 1983a, p. 181). Sinfulness or human evil ultimately involves not only the destruction of an individual's capacity to relate to self and/or to others, but the destruction of his/her very experience of self as a human being, as well (Heyward, 1982). Heyward (1982) elaborates:

> Evil is the violation of relation in human life. Radical evil . . . is the violation . . . of relation whereby the power in relation is transgressed so thoroughly as to be ineffective, dead, in human life.
>   . . . [It is] the extinction of the meaning and value of human experience; the nullification of human existence; that which is utterly without relation. (pp. 154, 80)

Historically, this rejection or destruction of mutual relation has been manifest as injustice which "has distorted the original equivalence of all human beings and has created instead hierarchical societies of privilege and deprivation, domination and exploitation" (Ruether, 1983a, p. 103). The systematic, hierarchical structuring of western society over time has increasingly undercut mutuality, becoming less relational and more destructive, more dehumanizing. The structural evils of militarism, racism, sexism, heterosexism/homophobia, and economic and ecological exploitation are all among the results (Heyward, 1982, Ruether, 1983b).

For feminist theology, passivity or indifference before these manifestations of evil is clearly a form of complicity in sin/evil (Heyward, 1984). Because humanity shares with God the responsibility for corrective, redemptive action, passivity, indifference, or any other form of turning from humanity "is the only certain negation of God, just as it is the only negation of humanity" (Heyward, 1982, p. 92, cf., Heyward, 1984). Once again we realize, therefore, that the so-called "death of God" is actually an indictment of human failures, insofar as shirked responsibility and indifference to social evil make God ineffective, negating or "killing" God (e.g., at Auschwitz or in homophobic violence). Moreover, passivity, the fear of freedom, and the rejection of liberation for oneself or for others are all equally complicitous (Ruether, 1985). Our passivity as gay people, for example, our frequent willingness to accept accommodation or to seek assimilation into the systemic structures of heterosexist hierarchies, not only contributes to our own oppression by those structures and hierarchies which posit us as "other"; our complicity in homophobic oppression is actually sinful.

The alternative to complicitous participation in social evil and human sinfulness is not, of course, some eschatological, otherworldly redemption. Just as sin and human evil are social and historical, so is redemption immediately possible in making right, just relation here and now, in restoring co-equal, relational mutuality between and among ourselves. Reconciliation and renewed cooperation with God in a "commitment to a struggle for a transformed social order where all these evils will be overcome" is redemption; the demand/command for social reform is redemption, not as an event in the distant eschatological future, but as a process occurring here and now (Ruether, 1983b, p. 19, cf., Ruether, 1983a, Heyward, 1982). For feminist theology the present possibilities of redemption/salvation are inseparably connected to our reclamation of our human responsibility for creating and making justice in history and here and now.

Heyward (1982) insists that we are ultimately responsible for creating a just world through our human choices and actions (cf., p. 3). She describes justice as the "fruit of human passion, deep love that is willing to bear up fear and tension and uncertainty in relation to persons, issues, and possibilities known and unknown" (p. 136); "justice is a . . . metaphor for the . . . establishment of love in human life" (p. 17). In her subsequent writing (Heyward, 1984), she continues to develop a set of tautologies whereby love and justice are one and the same, and, conversely, whereby the absence of justice necessarily entails the absence of love: "Love without justice is not love at all" (p. 22); "justice is the moral act of love" (p. 78); "God is justice" (p. 227, emphasis added); and, "a human act of love and justice is an act of God in history" (p. 108). Loving humanity is not romantic, not a matter of feelings; rather, it is our relational cooperation with other people, our recreation of "right-relationship between and among people" (pp. 30-31), in the activity of making love, of making justice, in this world. By so acting, we also cooperate with and truly love God, and this mutual relationship empowers our justice-seeking and -making efforts--for the poor, for women, for the socially outcast (e.g., gay people), and for the reaffirmation and resanctification of all human sexuality:

> We must begin to see that love is justice. Love does not come first, justice later. . . . We act our way into feeling. . . . Good feelings about love and justice may come later.
> . . . To really love is to topple unjust structures, bringing down the principalities and powers of domination and control at all levels of human social relations.
> . . . To live love is to be responsible for justice in society.
> . . . To profess love for someone, or for humanity itself, or for God, and to do nothing to bring those whom we love to life and power is to lie in the most shameful and cruel way, to make a mockery out of love, justice, humanity, and God. (Heyward, 1984, pp. 85-86, 92, 109, 124)

Ruether (1983a) provides a context for Heyward's (1982, 1984) strongly prophetic words on love and justice as the nexus of God's very being: Both women are firmly grounded in the prophetic tradition of Judaism. Ruether (1983a), for example, says that "Yahweh is unique as the God of a tribal confederation that identifies itself as liberated slaves" (p. 62); and, even as the ancient Hebrews exchanged first their slavery and then their nomadic wandering for the Davidic monarchy and the emergence of a settled, social class structure, the ongoing tension between rulers and prophets "established at the heart of biblical religion a motif of protest against the status quo. . . . God is seen as a critic of this society, a champion of the social victims" (p. 62). Subsequently, both the Synoptic gospels

and the pre-Pauline portrait of Jesus contain "a renewal and radicalization of prophetic consciousness now
applied to [all] marginalized groups in a universal
. . . context" (p. 63). Ruether (1983a) outlines four
elements of this biblical prophetic tradition with
which her own work and that of other feminists are continuous: (1) God's defense, vindication, and advocacy
of all oppressed people; (2) "the critique of the dominant systems of power and their powerholders" (p. 24);
(3) a vision of renewed social order in which present
injustice is overcome; and, (4) "the critique of . . .
religious ideologies and systems [which] function to
justify and sanctify the dominant, unjust social order"
and which thereby ignore "God's agenda for justice"
(pp. 24, 26).

Heir to both Judaism's rejection of a spiritualized redemption and to post-Christian feminist theology's rejection of a mainstream Christian spiritual-
ization of redemption "severed from historical change
in public ethics" (Ruether, 1985, p. 138), gay liberation theology must further encourage us to abandon any
reliance upon salvation from the outside or for some
other world. Instead, we must join with our Jewish and
feminist predecessors in a radical reassumption of human responsibility for saving and redeeming ourselves,
all people, and the very earth itself, here and now.
We must both strive against evil as failed human responsibility and act as compassionate, co-suffering embodiments of God before the tragedy of "natural" evil
(AIDS). As victims ourselves of both human evil/op-
pression (homophobia) and the devastation of AIDS--
which too often has hardened human evil against us as
well--we must assertively claim our right to justice
and reclaim our capacities to seek justice, to respond
compassionately, to create God's presence in the world,
and thus to restore our power in relationship both to
God and to others (cf., Heyward, 1982). These tasks
will not be easy, but grounded in our firm belief in
God's advocacy on our behalf, we can discover and engender the empowerment necessary to act. Writes
Collins (1979), for example,

> . . . Salvation for us is dynamic, this-
> worldly. . . . We were never promised a life free
> from fear and struggle. We were offered the hope
> that by committing ourselves to the struggle for a
> righteous society in solidarity with [all] the
> wretched of the earth we would discover the secret
> of life. (pp. 155-156)

If we will but grow into full maturity as human beings and as gay people, relinquishing our wishful thinking for easy solutions in either the sociopolitical or medical realms; if we will eschew assimilation into the norms, structures, and hierarchies of heterosexual acceptability and relinquish our frequently competitive and sometimes even self-hating attitudes toward one another, which undercut any real mutuality between and among us; and, if we will develop and nurture instead a deep and abiding, genuine compassion not only for our gay brothers and lesbian sisters, but for our very selves and ultimately for all people--grounded in God's a priori acceptance, love, and celebration/sanctification of who we are--we will find in this process an amazing and deep wellspring of energy, of empowerment, for demanding, seeking, and creating justice for ourselves and for others. God is absolutely with us in our efforts:

> . . . God is nothing other than the eternally creative source of our relational power, our common strength, a God whose movement is to empower, bringing us into our own together, a God whose name in history is love . . . that which is just, mutually empowering, and co-creative.
> . . . God . . . is nothing other than the power of love in history, the power for right relation in history, the power of justice in this world.
> . . . To the extent that anyone, or any group of people (such as homosexuals) are victims of injustice, God is with us precisely in our efforts to call into being a more just society. (Heyward, 1984, pp. 124, 146-147, 194)

The combined lesson of prophetic Judaism and feminist theology for our work in gay liberation theology, as our praxis, is that we cannot and must not wait for vertical intervention on our behalf; we must instead seize the offensive for creating our liberation and for responding to one another with compassion. We will be delighted to find in that process that we are buoyed up and empowered by a horizontally intimate and gently strong, divine embrace.

(iii) Developing a Gay Prophetic Standpoint

The emphases upon the unqualified value of this world and upon the importance of human responsibility for the creation of justice (or, conversely, injustice) in this world, as reflected in both our Jewish and our Christian feminist sources, are significant resources for those of us who are about the tasks of gay liberation and gay theology. While all too often gay men in particular have been accused of living "as if there were no tomorrow," our increasing experiences of homophobia and homophobic violence, as well as our collective experience of AIDS in the gay male community, have indeed made us realize that our tomorrows are certainly limited and that we must consequently live fully in our fragile present(s), both for ourselves and compassionately for others. This life, here and now, is the only reality we can know. Gay people and gay theology have thus already begun to reject a dualistic otherworldliness, and in so doing, we share with other liberation theologies a reaffirmation of this world, a reassertion of the good created value of our bodiliness and our sexuality (in the very face of AIDS and AIDS-phobic denouncements of all human sexuality), and a reclamation of our responsibility for seeking and creating justice. By these activities, as well as by our defiant refusal any longer to be treated as "other," we find that our particular claim to justice for gay people is solidly constructed upon the prophetic tradition and in God's historical advocacy of the oppressed. Our gay theology is indeed both a part of the spectrum of liberation theologies and our particular standpoint for a prophetic critique both of sociopolitical/cultural bias and of (institutional) religious exclusion. We must respond, act, and demand justice in all these realms.

God is clearly with us in our struggles to act, to seek justice, and to effect our liberation. Our a priori acceptance by God means we have the capacity and the responsibility to act justly with and for one another and to demand social justice not only for ourselves, but for all persons threatened by heterosexist hierarchies of power. Not surprisingly, for example, among the various demands of the October 1987 National March on Washington for Lesbian and Gay Rights were demands for reproductive freedom for all women and for an end to apartheid in South Africa. We can and we must join our voices to those other voices which are also seeking liberation in these times, in order to create an ethics not of exclusive spiritual or sexual purity, but of compassion and caring, of respect and mutuality. Thereby will we take responsibility for making/enabling God's power in the world and for effecting redemption, salvation, and liberation.

Our living fully committed to and responsibly in
the present of this world can also enable us to accept
our limits, our humanness, even our mortality. Our involvement with the AIDS crisis has taught us to be
angry, and that our anger is healthy and cleansing, as
well as inspired and sustained by divine co-suffering.
We are also learning, however, that we must move
through and beyond our anger to act and to respond compassionately, to use our limited lives most fully on
behalf of our community and others. As we synthesize
our activities in the quest of gay sociopolitical and
cultural liberation with our compassionate caring in
the face of AIDS, gay people may become paradigmatic
symbols of theology and praxis, seeking and making justice, making love, in the world. Importantly for us,
the anthropological understanding of theodicy, or the
problem of evil, explicated in our Jewish and feminist
sources here clearly focuses almost exclusively on human or social evil, upon sinfulness as failed human responsibility (cf., Rubenstein, 1966). Gay theology,
however, synthesizes or fuses both an understanding of/
response to natural evil and tragedy with the liberationist themes of justice and human responsibility, because as gay people we must reckon not only with the
systemic structures of homophobia, but with the painful
realities of AIDS as well. Ultimately, a synthesized/
fused understanding of both kinds of evil is necessary
for an adequate resolution to theodicy and for an appropriate response to the realities of evil, whether
"natural" or "social." This synthesis also informs our
efforts to create a theology which is our praxis of
action and compassionate response.
    Finally, our efforts to create a prophetic stand-
point in our theologizing must also include a perspective for appropriately engaging in tender self-criticism which, far from acting to blame the victim, actually acts to nurture our wholeness and to further our
liberation (cf., Ruether, 1972, Clark, 1987a). Our rejection of patriarchal heterosexism and its dualisms,
for example, means that we must avoid constructing or
sustaining we/they categories of dehumanizing and devaluing otherness in our own community. We must undo
our own value-laden hierarchies of opposites: gay men
vs. lesbians, whites vs. people of color, the economic
elite vs. blue and pink collar laborers, bar goers vs.
non-bar goers, singles vs. couples, monogamous relationships vs. polygamous networks, "sissies" vs. "real
men," "fems" vs. "butches," "straight looking and acting" vs. transvestites ("drag queens") and the leather

community. Such categories only divide us against ourselves and threaten to immobilize our justice- and liberation-seeking efforts. Our theology and our praxis
must instead celebrate our variety and nurture our
unity-in-diversity, not our sameness. While we must
absolutely eschew assimilation and too easy accommodation, or passivity and indifference among us, we must
also remain uncondescendingly compassionate toward
those individuals who, at least for now, feel they must
remain in the closet (cf., Boyd, 1984); even from their
closets, these individuals can be encouraged to find
ways to participate in the tasks of liberation. Thus
are we called simultaneously to heal our own community
and to seek and to create social change, or justice, in
the world.

Our tradition and its sources remind us over and
over again that both justice and our liberation are ultimately "up to us." Only when we act to create justice within our own community, as well as for our
people and for others in the world, is God also proactively effective with and for us. Our prophetic standpoint within our activity of gay liberation theology
will therefore build upon our religious tradition to
celebrate this life, to affirm our value as gay people,
to assume responsibility for demanding, seeking, and
creating justice in the world, and to nurture loving,
empowering community. Indeed, we must love one another
deeply, sustaining God-with-us. For surely as we do
so, we will again find ourselves empowered by a loving
divine embrace.

*   *   *

VI. Dechristologizing Jesus

(i) Exploring the Dilemma of Christology

Heyward (1984) argues that the activity of theology ("doing theology") must be grounded in the integrity of the theologian, in his/her own specificity,
limitations, and struggles. Doing theology in this way
is, consequently, largely a confessional activity; the
theologian seeks to resolve his/her own theological dilemmas and understandings in a public forum, hoping
thereby to engender dialogue, to raise questions, to
seek a broader synthesis of private and communal reflection and ideas. As such, theology is never final
or complete; it is rather a dynamic, perhaps even or-
ganic, and certainly a never ending process. Given
this confessional and dynamic understanding of the theologian's activity, Heyward (1982) also confronts the
inescapability of dealing with Jesus and with "Christology" in her own theological work. Both her upbringing
in a Christian home and her training within the Christian strand of our two-pronged Judaeo-Christian tradition require that she confront this historical and
mythical figure (cf., p. 196). Moreover, as a woman,
she must also deal with a male figure in history and
myth which has been used as a powerful tool against all
women (cf., p. 31f). Ultimately she confesses that
"Jesus matters because, for good or for ill, the titu-
lar name 'Jesus Christ' occupies center-stage in the
religious (and, I think, political) consciousness of
the larger portion of the Western world" (p. 31). Certainly, for an age in which the "Jesus freaks" of the
late 1960s and early 1970s have yielded to both "Jews
for Jesus" and, more significantly, to a resurgent fundamentalist Christianity capable of influencing American presidential politics in the 1980s, confronting the
mythic Christ, if not the historical Jesus, is unavoidable.
Wishing to ground these efforts toward a gay liberation theology in this same confessional and dynamic
understanding of theology as an activity and process,
I, too, must confront my own ambivalence toward and

connection with this historical figure and his mythologized image. As may already be apparent, I suspect that neither strand of our western Judaeo-Christian tradition has an unchallengeable grasp on Truth; illusive truth lies at once somewhere in between the two strands and beyond either of them, in our present participation and activity in the evolution of liberation theology and praxis. Nevertheless, the mythologization of a very Jewish Jesus into the Christ of Christianity places this man squarely in the middle of this two-pronged tradition within which I find myself doing theology. From United Methodist youth group leader and later seminarian, to occasional Unitarian, to cofounder of a gay and lesbian synagogue, I cannot authentically speak theologically apart from this tradition, as a whole two-pronged continuum, although I also cannot absolutely defend any particular institutionalized form on either side. Thusly both within and yet marginal to our western religious heritage, I must confront Jesus (and "Christ") because I further suspect that frequently neither side of the tradition has taken him seriously enough, as perhaps one historical example of reclaimed human responsibility, without first overlaying that image with the entanglements of mythology and religious faith requirements.

Christianity's fascination with a mythologized Christ, for example, hardly even needs the historical figure with which the mythic image is often only tenuously connected. Consequently, Judaism's self-defense against the antisemitism inherent in Christology has lead it also most often to ignore the, perhaps not unique, historical and Jewish Jesus. Fortunately, however, while the powerful image of Christ has frequently led both sides of our tradition to ignore or to distort the figure of Jesus, more recently both radical Judaism (e.g., Rubenstein, 1966) and even orthodox Judaism (e.g., Falk, 1985), on the one hand, and Christian feminist theology, on the other hand, have begun to reexamine the Jewishness and the historicity of Jesus while challenging Christological formulations and their impact. I find myself and my work as a gay theologian in the middle of all of this activity. Like Heyward (1982), by upbringing, training, and epistemological concepts and framework, I must confront and wrestle with this figure within our heritage, however idiosyncratically I may do so, simply as part of my efforts to derive meaning and to nurture dialogue for our efforts at specifically gay-sensitive liberation theology.

(ii) Deconstructing Christology and Resurrection

One way into the combined processes of deciding whether Jesus himself has any meaning for us and for (re)understanding that meaning for our work in gay liberation theology is to understand first how Jesus was transformed into the Christ and then to examine the problems which have resulted from Christology. Ruether (1983a) argues that while Jesus himself was firmly grounded in prophetic Judaism, calling Judaism back to its fundamental rootedness in the pursuit of justice, his immediate followers synthesized their "resurrection experiences," their denial of his brutal death and their cowardice before it, with traditional hopes for a Davidic messiah and with then popular Jewish apocalypticism. As this group moved through their guilt and grief and fear to realize that Jesus' death did not invalidate the importance and value of his life and teaching, as they remembered his love and continued his teaching, these excluded and marginalized men and women kept Jesus effective or "alive" in their own lives and experienced God's co-empowerment in their reconstitution as a "Jewish-Christian" community. Unfortunately, however, as they sought to communicate their cathartic experiences of Jesus' death and of his continuing influence in their lives to others, particularly amidst the conflict between James' Jewish commitment and Paul's gentile orientation, the power of Jesus' life and teaching beyond his death became literalized, especially when communicated outside Palestine to Greco-Romans whose native religions were both dualistic and replete with dying/rising gods (cf., Clark, 1986a, 1987a). Finally, the fall of Jerusalem in 70 C.E. severed the Jesus tradition from any rootedness in Judaism; developing Christianity became instead, first, an Hellenistically/ dualistic salvation religion, and ultimately, the imperial religion of Rome. The historical, Jewish, and justice-seeking Jesus was utterly displaced by an imperial Christos who sanctified Caesar and who saved individual souls for the next world. Christianity thus became the very kind of religious power and authority against which Jesus had taught, and the Christ became not a "suffering servant," but an oppressive mythic image (Ruether, 1983a, cf., Heyward, 1984).

One of the major problems with Christological development, with the divinization of Jesus as Christ for any liberation theology, is the way in which that process became oppressive. Displacing Jesus with Christ

provided an image of male Lordship (the Kyrios Christos) which was no longer liberating: "Masculinist imperial Christology" used this image to sanctify patriarchal dominance, to bless dominant hierarchies, and to
sustain the status quo of those in power (Ruether,
1985, p. 110, cf., p. 160, cf., Heyward, 1984).   It
spiritualized justice as only an otherworldly hope and
systematically excluded Jesus' own people, the Jews, as
well as any other nonconformers: "Christology [became]
the apex of a system of control over all those who in
one way or another [were] 'other' than this new Christian order" (Ruether, 1983a, p. 125). Furthermore, the
combined force of spiritualizing justice and divinizing
Jesus as Christ devalued and discouraged any commitment
to social justice, to human action in history, and effectively severed religious faith from the experience
of God's intimate nearness, particularly with the oppressed (Heyward, 1984, cf., 1982).   By further bol-
stering dualism, Christology also reaffirmed the Hellenistic rejection of the body; developing Christian
spirituality rejected the body as nonspiritual and all
human sexuality as sinful (Ruether, 1985).

As an oppressive force, the development of Christology came down especially hard on Jesus' own people.
Monotheistic nonconformers both to developing trinitarian ideas and particularly to the divinization of Jesus
as Christ, the Jews were not only labelled as "other";
they were held corporately responsible for the death of
Jesus and, by implication, for the murder of God (as
Christ). Writes Heyward (1984),

> . . . The significant difference (between
> Jesus and orthodox Judaism) was not necessarily
> violent . . . and exclusive--until Christians be-
> gan . . . to characterize this break with Judaism
> . . . as God's particular and unique interruption
> of Jewish history . . . rather than as . . .
> rooted in Jesus' commitment to a way of life Jesus
> understood to be Jewish. (p. 219)

The Jewishness of Jesus was dismissed by Christians
who, rejecting normal human responsibility for evil,
projected the tragedy of the crucifixion onto a cosmic
scheme. Nonconforming Jews became the scapegoats in a
cosmic drama of the death (and rebirth) of God (as
"Christ"). Rubenstein (1966), however, argues that if
we do not make Jesus into a Christo-divinity, and if we
instead see Jesus as continuous with Judaism and his
death as a tragic miscarriage of human justice, wherein

God is a co-sufferer and not an absent (or temporarily murdered) self-rescuer, then there is no deicide and no religious basis for antisemitism. Cosmic drama and genocidal scapegoating are appropriately and realistically replaced by a human tragedy, by a victim of human injustice, and by a God who shares tragedy and who demands human responsibility and justice.

Feminist theology similarly rejects Christology both for its oppressive quality and for its idolatrous and dualistic misappropriation of Jesus' this-worldly Judaic commitment to human justice and human responsibility. Daly (1979a), for example, rejects both the idea of a single incarnation of the divine, as well as any superiority sanctioned by an exclusively male incarnation. She wants to free Jesus from the chains of trinitarian divinity and simultaneously to enable all people to embody God's presence in the world. Heyward (1982) goes so far as to say that "Jesus matters only if he was fully, and only, human. Otherwise we are speaking of something/someone who bore no fully . . . human relation to God or his sisters and brothers" (p. 31); moreover, "to affirm the divine Lordship of Jesus is . . . to negate the full and simple humanity of this person who was born--like us all--with a choice to make regarding . . . acceptance of relationship to God" and/ or to all humanity (p. 198). In short, to impune Jesus' humanity is to invalidate his exemplary force; we are not God and thus cannot be expected to follow the example of a Jesus who was. The real revelation in Jesus' life, then, for Heyward (1982) is that "when God and humanity act together in the world, human action and divine action are the same action" (p. 199). Conversely, to insist upon Jesus' divinity is not only idolatrous, displacing God-with-us with an otherworldly, saving Christo-divinity; it encourages us to neglect our responsibilities for effecting right relation and for seeking justice here and now. Reflecting Daly's (1979a) concerns, Heyward (1982) elaborates:

> The shift on the part of Christian theologians from an image of Jesus' own knowledge of the in-breaking of God's realm among lovers of humanity to an image of Jesus himself as Lord of an otherworldly realm is tantamount to a movement from God to idolatry, or the making of Jesus into an image of all that he did not represent in the world.
> . . . God's incarnations are . . . many and varied. . . . To focus messianically on any one

person . . . is to deny the movement of power in relation through many incarnations in history. To worship a messianic figure is to lose touch with our power in relation. It is [actually] to distance ourselves [idolatrously] from God. (pp. 49, 164)

With Rubenstein (1966), Daly (1979a), and Heyward (1982, 1984), gay liberation theology may also want to reject divinizing Jesus, to reject making Jesus or anyone/thing else a tyrannical Lord over us. Thus, while Ruether (1985) argues that the theological development of trinitarian language was necessary to enable us to "think in terms of relationality within the divine, history, the created world, and human persons" (p. 21), we may argue instead that a radically monotheistic God can be self-conscious, self-reflective, and self-interrelated without being split or divided against godself. The analogy of human self-relatedness and the experience of God's horizontally intimate relation in history are sufficient. We do not need the multiple personalities of the trinity: Why should God be any less unified and integrated than people? The ideal (i.e., God) would indicate greater unity, in fact, and the ability to integrate more diversity of human variety, of sexuality, and of all created possibilities. Moreover, if incarnation is not a single trinitarian event for us, gay theology can enable us not only to appreciate and respect Jesus' embodiment of God's horizontal energy on behalf of the oppressed, but also to recognize and celebrate the similar embodiments or incarnations of liberational energy in Ghandi, in Martin Luther King, in the four nuns slain in El Salvador, in our own Harvey Milk, and even more importantly, in every man and woman, every gay man and lesbian, whose life is dedicated to the pursuit of justice, love, and right human interrelationship, here and now.

If in continuity with feminist theology, gay liberation theology can penetrate the process and the problems of Christology to affirm the utter humanness of Jesus and the radical oneness of God horizontally and intimately with us, we are also free to (re)consider--and to set aside--one other idolatrous element of dualistic otherworldliness in our tradition, one other stumbling block to a theology of praxis in the tasks of this-worldly liberation--belief in a literal resurrection. If Jesus is utterly human, if his life requires no external vertical validation, then resurrection is not only unnecessary; it may actually reinforce the effects of oppressive Christology. Ruether (1983b), for example, acknowledges that "too often Christians use the resurrection as a way of not taking the unresolved evils of history seriously" (p. 29).

For those who suffer, for those who are marginalized, for those who are oppressed, the human tragedy of Jesus' death is redoubled insofar as post-Pauline Christianity weakened the powerful message of the cross and made a literalized resurrection the crux of Christian belief. The this-worldly message that God is not an all-powerful vertical rescuer but is instead a horizontal, co-suffering power, strongest on our behalf in our experiences of (vertical) god-forsakenness and insistent that we assume responsibility for justice, was displaced by a cosmic/mythical salvation event. And, despite subsequent theological interpretations of a crucified, suffering divinity (Christ), literalizing the metaphor of resurrection has provided a stronger, subliminal message that an all-powerful god does "fix it all in the end," or worse, that a selective god rescues one special victim while the rest of the world languishes, all of which has consistently pointed believers toward an otherworldliness which contradicts both Jesus' own insistence upon God's immediate nearness and his demand for social justice in this world. Literalizing resurrection only functions as a further denial of the real tragedy in the world. Neither the tragedy of Jesus' martyrdom nor contemporary tragedy such as the pathos of AIDS can be so easily canceled! The God of Job, the God at the cross painfully aware of his/her own limitations, is the co-suffering and quietly empowering God and not a deus ex machina rescuer or an Hellenistic dying/rising God (cf., Clark, 1986a, 1987a). Ruether (1983b) similarly argues that the "whole concept of God as omnipotent sovereign [or all-powerful rescuer] is thrown into question by . . . the martyrdom of the just" (p. 29); rather, God identifies with the victims of human injustice here and now: "God abandons God's power into the human condition utterly and completely so that we might not abandon each other. God has become a part of the struggle of life [justice and liberation] against death [the systemic structures of oppression and dehumanization]" (p. 29). The resurrection as the focus of faith can in fact be displaced by the crucifixion as a symbolic locus of God's co-suffering activity; the struggle for justice continues, empowered in the face of and in spite of oppression and even tragedy and martyrdom (Ruether, 1983b).

Heyward (1982) also shifts the theological focus from any literalized resurrection back to the crucifixion, to the real tragedy of Jesus' death. In so doing, she again rejects otherworldly rescue and consequent human passivity and reemphasizes the demand for human responsibility in the creation of justice (or injustice), in the creation (or destruction) of right relationship:

> The rejection and, finally, the crucifixion of Jesus was the denial and death of God not because Jesus was God, but rather because his [empowering influence] disrupted so radically the good order of social and religious structures as to alarm those whose high institutional stakes were cemented in conformity, expediency, and the shallow secularity promised by established [authority]. The rejection and crucifixion of Jesus signaled the extent to which human beings will go to avoid our own relational possibilities. God dies when[ever] a person is put to death because he/[she] loves humanity too intimately, too powerfully, too well.
> . . . Jesus' death was an evil act, done by humanity to humanity, no more and no less evil than that which is always done to persons who are tortured and killed because they take justice seriously. . . . There is nothing . . . penultimate about the death of Jesus. His is an unnecessary, violent, [and] unjust death. (pp. 48, 56-57)

A resurrection was not necessary to validate Jesus' life and it certainly could not nullify the real experience of his suffering. Moreover, our ability to relinquish this artifact of cosmic drama and to take seriously Jesus' death, instead, forces us also to take seriously the reality and tragedy of all human injustice and cruelty, of all human passion and suffering, and thus to take responsibility for healing, for creating justice out of tragedy (Heyward, 1982).

Albeit colored by contemporaneous eschatological hopes to some extent, Jesus' message, as was the man himself, was grounded in the human community of his native Judaism and addressed to both the Roman and the Jewish oppressors and rulers of his own community. His crucifixion at their hands was/is a tragedy of the human inability to assume responsibility, to eschew power for justice. Jesus died on the cross. Period. Human tragedy is enough; we do not need a cosmic drama.

We do need, however, to see God's co-suffering limits and compassion in this paradigmatic tragedy of the human failure to seek justice. No miraculous validation of the historical demand for justice is necessary, particularly in Jesus' prophetic Jewish context; that demand is already established and validated a priori in the very nature of the covenantal history of that tradition. "Resurrection" is not an historical or cosmic event, deus ex machina. Metaphorically it bespeaks not only Jesus' friends' refusal to relinquish an intimate relationship and their experience of God's immediacy for justice; it also bespeaks the experience of any community whose charismatic leader is killed (e.g., Harvey Milk) or whose numbers are decimated by genocide (e.g., the Holocaust) or by disease (e.g., AIDS), when that community refuses to die as well, but instead finds itself re-empowered as a community, in the very face of death, to continue struggling for justice. "Resurrection" should not be literalized, spiritualized, or made otherworldly; its metaphorical force points to group empowerment, rather than defeat, in the face of oppression and tragedy (cf., Ruether, 1983b, Heyward, 1982). If we cannot, however, refrain from literalizing the metaphor, if we cannot resist focusing upon "Easter" as an historical/cosmic event instead of appropriately focusing upon "Good Friday," then as with Christology and all its oppressive, dualistic baggage, we must also completely set aside the concept of resurrection and in its place develop other, less ambiguous metaphors for describing hope and empowerment in the midst of defeat, life in spite of tragedy and death. Our this-worldly images must recognize both the fragility and the tenacity of life and bespeak both renewal and empowerment, after mourning and catharsis.

The anthropological and this-worldly focus of our efforts toward a gay liberation theology thus lead us to reject not only the eschatological escapism of patriarchal (and heterosexist) dualism, but, in a thoroughgoing fashion, to reject as well the Christolatrous divination of Jesus and the miraculous rescue/validation of his particular human life, insofar as both these concepts simply reinforce the world-denying and responsibility-avoiding dualism we first rejected. Jesus lived and died and yet the value of his life did not die with him. That is our theological dilemma. Or, as Heyward (1982) has suggested, the prophetic corrective for developing a liberation theology lies not in who or what Jesus was (Logos, Son of God, a trinitarian member of godhead, a resurrected/returning

savior), but in what he did; unfortunately, as she also
readily admits, reconstructing what he did is the far
more difficult task, because even the most historically
reliable layers of texts in the Synoptic gospels are
already shaped by frequently anti-Jewish and pro-Chris-
tian theological concerns. Nevertheless, within our
feminist, gay, and even our Jewish sources for a gender-based and gay-sensitive liberation theology,
Ruether (1978, 1983a, 1983b, 1985), Heyward (1982,
1984), and others have been able to reconstruct and to
expand upon a reliable portrait of the Jewish Jesus
which may have some significant meaning for us far beyond that of any Christological images.

(iii) Reconstructing a Jewish and Gay-Sensitive Jesus

Both Heyward (1982) and Ruether (1983a) agree that
Jesus was in no way attempting to break with his own
ethnic and religious Judaism. Moreover, as regards the
sociopolitical climate of his day, he was interested
neither in transforming Judaism into a nationalistic
campaign to overthrow Roman occupation per se nor, conversely, in imbuing Judaism with an otherworldly escapism which would encourage passivity before that oppression. What he was doing was radicalizing the Jewish
concepts of God's covenantal and immediate advocacy of
the oppressed and God's demand for justice in the present; as such, he both embodied and extended the prophetic tradition already integral to Judaism:

> [Jesus] was not attempting to undo Judaism. . . .
> He was not trying to negate the covenant, but
> rather to radicalize it. What was new in Jesus'
> realization of the covenant was the intimacy and
> immediacy of God's activity through human [power
> and agency]. (Heyward, 1982, p. 42)
> Jesus seems to express a radicalized view of the
> [Judaic] concept of a coming reign of God as a
> time of the vindication of the poor and the op-
> pressed [the religiously and socially marginal-
> ized]. (Ruether, 1983a, p. 120)

How Jesus understood and used his Judaism prophetically to critique his society from within, rather
than how he developed some radically new revelation,
thus becomes critical. Ruether (1983b) argues, consequently, that prophetic criticism, such as Jesus', was
always that of one loyally committed to Judaism, that
of one perhaps marginal to institutionalized

(hierarchically powerful or authoritative) Judaism, but one nevertheless totally within the overall tradition. Specifically, then, Jesus combined both the messianic and prophetic themes, both the religious and sociopolitical elements, both the transcendent and this-worldly demands of Judaism, in order to oppose any oppression of the poor and the marginalized by the local ruling classes; Jesus did thereby indirectly indict the political domination of Palestine by Rome, insofar as it contributed to this prior (more fundamental) oppression. In more general terms, Jesus simply reiterated or reemphasized the prophetic Jewish belief that reconciliation or right relationship with God and justice or right relationship on earth (regardless of who holds religious or political power) are one and the same:

> Reconciliation with God means revolutionizing of human social, political relations, overthrowing unjust, oppressive relationships. The sociopolitical dimension is never lost in [prophetic or messianic] Judaism, but always remains the central expression of what it means to obey God. (Ruether, 1983b, p. 11)

At the individual or personal level, Jesus' concerns similarly reflected an ethical norm of justice as right relation: Love of God and love of neighbor were (and are) one and the same (Heyward, 1982). Even with this personal norm, however, Jesus was still not developing a new idea, but simply espousing and reiterating a Jewish concept earlier articulated by Hillel: "Leaders of the Pharisaic schools, such as Hillel, were making some of the same interpretations of the Law as did Jesus; i.e., that love of neighbor is the essence of the Law" (Ruether, 1983b, p. 37, cf., Falk, 1985).[11] Falk (1985) even goes so far as to contend that, within the sometimes violent conflict between the followers of Shammai and the followers of Hillel over whether and how Judaism should be extended to Gentiles in Palestine, Jesus was,

> . . . actually a follower of the School of Hillel. . . . Any criticism of the Pharisees attributed to him was in reality directed against the opposing School of Shammai, who were in control of the Pharisees at the time. By attempting to bring salvation to the non-Jewish world [by demanding justice of Romans, Jews, and others

alike], he would have been following the teaching
of Hillel. (p. 86)

Because, according to Falk (1985), Jesus was himself
clearly Jewish identified and even closely aligned with
the Pharisaic School of Hillel, and because earliest
"Christianity" (pre-70 C.E.) was intended merely as a
branch or movement within Judaism, neither Jesus' negative pronouncements against the Pharisees, nor any of
his other teachings, should be distorted to justify
antisemitism.[12]
    That Jesus' personal ethics and social justice
concerns were sometimes also overlaid with an eschatological fervor stems from yet another part of first
century Judaism, then current apocalypticism, and
Jesus' own possible early involvement with the Essenes,
an apocalyptic sect (cf., Falk, 1985). In Jesus' actual message, however, eschatological otherworldliness
never overbalanced the demand for this-worldly justice.
In fact, Jesus' synthesis of messianism/apocalypticism
and Hebrew prophecy made eschatology not a future hope,
but a present possibility dependent upon human action
and not upon miraculous divine intervention. The es-
chaton as an era of human justice and earthly peace
could be/can be created here and now by human action.
Jesus' seeming eschatological fervor, as a powerful demand for an immediate and revolutionary in-breaking and
creation of a "messianic age" of utter justice, by humans cooperating with God horizontally and here and
now, thus remained both sociopolitical and theological.
Moreover, the full actualization of such a vision would
indeed have been a real threat to those individuals,
whether Roman or Jewish, whose power was dependent upon
an oppressive status quo. In this light, Jesus' death
was not just a mistake; it was a political expedient in
opposition to justice, a tragedy of failed human responsibility. Those Roman and Jewish leaders whose positions were threatened by the potential of Jesus' prophetic message collaborated in his death. The power
holders in the oppressive hierarchy, regardless of
race, ethnicity, or religion, and not the Jews as a
category, were thus responsible for his death (cf.,
Ruether, 1983b, Rubenstein, 1966, Falk, 1985, Heyward,
1982). Ruether (1983b) goes on to say that subsequent
non-Jewish Christianity has been equally culpable of
betrayal whenever it has similarly acted as a powerful
oppressor and excluder of any people.
    Upon this understanding of the prophetic, ethical,
and thoroughly Jewish context of Jesus' life, teaching,

and death, Ruether (1983a, 1983b, 1985) and Heyward (1982, 1984) continue to interpret and to reconstruct an understanding or portrait of Jesus which is at once grounded in tradition and exemplary for all liberation theology. Convinced that Jesus' message is this-worldly and sociopolitical as well as religious, for example, Ruether (1983a, 1983b) contends that the Synoptic Jesus' renewal of prophetic vision, his criticism of religious and social hierarchies, and his insistent message that God is on the side of marginalized and despised people did not and do not seek a simplistic reversal wherein the oppressed become the oppressor. Instead, his vision aimed "at a new reality in which hierarchy and dominance are overcome as principles of social relations" (1983a, p. 136, cf., 1983b, pp. 17, 53). Jesus simultaneously perceived the interconnectedness of all those things (whether economic, classist, religious, or [hetero]sexist) which are used to oppress and exclude people; called for a renunciation or dissolution of the "web of status relationships by which societies have defined privilege and deprivation" and sought instead a "new humanity of service and mutual empowerment"; and, "announced that God's favor [was/is] upon those who [had/have] no chance in the present system of social status and religious observance . . . the humiliated of society," including all marginalized people (Ruether, 1983a, p. 137, 1985, p. 108). By renouncing systems of domination and dehumanization, Jesus embodied in his person and life both the corrective shift from hierarchical/vertical models of divine/ human and human relationships to communal/horizontal models, and thereby, his own understanding of a "new humanity of service and mutual empowerment" (Ruether, 1983b, p. 56, cf., 1983a). He envisioned,

> . . . a new kind of power, . . . exercised through [mutual] service, which empowers the disinherited and brings all to a new relationship of mutual empowerment. . . . All power and domination relations in society are overcome by overcoming the root metaphor of relationship to God modeled on King-servant relations.
> . . . [He envisioned] a time when [the] pattern of power over others would be overcome by a new pattern of relationship. (Ruether, 1983a, p. 30, 1985, p. 108)

Rejecting power to rule for that power which instead empowers and liberates the oppressed of any system (i.e., including gay people), Jesus re-invoked the empowering image of God as liberator in history, in order to seek both the "conquest of human historical evil" (as failed responsibility to seek justice) and the correction or righting of divine/human and human interrelationships (Ruether, 1983b, p. 15, cf., p. 54f).

Heyward (1982, 1984) similarly continues to develop this portrait of Jesus' concern for justice and right relationship when she recognizes that Jesus "seemed to perceive that his work would involve a radical shift in consciousness . . . from an emphasis, for example, on ritual to right-relationship" (1984, p. 17). She further contends that, as fully (and only) human, Jesus' actions are exemplary insofar as they were <u>voluntary</u> in his assuming responsibility for creating justice and enabling God-in-the-world; not compelled from above, his actions were a matter of choice and decision, of cooperation and mutual dependence (cf., 1982). The other exemplary elements of Jesus' life and ministry which she reemphasizes are his sense of immediacy and radical presentness in this world ("an urgent sense of investment in the present" [1982, p. 49]), his concern that other people also (re)claim their <u>own</u> "capacity to make God incarnate--immediately" (1982, p. 53), and his belief that, in so doing, we also reclaim our shared participation in the justice-making activity about which God has been all along and for which God absolutely depends upon our help:

> The image of a Jesus who contravened unjust relation, who suffered pain rather than compromise . . ., who hated . . . unjust death, including his own, can push us beyond our temptations to make easy peace with injustice [or with] our own hesitation.
> Fulfillment . . . did not begin [or end] with Jesus. . . . The fulfillment of God's reign . . . is the constancy of empowerment of God's people by God <u>and</u> the ongoing empowerment of God by God's people to break the yokes of oppression wherever they exist. (1982, p. 168, 1984, p. 178)

In addition both to Jesus' urgent concerns for immediate and this-worldly human justice and right relationship, which are clearly exemplary for any liberation theology (the question of their uniqueness notwithstanding), and to his reiteration that God is radically present on behalf of any marginalized group responsibly seeking liberation (including gay people),

another question about this man which is of critical
importance for our efforts toward a specifically gay
liberation theology is that of where Jesus might have
stood regarding human sexuality. Fortunato (1987) ten-
tatively suggests, for example, that Jesus seemed to be
saying that "all of creation is holy; that all that can
be apprehended sensuously [i.e., including sexually] is
sacred; and that God is known potently [even fecundly]
in all that God creates" (p. 62).   Elsewhere (Fortunato, 1983), he has elaborated on the traditional response to this issue which gay liberationist Christians
have generally developed:

> Although scripture never quotes Jesus as saying
> anything about homosexual people, he did spend a
> lot of time with social outcasts. . . . His atti-
> tude toward those rejected by society was always
> one of incredible compassion. . . . He identified
> with them, accepted their lot as his own, and
> loved them as they had never been loved before.
> (pp. 124-125)

While Jesus' unabashed identity with the socially outcast of his day is clearly important for us, many of us
may nevertheless remain uncomfortable with only the
general inclusion and the seemingly specific omission
of sexuality and of gay people with which this widely
held, apologetic view contents itself.   One alternative, then, is to examine our own phenomenological experience, as gay people, of Jesus' life and person.
     Cosmos (1984), for example, develops an eroticized
understanding of Jesus which may be quite meaningful,
specifically for gay men.   Through the eroticization of
the often same-sex identified Jesus, he makes a spiritual, empathetic connection with sensual, suffering,
male bodiliness and thus with gay oppression. A sexual
longing for the wiry, powerless, and virtually naked
Jesus of crucifixion portrayals has the potential, he
argues, to connect us as gay men with Jesus' experience
of (vertical) god-forsakenness and with his faith in a
(horizontal) co-suffering God at the margins.   Eroti-
cizing Jesus discloses his love for all people and nurtures our love for him and in turn for God (and for
others).   Our erotically empowered love for Jesus, and
thus for the God proactively present in pain and suffering, can undergird our capacities to love one another, to join against the forces of gay oppression,
and to help persons-with-AIDS.   For Cosmos (1984) an
eroticized, sexual/sensual Jesus is a powerful symbol,

at least for gay men, of God's presence and empowerment
in gay sexuality, gay relationships, and gay struggles
for liberation:

> I always felt sorry for Jesus, hanging up
> there on the cross, his body all stretched out and
> twisted in pain, his genitals barely covered. I
> imagined how his naked body would feel against
> mine.
> . . . that image of pained, naked maleness,
> who hung out with other men and spoke of love and
> sharing.
> . . . Hanging limp and hurting and mostly
> naked in plain view, Jesus was all alone. (p. 32)

For gay men according to this view, our sexual yearnings toward and our compassion for Jesus interweave as
we reach toward him, toward God, and toward others to
heal pain correctively with justice. However, while
the idea of a sexual pull toward Jesus and through him
toward God is akin to Heyward's (1984) belief in our
each having a sexually motivated drive toward mutual
relation and justice, a fixation solely upon the crucifixion borders upon sadism and a sexual focus upon a
male-identified Jesus both excludes our lesbian sisters
and distorts the extent of his relationships with women
as well as with men in the scriptural record. Jesus
the rugged carpenter, sunburned fisherman, and wandering prophet may indeed conjure sexual feelings which
have broader implications for gay men; however, our inclusive efforts toward a gay liberation theology require something more, something deeper, than either
Jesus' general identity with the socially outcast or a
male-eroticized experience of him. Fortunately, Ruether (1978) has provided just such an in-depth look at
Jesus and sexuality in both canonical and noncanonical
sources. Her study may therefore prove an invaluable
resource for our work (cf., Clark, 1987a).
    Ruether (1978) argues that while the traditional
image of Jesus is one of holiness divorced from sexuality, the most historically reliable layers of the Synoptic gospels do not imply that sexuality is the heart
of sinfulness. Jesus himself was far more concerned
with the "sins of religious hypocrisy [and] the sins of
the powerful among the religious and economic elite
against the little ones" (p. 134). Indeed, she has
discovered the possibility that Jesus' own sexuality
was channeled in neither acceptable direction insofar
as "he appears to be neither married nor celibate" (p.

135).   She consequently pays equal attention to both
Jesus' primary relationships, with Mary Magdalene and
with John.   Of Mary as portrayed in noncanonical writings, Ruether (1978) says that her "role is affirmed as
a way of castigating religious male chauvinism and up-
holding the equality of women. . . . Jesus is even portrayed as having a special love relationship with Mary
Magdalene.   She is his beloved disciple.   She under-
stands him better than the others, and he responds with
physical caresses" (p. 135).   Equally clear within the
canon, Jesus' relation to John was also one of love
which included physical touching and signs of affection.   John is "repeatedly referred to as the one who
laid his head on Jesus' breast" (p. 136).   Ruether
(1978) uses this apparently bisexual potential within
the person of Jesus as a standpoint for criticizing patriarchal machismo:

> There is much in the model of Jesus in the New
> Testament which makes him decidedly a male who
> was, if not unmasculine, at least iconoclastic to-
> ward male models of power and authority.
>   . . . The striking fact about the Synoptics
> is the lack of [sex-role] stereotyping. . . . His
> is an authority that overthrows conventional
> models of patriarchal, hierarchical, religious,
> and political power systems; that champions women,
> the poor, the . . . outcasts [and] that rejects
> the power games of the male leadership classes.
> (p. 136)

Ruether's (1978) conclusions thus appropriately
criticize the patriarchal obsession with sexuality,
while simultaneously elucidating Jesus' own proper pri-
oritizing of sexuality:

> Jesus' life gives no exclusive sanctification
> to a particular sexual lifestyle, whether celibate
> or married, hetero- or homosexual, as the norma-
> tive model. . . . None of these options is en-
> shrined, none is ruled out. . . .
>   If there is anything at all to be said about
> the sexuality of Jesus it is that it was a sexual-
> ity under the control of friendship.   He could
> love both John and Mary Magdalene, physically em-
> brace and be embraced by them, because first of
> all he knew them as friends, not as sexual ob-
> jects. (p. 137)

While no real evidence either for sexual activity or for its particular absence (celibacy) exists per se in the sources and texts, the picture which does emerge is that of a Jesus who was not obsessed with sexuality, but who instead was able to relate intimately, tenderly, and equally with both men and women in ways which also included physical affection and in ways always guided not by sexual objectification or exploitation, but rather by friendship. Jesus was, according to Ruether (1978), a fully sexual (and probably actively sexual) individual whose relationships were nevertheless "controlled not by sexuality, but by friendship" (p. 137). That priority can be a part of his exemplary force for our efforts in gay liberation theology, insofar as we seek to affirm and to celebrate our sexuality in responsible and compassionate ways as lesbians and gay men, in the very face of AIDS, while also responding to both our sick and our well friends as friends first and not just as sexual objects.

Barrett (1978) anticipates such a perspective when she extends Ruether's (1978) conclusions to affirm that restoring sexuality to our understanding of Jesus, as to our (re)conceptualization of God, affirms and uplifts those people who have been marginalized because of our sexuality. A fully human and fully sexual Jesus is thus an especially important image for us as gay people: Our capacity to embody God, to make God effective in the world through our love-making/justice-making (cf., Heyward, 1984) has nothing to do with what is "technically and literally the accident of sex. . . . We human beings are not just souls, we are bodies as well, and God participate[s] in our bodily life, dignifying and sanctifying it forever as an instrument of love" (Barrett, 1978, pp. 331-332, cf., Clark, 1987a). Moreover, Jesus can only be important for us if he was not only fully human, but also a full participant in bodily, and hence sexual, human existence.

Overall, the importance and/or place of Jesus in our efforts at gay liberation theology remain tentative, provisional, an open question. While we discover that the Christological divinization of Jesus and the mythico-eschatological resurrection of Jesus both reflect and sustain the same dualistic structures which devalue this life and which exclude gay people, we also find that what he did is more important than who/what he was, anyway (cf., Heyward, 1982). Similarly, while we find that his prophetic insistence upon human responsibility for justice and upon God's radical advocacy of the oppressed is not unique, but is grounded in

his native prophetic Judaism, we also still find him
having some exemplary force for us, in terms both of
his this-worldly obsession with justice and his understandings of human sexuality and friendship. We do not
in fact have to make Jesus a Christ, or even particularly unique, to understand God's radical incarnation-
ality in and through all of us, or to understand God's
absolute presence in the stuff, the energy, and the in-
terrelatedness of this world, of real history, and of
real people, as these concerns were reiterated by
Jesus. Historically, God is most effective in human
right relationships, in the struggles and suffering for
justice, in divine limitation and human justice-seeking
and -making; God depends upon us to make godself effective and real--in our love-making, in our physical and
sensual experience of the world, in our awareness of
the erotic power in nature, and in our ability to sense
and to imbue the very cosmos with dynamic/erotic/fecund
power (cf., Fortunato, 1987). The locus of belief,
then, need not be in the person of Jesus, much less in
the discontinuous and oppressive image of Christ, but
rather generally in the unity of Judaism with earliest
Palestinian Christianity and specifically in the unity
of God's co-suffering advocacy of all marginalized
people and God's demand for justice and mutual/healing/
reconciling human relationships here and now, which is,
after all, the very heart of the message shared by both
Hillel and Jesus.

* * *

* A Gay Celebration *

VII. Resanctifying Gay Being

(i) Coming Out to Empowerment

The activity of developing a thoroughgoing and systematic gay liberation theology, as well as the sources for this process, consistently shift our attention from contemplating the divine nature or focusing idolatrously upon any single incarnation of the divine, toward reexamining humanity instead. Such an anthropological focus for gay liberation theology further entails relinquishing any eschatological or otherworldly hope for divine intervention on our behalf and reclaiming, instead, our responsibility, not only for our own lives and relationships, but for our very liberation itself. Indeed, for us as gay men and lesbians, theology and praxis conflate; we are responsible for seeking, demanding, and creating justice and liberation. Conversely, our failures to assume responsibility, our fearful refusals to claim and to use our power to effect liberation, not only function to forestall our liberation; such failures and refusals may actually undercut our very humanity. Speaking for both women and gay people, for example, Heyward (1984) contends that the "greatest sin" of an oppressed and marginalized people "has always been our failure to take ourselves seriously as strong, powerful, autonomous and creative persons" (p. 3); moreover, "our fear of our strength may be our undoing. And our learning to stand and speak up for ourselves may well be our salvation" (p. 131, cf., Morton, 1985).

While we clearly have the capacity to claim and to assert our power and our full humanity, to create redemptive and liberating justice for ourselves and for others, we can still choose passivity and inactivity instead. Whenever we accept the heterosexist devaluation of ourselves as merely one-dimensional and purely sexual beings, whenever we pursue assimilation into the hierarchies of heterosexist acceptability and power instead of pursuing radical/systemic/structural change, whenever we believe government or institutionalized religion or the medical research system will altruisti-

cally protect our best interests, and whenever we fail
to participate in celebrations of gay/lesbian pride or
demonstrations for gay/lesbian rights because someone
else will "do it for us," in all these instances we abdicate our power. Such passive inactivity, like expecting some deus ex machina to rescue us or waiting
for governmental leadership or the emergence of some
new gay/lesbian hero/martyr (another Harvey Milk) to do
the hard work of liberation-seeking and -creating for
us, always shifts the responsibility for our liberation
onto others. Moreover, as long as we do so, we will-
fully forfeit our full humanity as gay people before
the forces of oppression: "To the extent that we seek
heroes [gay martyrs or a divine deus ex machina] to do
it for us--someone else to incarnate the power . . . we
give up our birthrights to . . . walk in the world
. . . and [to] claim our own power to do something--
simply because we believe that we must" (Heyward, 1984,
pp. 119-120).

The obvious alternative to such passive forfeiture
of either our full humanity or our liberation as gay
men and lesbians is for us to (re)claim our power, our
traditional/historical strength, and our in-born, created goodness. We can (re)claim what has been within
us all along, including not only our value and worth,
but our capacities to effect change as well (cf., Heyward, 1984). Not surprisingly, Judaism provides the
best historical example, within our western religious
heritage, of both the refusal to accept powerlessness
and the consequent empowerment of active and assertive
endurance. The collective Jewish experience, as a frequently threatened and oppressed people, has developed
a moral obligation not to encourage oppressors with
passivity, but to eschew martyrdom by an assumption of
protest and action against human injustice (Fackenheim,
1970).

Speaking from the historical standpoint of accumulated antisemitism and virtual genocide, Fackenheim
(1970) writes that "the voice of Auschwitz commands
Jews . . . to accept their singled out condition, face
up to its contradictions, and endure them. Moreover,
it gives the power of endurance. . . . The Jew of today
can endure because he [sic.] must endure, and he [sic.]
must endure because he [sic.] is commanded to endure"
(p. 92). Through the historical perspective of Auschwitz, both Fackenheim (1970) and Rubenstein (1966) have
come to recognize the radical powerlessness (and even
death) of God before human failures, injustice, and
cruelty, and to experience therein both the co-suffer-

ing compassion of God for the victims of injustice and
the demand of God that the oppressed themselves refuse
to be victims. Fackenheim (1970) consequently describes a number of duties, the fulfillment of which empowers the oppressed, duties (1) to remember and to
tell about (antisemitic) persecutions, (2) to survive
rather than to seek or to accept martyrdom, (3) to
refuse either cynicism or otherworldliness ("not to
abandon the world . . . but rather to continue to work
and to hope for it" [p. 87]), and (4) to continue to
wrestle with God and to bear a kinship will all other
victims of oppression.

According to Fackenheim (1970), then, Jews are
commanded to persevere, to sustain the continuum from
past to future, by living fully (actively, not passively) in the present, by embodying the divine covenant with all marginalized people, and by compassion-
ately/empathetically sharing the agony and even death
suffered by those who are different. At the same time,
remembering God's demand for human justice, when
coupled with the memory of Auschwitz, empowers ongoing
Jewish efforts for justice, efforts to create hope and
to (re)create God's presence in just human relationships. For gay men and lesbians, as well as for gay
theology, Jewish experience can be paradigmatic for our
(re)discovering not only God's presence in suffering
(whether in the anti-gay genocide in our own history,
or in current homophobic violence, or in the tragedy of
AIDS), but God's demand for justice as well (against
heterosexism, homophobia, and AIDS-phobia). Much like
for the Jews, our gay survival throughout history, our
adamant refusal before anti-gay violence and politics
to simply "go away," our refusal before AIDS to quit
loving one another--in fact our loving each other even
more deeply, and our persistent presence and visibility, are together the very sources of our power, of
our capacity to act and to effect our liberation.[13]

Moreover, as conservative politics and religion
have exploited the AIDS crisis to feed an already increasing homophobia, the command/demand that we claim
and use our power has in turn become even more persistent. As the half-million participants in the October
1987 March on Washington for Lesbian and Gay Rights
made clear, the time is past for wasting our energies
in gay self-justification and in gay apologetics; the
time is past for arguing scripture and seeking assimilation into established churches and synagogues or into
the clergy on "their" terms; and, the time is certainly
past for passive inactivity, whether in regard to the

sociopolitical or the religious realms. We must, instead, take up the tasks of forthrightly doing and enacting/embodying a gay theology-as-praxis, absolutely and without apology. We must take up the tasks of our own liberation, all of us, together. As Heyward (1984) has said, "The time has come . . . to channel our . . . energies into the active realization of our power . . . and to make no apologies for being who and what we are" (p. 3); in fact, "to be oneself is the only truly responsible way to be" (p. 17). We must claim and use our power to effect liberation; and claiming our power means we must first (re)claim and (re)affirm ourselves. Only in claiming ourselves, in coming out, do we really begin to glimpse the immense power we actually have.

Fox (1983) has described the "sacrament of 'coming out'" as a "kind of letting go: a letting go of the images of personhood, sexuality, and selfhood that society has put on one in favor of trusting oneself enough to let oneself be oneself" (p. 198). Those powerful images of heterosexist enculturation, however, are very strong ones which often make coming out a difficult process of anger and mourning over estranged familial relationships and lost professional possibilities, a process of grieving for what life "might have been" otherwise, a process of often painful spiritual deepening and "letting go" in order to accept and to affirm one's gay or lesbian identity and to embrace one's exile on the margins of sociocultural acceptability (Fortunato, 1983, cf., Clark, 1987a, 1987d). Moreover, those of us determined to create a gay liberation theology, as well as those of us equally determined to nurture the ongoing pursuit and creation of gay liberation, face a double bind. We must advocate and nurture compassion, without condescension, for those numerous individuals who feel that pressures of whatever sort warrant keeping the closet door closed for now, while at the same time we must insist that coming out en masse is both the only sure route to authentic living as gay men and lesbians and the best means for discovering and claiming our collective power to seek our own liberation (cf., Boyd, 1984). Albeit a process without the benefit(s) of culturally ritualized support (or "rites of passage"), coming out is nevertheless a vitally important process of discovering and constructing an authentic self-identity "from within," of discovering one's own truths, and thus of building "ontological security" upon one's "own myths" (Walker, 1980, pp. 18-19). As such, coming out requires penetrating one's depths, discovering one's center of meaning, being, identity, and values, and beginning to live from this newfound center or grounding as one's spiritual empowerment. The process may also include confronting and resolving opposites, discovering the genuine balance or androgyny of the unity-in-plurality of God/cosmos, and imploding the enculturated heterosexist/patriarchal divisiveness of the self, thereby penetrating, confusing, and reconciling the opposites (Walker, 1980). For a gay man, in particular, these aspects of the coming out process require a commitment to "ending male dominance within himself" (Walker, 1980, p. 88).

For any individual, then, the deepening required by coming out, the process of discovering and constructing an authentic and centered self, can yield an "infinite enspiriting empowering source" or grounding for being gay or lesbian in a homophobic society (Walker, 1980, p. 90, cf., Fortunato, 1983). That process and its individual empowerment can further enable an individual to join with other gay men and lesbians in community. In other words, coming out exchanges the isolation of the closet for the nurturance of community, whereby the empowerment of the freed and centered self can be endlessly multiplied and further nourished for our joint efforts at liberation. Coming out, therefore, not only functions to free the individual from the closet, but on its communal side, also functions "to name social reality and to participate in its re-imaging. It is to lift up for reassessment a piece of covert public policy which needs overt public attention" (Heyward, 1982, p. 134). Coming out is to move both toward claiming our responsibility for right and just relationships and toward engaging in corrective action. Coming out is, thus, not only an intensely personal act, but a social, political, and spiritual act as well:

> Coming out is a protest against social structures that are built on alienation between men and women, women and women, men and men. Coming out is the most radical, deeply personal and consciously political affirmation I can make on behalf of the possibilities of love and justice in the social order. Coming out is moving into relation with peers. It is not simply a way of being in bed, but rather a way of being in the world. . . . Coming out is an invitation to look and see and consider the value of mutuality in human life. Coming out is simultaneously a political movement

and the mighty rush of God's spirit carrying us on. (Heyward, 1984, p. 82, emphasis added)

Coming out moves us beyond isolation and "mere homosexual acts" to the realization of our gayness as an all-encompassing existential standpoint for being in the world, for shaping/nurturing community, for joining with God's empowering advocacy and companionship, and thus for effecting our liberation. Coming out is the way into our empowerment, as a liberation-seeking and -creating people (cf., Goodman et al., 1983).

Fortunato (1983, 1987) has been most astute to the ways in which coming out brings us to empowerment by first confronting us with the personal costs involved and with the realities of homophobia and anti-gay oppression. Only as we are able to deepen, to penetrate, our personal and collective experience(s) of oppression do we come through or come out to empowerment. He says that "being exiled puts us intimately in touch with our powerlessness [our experience of oppression]. . . . But precisely because we are confronted with that awareness, we [discover therein] spiritual empowerment," the empowerment required to act and to be (1987, p. 27). Ironically for those of us indoctrinated to the "sinfulness" of anger, our anger experienced in grieving and later embracing our marginality, as well as our collective anger as a people embattled by homophobic oppression and even violence, can be an important resource for this empowerment. Ruether (1983a), for example, argues that our anger can be liberating and grace-filled insofar as it empowers us both to break from our socialization and to demand our liberation: "Only by experiencing one's anger and alienation can one move on, with real integrity, to another level of truth" (p. 188). In other words, whenever we take responsibility for our lives and our liberation in the absence of any deus ex machina, genuine divinity is revealed as the empowerment and sustenance which can enable us to transcend self-pity and fear. We further discover divine empowerment as we realize the righteousness of our anger and the consequent need for prophetic, corrective activity in the face of oppression. In fact, our anger at life's seeming unfairness or at human injustice and cruelty is not opposed to God; it is actually nurtured by the divine presence on our behalf (cf., Clark, 1986a, 1987a). Heyward (1982) similarly describes God as an "indignant" or angry power against injustice and asserts that "without our crying, our yearning, our raging, there is no God" (pp. 55,

172). Our righteous and divinely nourished anger further enables us to transcend self-doubt, depression and madness and to develop self-esteem and gay pride instead, virtues without which we can have no sense of self or of community (Heyward, 1982, Ruether, 1983a).

Our anger alone, however, is not itself liberating, unless we are able to deepen and to temper our anger with a compassion equally borne of our experiences of oppression and of God-with-us therein. Much like Fortunato (1987), Edwards (1984) contends that insofar as gay men and lesbians know human oppression and hatred, we also have a capacity for knowing the depths of God's love, for discovering God's empowerment at the margins. Our excluded gay and lesbian sexuality itself can actually become the very source of our compassion: "Love, without becoming antisexual, is carried beyond the [narrow] perimeters of sexuality . . . into the total arena of the liberation struggle" (p. 125). Heyward (1984) further extends this understanding of our compassion, borne at once from our anger at injustice and from our exiled sexuality, when she says that,

> . . . we, as lesbians and gay men, have some particular resources for faithfulness: our experience as victims of injustice; our knowledge of the sham of sex roles; and our elusive and bittersweet awareness of the moral power and value of our bodies. . . .
> [Moreover], our concrete faith as lesbians and gay men will reflect (1) awareness of our common situation as victim; (2) commitment to making right this situation, to creating justice; and (3) solidarity with other victims of injustice, oppression, and discrimination. (pp. 199, 193)

Our anger, our capacity for compassion, our marginalized sexual loving, and God's absolute nearness with and for us--all of these resources constitute our particular power as lesbians and gay men (cf., Morton, 1985). As such, our communal spiritual power is very different from a patriarchically conceived, hierarchically structured power of domination and subordination. Our same-sex love at the margins is, instead, a balancing, horizontal, mutually relational force in opposition to vertically distributed power, a love energy which champions and empowers the powerless, and thus a socially democratic power (Walker, 1980, Morton, 1985). Our power is horizontal, reciprocal, shared/held in common and within our marginalized community; our power simply awaits our collective realization, reclamation, and shared enactment to create significant liberational change (Heyward, 1984). Our power is not something we can possess as a tool or as a weapon; it is rather an abstract quality of our liberation, not as a goal which can be achieved once and for all, but as a process or communal journey in which we simultaneously celebrate what we have already achieved--"the vision we have seen, the power we are sharing, and the justice we are making"--while continuing to struggle (Heyward, 1984, p. 181). Says Heyward (1984), "Our strength is our commitment to do something about what we have experienced, to celebrate the just and change the unjust. . . . Our strength is our commitment to live our values" (p. 128).

Heyward (1984) also continually reconnects us to the reality that our power, our capacities to reclaim and enact our power in the sociopolitical and religious realms, does not and cannot depend upon anyone or anything other than ourselves. We alone are responsible for claiming or failing to claim our power. Not only is our power not vertically given; God in fact depends on us in order for God to empower us in turn. Thus is our power utterly horizontal and mutual:

> We cannot fool ourselves . . . that someone else is going to liberate us. . . . We need to realize the inseparability of our efforts and our commitments and our lives from the activity, and love, and life of God who lives and moves through us, and with us, and in us, and among us.
>   . . . God needs us. Our commitments. Our hearts. Our touching and our pleasures. Our bodies. . . . God is our liberator. . . . And, just as surely, we are the liberators of God. (pp. 182, 183)

The utterly horizontal, mutual, and communal nature of our power as gay men and lesbians, a power interdependent with divine advocacy and companionship, also constitutes our "faithfulness" as gay people, according to Heyward (1984). Insofar as we are able to synthesize both our experience(s) of oppression, our individual and collective anger, and our deepened compassion, and are thereby able to shape, claim, and enact our power in the ongoing process and tasks of liberation, through all of this do we emerge as a faithful liberation community. A faithful people is a committed, participating, and empowered people:

Faith is our commitment to participate, with and by the power of God, in the ongoing creation, liberation, and blessing of the world.

. . . Our faith will reflect some pain, some alienation and, as we grow stronger . . . some anger in a commitment to loosen the bonds of oppression, to break the yoke of victimization. . . . Our experience of victimization stands us alongside many other victims in this world. . . .

[Moreover], to be faithful . . . is to touch and be touched--whether physically or otherwise--with a depth and quality of tenderness that actually helps create life where there is death, comfort where there is despair. To be faithful in our sexualities is to live a commitment to mutual, reciprocal relations between and among ourselves in which no one owns, possesses, dominates, or controls . . . but rather in which [we participate together in the tasks of liberation]. (pp. 190, 192)

Over and over again are we reminded theologically of our responsibility for our own liberation. Our sources for a gay liberation theology insist and exemplify a demand/command that we refuse passive victimization and that we take up the tasks of liberation instead. We are commanded not only to endure, but to act, to come out, to claim our individual power and to nurture our communal power, as lesbians and gay men (cf., Morton, 1985). As we confront the pain and losses of coming out, as well as the realities of anti-gay oppression, we discover in our anger and in our capacities for empathy and compassion a peculiar, divinely nourished power. Moreover, we discover that we can not only accept, but actually embrace and prefer our place at the margins. We find there that our particular sexuality is not only the source or cause of our ostracism; rather, our gay/lesbian sexuality is a blessing which enables mutuality and reciprocity, and which consequently nurtures our horizontal and shared power to effect liberation as a people faithful to our created goodness, to God's a priori acceptance of us, and to God's intimate presence with and for us. Coming out and reclaiming our power to demand, seek, and create liberation transcends the heterosexist devaluation of our sexuality and instead lifts up our sexual mutuality as the sacred source and grounding of our power as a liberation community.

(ii) Reaffirming Human Sexuality

The history of western religious, and hence moral, thought has more often affirmed a dualistic Christian denigration of the body and of human sexuality, rather than affirming with Judaism the goodness of sexuality and the wholeness of bodiliness and spirituality (cf., Waskow, 1983, Fortunato, 1987, Saslow, 1987). Speaking from the latter perspective, Rubenstein (1966) contends, therefore, that human sin does not lie in our fundamental/original bodiliness or sexuality, but rather in the prideful refusal of passion, in the embarrassed estrangement from nature, and in the guilt-ridden spirituality which destroys pleasure and drives people to excess. He writes, "Only hubris is man's [sic.] real sin [which] characterizes [our] refusal of the ecstasy and power of existence. . . . Hubris characterizes [our] refusal of [our] limits . . . [our] sin against [our] own being, [our] pathetic refusal to recognize and be [ourselves]" (p. 137). For even the most openly and self-acceptingly gay among us, who were nevertheless first enculturated into the puritanical sexual ethics which pervade our society, our sexuality as gay men and lesbians may not be quite comfortable even for us. Our sexual relationships and our particular sexual activities may be shaped and restrained not by our mind/body's limits or capacities for pleasure, love, and self-giving, but by our own sense of guilt, by our qualms about sexuality itself, as well as by some lingering guilt about our homosexuality. Especially in the face of AIDS and conservative AIDS-phobic pronouncements do we find affirming sexuality and/or bodiliness (hence, mortality) very difficult (cf., Fortunato, 1987).

What is perhaps most disturbing about this uncomfortable dilemma is that our lingering distrust of the full range of our sexual capacities and our lingering fear of our bodies together connect us with the most homophobic of persons. Heyward (1984) pointedly says, for example, that "homophobia is rooted in a fear of the body" (p. 143); moreover,

> . . . for a man to touch and love another man's body is intolerable within the sociotheological walls of an ideology constructed on the definition of a man as a disembodied, rational mind/spirit that is ever in control and always "above" body. Thus as a sociopolitical institution, male homosexuality--far more than lesbianism, because

women's power is not taken seriously--threatens to bring down the sacred canopy of an economic, sexual, and racial order founded on the assumption that the "real man" is a disembodied, dispassionate agency of control. . . . [Consequently], gay men who experience, and choose to celebrate, the value of their bodies and those of other men have a remarkable opportunity to join in the reshaping of a radically incarnational faith. (pp. 198-199)

Our gay male (as well as lesbian) sexuality and bodiliness allow us such a radical opportunity because God in godself is not homophobic; God created, sanctified, and continues to celebrate the entire spectrum of human sexuality.

Gay men and lesbians are, absolutely, a part of God's good creation and our capacities for sexual love are absolutely not sinful. In fact, our various sexual differences, "like other signs of uniqueness in our lives, need to be celebrated, not castigated," as part of God's own delight in the plurality and variety of creation (Boyd, 1984, p. 129). McNeill (1987) similarly elaborates:

God so created humans that they develop with a great variety of both gender identities and sexual object choices. . . . Homosexuals or lesbians . . . should be considered as part of God's creative plan. Their sexual orientation . . . is a gift from God to be accepted and lived out with gratitude. God does not despise anything that God has created. (p. 243, cf., McNeill, 1988)

He goes on to contend that not only does every human being have a "god-given right to sexual love and intimacy" (p. 243), but that "only a sadistic God would create hundreds of thousands of humans to be inherently homosexual and then deny them the right to sexual intimacy" (p. 244, cf., Barrett, 1978, McNeill, 1988). If God is not primarily a sadistic judgmental energy, but a horizontal co-creative power of responsible loving mutuality, as gay liberation theology contends, then denying our loving sexuality is clearly not required of us. The proper issue becomes not that we are sexual, but how we are sexual, how responsible are we with/in our sexuality (cf., Barrett, 1978, McNeill, 1987). God created all human sexuality and God sanctifies all responsible, caring, loving, mutually pleasuring sexuality. God accepts gay men and lesbians a priori. But

God is concerned, however, "whenever sex with another person is exploitative, unloving, undertaken for purely selfish reasons and with absolute indifference to another person's feeling and needs" (Boyd, 1984, p. 151). Nevertheless, the shift from (homo)sexuality as sin to a focus on responsible, mutual sexuality allows us a far broader range of sexual possibilities than our sex-negative and guilt-inducing enculturation would have us believe!

The way out of our puritanical sex-negativity, then, the means for overcoming our learned estrangement from earth/nature/cycles/limits, may in fact lie in our ability to resanctify our bodiliness and our sexuality, in our ability to transform the profane into the sacred by sanctifying the "physical/sexual" (cf., Satloff, 1983, p. 202). Revaluing our sexuality as wholeness-making and loving can thus (re)connect us to God's love for creation and can thus in turn enable us to revalue our gay and lesbian selves. If (homo)sexual sin/guilt is no longer a power over us, then we are free to celebrate both our sexuality and our self-worth as equally gifts from God (cf., Boyd, 1984). Such a radical reaffirmation of both all human sexuality and especially gay/lesbian sexuality has never been as important as now, before the spectres of AIDS and AIDS-phobically strengthened sex-negativity and homophobia in our western society.

As lesbians, and gay men in particular, we must absolutely refuse to allow AIDS to destroy our sexual energy or our sacramental capacities for loving mutuality, borne in and nurtured by our particular sexuality. Instead, we must responsibly and thoroughgoingly adopt, and adapt to, "safe-sex" practices, while insisting still upon the sexual/spiritual interconnectedness and empowerment we experience in our sexually deepened relationships. Our loving one another now, even more deeply and passionately (and safely), can in fact strengthen our mutuality in community and our shared, caring response to those who suffer with AIDS, while also informing our every effort against homophobia and for our liberation. And yet, to make such a radical affirmation of our bodiliness and our sexuality in these times will not be an easy task. Our gay liberation theology must again enable us to confront and to heal the dualisms of body/spirit and of sexuality/spirituality whose rigidity falsely attempts to protect heterosexist patriarchy from the mortality which AIDS makes plain. We must penetrate and heal these dichotomies in order to fully understand the mutuality and empowerment at the heart of our exiled and often despised sexuality.

Feminist theology has consistently been at the forefront of such liberational efforts to dissolve the dualistic separation and devaluation of body from spirituality/intellect. In so doing, feminists insist that our bodies, our selves, and our spirits are one, that we are our embodiedness (Heyward, 1984). Christ (1980), for example, argues that,

> . . . rather than ignoring or denying feelings of connection to nature, women (and others) need to develop a new understanding of being human, in which the body is given a more equal footing with the intellect and the human connection to nature is positively valued at the same time that the awesome (but not unlimited) human capacity to manipulate and control nature is recognized. (p. 129)

Similarly, Heyward (1984) insists that "all liberation theology reveals a bias for the spirituality in physicality, the spirit in flesh, the God in humanity" (p. 173). Ruether (1983a, 1983b) is equally clear in her assertion that the rejection, domination, and exploitation of nature, of other people, and of our bodies are all connected. Dominated people, for example, are always devalued as closer to nature, more bodily and sensual, and less spiritual (i.e., less valuable). Ultimately, she argues that both a "world-fleeing spirituality" and the "fear of embodiment as moral debasement" reflect our fear of death, our refusal to accept our limits (1983a, p. 79, 1983b, p. 61). Again, the irrational quality of AIDS-phobic sex-negativity is invoked.

The clear alternative which feminist theology offers for this dilemma is "an explicit and unequivocal commitment to the liberation of the body [and nature] from disrepute, the liberation of sexuality from contempt and embarrassment, the liberation of feelings from trivialization, and the liberation of death and dying from shame and denial" (Heyward, 1984, p. 174). Feminist theology thus makes concerted efforts to reconcile both spirit/intellect with the body and people with the environment or nature, to reclaim/revalue the material or physical, and to understand body and spirit as one (Christ, 1980, Ruether, 1983a). The ultimate goals of these conciliatory efforts are both "eco-justice" and human interpersonal justice--"the realization of spiritual insight in social reality" (Christ, 1980, p. 130, Ruether, 1983b, p. 66, cf., 1983a, cf., Waskow, 1983). In short, feminist theology makes a "radically incarnational affirmation" that the body is good and that full (i.e., sexual) participation in bodily existence "is to participate in the movement of divinity" (Heyward, 1984, p. 172). Outside feminist theology, Rubenstein (1966) has anticipated these same concerns when he admonishes us "to acknowledge our temporality and mortality without illusion" (p. 238), as well as "to learn how to dwell in our bodies. . . . Fewer capacities come harder to Americans," he adds, "than the capacity to dwell in [our] bodies with grace, dignity, and gratification," and without guilt (p. 239). Our efforts to develop a gay liberation theology upon these sources consequently call us also to affirm, again in the very face of AIDS, both the goodness of our limits or mortality and the absolute sanctity of our bodies and of our bodiliness (cf., Fortunato, 1987). If we are able to affirm that our bodies and spirituality are unitary and good, we can then move to free not only our bodies, but our sexuality as well, from repression (cf., Waskow, 1983).

As with penetrating/dissolving the dualism of body/spirit, our extended efforts to break down the related dualism of sexuality/spirituality, and thus to free our repressed and marginalized sexualities, can begin in the insights and analyses of feminist theology. Lesbian/feminist theologian Heyward (1984), for example, simply rejects a dualistic theological tradition which separates sacred and profane, spirit and body, a god "up there" and human embodiment "down here." She insists instead upon an "integrity in which spirituality and sexuality are realized as one flow of being, relating us both to God and to sisters and brothers, enabling self-validation. [Sexuality] is God-with-us" (p. 45). Spirituality and sexuality, together, reflect a "fundamental human yearning" for spiritual meaning in relationships, a spiritual yearning which is inseparably linked to our sexually and physically yearning for one another (p. 35). Numerous gay male religious writers have extended and/or elaborated this feminist message that to affirm bodiliness also entails affirming sexuality and that bodiliness, sexuality, and spirituality are all one. Boyd (1984), for example, insists that the "sacred and the secular are truly knit together" whenever we make sexual love "in the sincere hope of sharing communion" (pp. 140, 144). Similarly, Fortunato (1983) not only insists

that both (homo)sexuality and spirituality are equally
gifts from God; he also contends that gay men and lesbians can heal "the cruel gash" separating sexuality
and spirituality in western culture (p. 18). And, Fox
(1983) urges gay men and lesbians to pursue an intrinsic understanding of love and sexuality as unitary--a
"recovery of the body as spirit, of sensual spirituality"--rather than remaining frustrated by the utilitarian, procreative understanding of sexuality inherent in
heterosexism, and thus to recover the "mystical side"
of our sexuality (p. 202).
    Both Uhrig (1984) and Edwards (1984) also echo
feminist concerns when they reiterate the fact that the
sexuality/spirituality dualism has not only distorted
sexual love as sinful, but has actually alienated gay
men and lesbians from our inherent spiritual capacities
because we are seen (and we gay men, at least, too often see ourselves) as only sexual. The schism of sexuality and spirituality "has prevented us from becoming
part of any organized spiritual community and indeed
from being able to claim our own spirituality" (p. 79).
The result has been that a latent, unresolved sexual
shame has heretofore precluded our aggressively pursuing the development of any gay liberation theology
(cf., Goodstein, 1985). Defiantly rejecting this
schism in an effort to heal its resultant alienation,
Uhrig (1984) argues that our gay/lesbian sexuality is
actually the very locus of our encounter with divine
acceptance and empowerment; moreover, "lesbians and gay
men now have a prophetic function to fulfill. . . .
Consistent with the [fact] that God always chooses a
rejected people through whom to act, gay people are re-
vealing the reunion of sexuality and spirituality" (p.
80). Edwards (1984) adds that the "moral task" for gay
liberation theology is to "exemplify and teach the fulfilling of sexual love in . . . a mutuality that no
longer seeks surrender and self-sacrifice from the
other [and] pleasure and domination for the self" (p.
111).
    Our efforts in gay theology, then, must not fail
to include our opportunity, and our responsibility,
both to advocate and to embody/enact a conciliatory return to divinely intended sexual/spiritual integration
and wholeness and to both reconceptualize and reunder-
stand that sexuality is a means to communion with God
by way of communion with another person (cf., Uhrig,
1984). As we discover minority group co-empowerment
with the God of the oppressed at the very point of our
marginalized sexual difference, we as gay men and les-

bians can be the vanguard of fundamental change (cf., Uhrig, 1984, Edwards, 1984). As we are able to penetrate/dissolve/reconcile the dualisms of body/spirit and sexuality/spirituality, we may also be able to discover God with us in our sexuality and thus also to realize that our sexuality may be the very ground of our spiritual and sociopolitical power. From these discoveries will we be able to set aside our limited and limiting understanding of sex as sinful, and instead, seek to develop a broadened and resanctified understanding of sexuality in all its liberational potential.

Numerous gay and lesbian writers have already begun this reclaiming and resanctifying process as they advocate freeing sexuality from the confines either of utilitarian procreation or of rigid gender roles. Freed from function, role, and even mere orgasm, our sexuality can instead be our mutual and egalitarian means for rediscovering intimacy and reestablishing the importance of love in our relationships (cf., Edwards, 1984, Fox, 1983, Goodman et al., 1983). Apart from procreative roles and functions, for example, the open, active, unfettered sexuality of gay men and lesbians "may be the means for us to finally learn to go beyond orgasm to much deeper levels of intimacy," thereby allowing us the freedom to enjoy "varied levels of intimacy and . . . intensities of relationship . . . beyond the genital sexual experience" (Uhrig, 1984, p. 82). Similarly, McNeill (1987) writes,

> . . . What is unique to human sexuality is the fusion that God has made of biological sexuality with the uniquely human vocation to, and capacity for, love.
> . . . The relational aspect of sexuality has primacy and, when appropriate, can be separated from the procreational aspect. (p. 245)

Not only may we (re)discover our capacities for deepened interpersonal/psychic intimacy; we may also be able to (re)learn appropriate ways for physically expressing affection. Goodman et al. (1983) contend, for example, that "sexuality and sensuality need to merge into a continuum, as affection and touching are recognized as necessary and desirable for human health and sex loses its genital and orgasmic preoccupation" (p. 47). In other words, as our gay/lesbian sexuality (and ideally all human sexuality) ceases to be repressed, but is rather accepted and blessed as natural and healthy, sexuality will cease to obsess us. Then we can properly prioritize our sexuality as a part of, an expression of, but not all of, loving human intimacy. Thus, Edwards (1984) goes on to say that the "task of liberating love is to transcend [sexual and gender role] reductionism . . . and to underline the confluence" of God's love with the "totality of human passions for freedom" (p. 125). While the anti-sexual biases or pervasive sex-negativity of western consciousness have repressed our bio-erotic need for intimacy and relationship, leading to brokenness, alienation, injustice, and exploitation, our sexuality as a drive toward relationship and mutuality with one another, and with the divine in turn, may actually be the "most important reality we have" (Rubenstein, 1966, p. 78).

Ironically, such a radical understanding of sex as a drive toward human intimacy and potential communion with an empowering, horizontal God, rather than as a sinful and procreatively necessary function, has an historical precedent--in the long overlooked "theology of passionate friendship" of a gay twelfth century monk, St. Aelred of Rievaulx (Clark, 1987a). Aelred insisted that human love and relationships, grounded in erotic and even same-sex attraction, evoke God's presence. Human friendships are a route to union with God and not ends in themselves; intimacy, love, and even sexual sharing create encounters wherein God is also present. Aelred also stressed the utter loyalty and self-sacrificial quality of (same-sex) friendships; one is expected never to violate the trust, confidentiality, and love of one's friend and always to embody humility and loving forgiveness before one's companion. The implications of Aelred's theology for a contemporary gay liberation theology are that sexually active gay people must live with both our sexuality and our spirituality, as a whole; both the love of God and a responsible sexual love must be rightly ordered. In Aelred's writing, while an irresponsible or dehumanizing or impersonal promiscuity is precluded, a responsible gay orientation is clearly affirmed. Sexual love should simply facilitate rather than circumvent or distract from communion with the divine in the encounter with another person (cf., Clark, 1987a, Hallier, 1969, Russell, 1982, Squire, 1981).

This same radical affirmation of sexuality is taken up and extended most adamantly for our purposes by Heyward (1982, 1984), who further insists that "sexuality is our experience of moving toward others: making love, making justice in the world. It is the drive

to connect. . . . Sexuality is our means of making
love, justice, in the world" (1982, p. 220); moreover,
"our passion as lovers is that which fuels both our
rage at injustice . . . and our compassion. . . . Rage
[the anger which empowers corrective action] and compassion belong together," lest we merely reverse the
present order and become oppressors ourselves (1982, p.
221). This basic affirmation in her doctoral disserta-
tion (1982) subsequently becomes an elaborate cornerstone for her particular feminist liberational theology
(1984). Much like St. Aelred, for example, she writes,

> . . . The yearning within me for meaningful
> relationship . . . is, in fact, simultaneously a
> sexual and a spiritual yearning for relationship
> [which] is not only good, but . . . which brings
> me to life, to risk, to courage, to commitment, to
> passion, to vocation, to feelings, to sisters and
> brothers, and, yes, to God. (1984, p. 44)

Unlike St. Aelred, however, for whom coming to God
through sexually motivated human intimacy was confined
to the isolated, contemplative monastic life, Heyward's
(1984) radically participatory liberation theology
links sexual enspiritment/empowerment not with contem-
plation but with social action. Sexuality is an extension, a deepening, and an expression of both human intimacy and our commitments to action. Because our sexuality drives us toward mutual relation, toward just
and loving human intimacy, it simultaneously drives us
toward just relations, toward justice, in all areas of
human life. As our drive toward loving human interrelationship, our marginalized gay/lesbian sexuality is
the very ground and empowering source for our efforts
to make justice and to effect liberation in this world,
here and now:

> In its nonperverted, most radical dimensions, sex-
> uality is our socio/psychophysical drive toward
> right, mutual relation. It is loving. It is
> just. It is co-creative. Sexuality is, I be-
> lieve, our impulse to seek and find what we, and
> all creation, need in relations, both to one an-
> other and to the source of all creative power,
> that which is God. (1984, p. 130)

Not only is sexuality "the undercurrent of the love
that flows as justice" (1984, p. 36), but "to celebrate
our sexuality is to make a theological and anthropolo-

gical affirmation of the pulsating dynamic of created life, the force within us that moves us beyond ourselves toward others" (1984, p. 76).

As gay men and lesbians marginalized because of our particular sexuality, we are peculiarly able to imbue the earth and cosmos with erotic power. And yet, we discover with Heyward (1984) that divine/cosmic fecundity is not merely procreative; rather it yearns for and creates just, interpersonal relationships. Far from merely orgasmic and procreative, our sexuality, the "sanctity and value of the body," is the "ground of all holiness," the source of our empowerment to seek, demand, and create justice, to effect liberation (p. 139):

> The ecstatic power of the sex act can lead us to identify it wrongly with the whole of sexuality, when in truth sexuality is . . . the one most vital source of our other passions, of our capacities to love and to do what is just in the world . . . to court peace, instead of war; justice, instead of oppression; life, instead of hunger, torture, fear, crime, and death.
> The power of mutual relation [transcendent divine co-empowerment] is creative sexual power, which . . . carries us into lovemaking with our partners, but [which] is moreover present and active in all creative, mutually empowering relations. (1984, pp. 78, 247)

Our sexuality is nowhere more powerful or more sacred and resanctified than in our compassionate, loving, fecund efforts toward justice and liberation.

As gay men and lesbians in an erotophobic and, yes, AIDS-phobic sociocultural time and place, we have a unique vocation, both an opportunity and a responsibility, regarding our sexuality and all human sexuality. As we are able to set aside our lingering (homo)-sexual guilt, to penetrate and resolve the dualisms of body/spirit and sexuality/spirituality, and thus to resanctify and celebrate our sexuality in safe and responsible ways, apart from the procreatively functional and gender role reinforcing patterns given by our heterosexist enculturation, we may also be able to discover both a heightened awareness of the value of our sexual partners and a deepened sense of human intimacy and affection--for one another and for our whole community. We may also be able to recognize and to touch the spiritual power latent in caring acts of sexual

love. By reaffirming and reclaiming our marginalization as the locus of our liberational encounter with
horizontal divine empowerment, and by resanctifying our
particular sexuality both as the means to divine and
human intimacy and as the source of our passions for
community, for right relationships, and for justice,
therein do we find with Rubenstein (1966), Aelred (cf.,
Clark, 1987a), Heyward (1982, 1984), and others the
fecund communal empowerment for the tasks of liberation. Moreover, in reconceptualizing sexuality in such
a healing, empowering, and wholistic fashion, our gay
liberation theology enables us to assume our larger
roles as creators and sustainers of balance and wholeness as gay men and lesbians.

(iii) Creating Gay Wholeness and Balance

Our gayness as an all-encompassing existential
standpoint for being in the world entails not only the
possibility/responsibility for us to reconcile and reunite our bodiliness and our spirituality; it also enables us to cut across, to destroy, confuse, and conflate, all polarities and dualistic hierarchies, and
thus to stand prophetically, symbolically, and actually
over against the predominant mythic structures of the
west (Walker, 1980). Our gay and lesbian being allows
us to embrace and to embody androgyny in its broadest
possible sense, not only by affirming that spiritual
existence is only possible through bodily and sexual
existence, but by balancing, compromising, and mediating extremes or opposites, as well; our spirituality is
that in us which seeks to uphold the middle ground between the demands of homophobic enculturation to the
"real world" and the yearnings of our deeper, more
basic, sexual/mythic being, our "primal humanness"
(Wright and Inesse, 1979, pp. 41, 43). Wright and
Inesse (1979) have even argued that our "true spiritual
function" is to lead others also toward a reunion of
the opposites (p. 86), while Boyd (1984) has similarly
suggested that "perhaps the chief contribution gays can
make to the rest of society is in relation to the human
search for wholeness" (p. 167). Spirituality, bodiliness, sexuality, and the drive toward balance and
wholeness are one, grounded in the horizontality of
God-with-us:

I believe that God possesses the wholeness and
fullness of what we understand to be body and
soul. This completeness incorporates all of femi-

ninity and masculinity. . . . Soul is neither superior to body nor can it be separated from it.
. . . The experience of loving sexuality brings me
closer to God and also to other people.
    . . . God is experienced in orgasm as much as
in . . . nature, human friendships, meditations,
religious rituals, and acts of charity. (Boyd,
1984, p. 144)

As gay men and lesbians, our standpoint between
the rigid poles of gender, our refusal of the roles and
sexuality of opposites, thus also functions to undermine all other fundamental dualisms--transcendence/im-
manence, spirit/matter--which are fundamental to hierarchical heterosexism, and to evoke and create fundamental wholeness and balance instead (cf., Ruether,
1983a). Our efforts in gay liberation theology are
called thereby to join all liberation theologies in articulating "a wholistic understanding of human beings--
a unity between matter and spirit, mind and body, will
and emotion," and an androgynous balance which affirms
the goodness of creation through both ecological and
human justice (Collins, 1981, p. 345). Moreover, our
capacities for such balancing, for constituting unity,
are not merely whimsical or imagined; they are in fact
grounded in the mythico-psychic images of our very being as gay people.
    Those of us who are gay men, for example, and gay
men within a frequently ghettoized subculture at that,
can archetypally unite life, death, and rebirth by consciously penetrating the dark, unconscious world of bar
time (the mythic Underworld or Hades) and then re-
emerging to rejoin dayworld activities, thereby balancing the "chaotic unreason of the Underworld" (night)
with the "expiatory reason of the dayworld" (Clark,
1987a, p. 9, cf., 1987b, cf., Hillman, 1979). The
archetypal reunion of opposites can also occur for gay
men in the acceptance and integration of our gay selves
(the Heroic freeing and wedding/merging of Anima/Psy-
che), as well as in the interchangeability or confusion
of socially enculturated gender roles in sex and elsewhere, through our clothing, mannerisms, and "camp."
The full panorama of Jungian/post-Jungian mythico-psychic images shows gay men, in particular, with the potential for balancing "unconsciousness [Oedipus and Or-
pheus] and self-consciousness [Narcissus], rebellious
Youth and reforming maturity, nightworld amorality and
dayworld morality, masculinity and femininity" (Clark,
1987a, p. 12, cf., 1987b). Thus, in the visions of

male gayspirit writers and feminist theologians, as
well as in the depths of mythic history and of our own
psyches, do we discover the possibility/responsibility
of our gay being as an existential standpoint for balancing the opposites. Moreover, our balancing act to
create and sustain unity by holding opposites in a conciliatory tension is nowhere more plain then in our
place between the gender and gender role polarities.

While Heyward (1984), for example, argues that all
same-sex relationships may just offer the best opportunities for real mutuality apart from gender roles,
within our present heterosexist culture, Goodman et al.
(1983) have said that,

> . . . gayness, on a personal level, has to do
> with love, commitment and energy as well as sex,
> and on a societal level, with breaking out of con-
> ditioned behavior and sex-role stereotyping. [In
> fact], to reduce gayness to a simple question of
> sexuality is to [homophobically] belittle its im-
> pact both on the individual and on society. (p.
> 15)

Similarly, McNeill (1983) contends that gay people can
significantly help in "leading the whole human family
to a new and better understanding of interpersonal love
between equals [in mutuality and friendship] . . .
rather than the patriarchal role-playing of tradition"
(p. 55). In each of these sources for our gay theological activity, we again find that our balancing position between the gender and gender role opposites is
both a possibility and a responsibility (command/de-
mand). McNeill (1983) further makes plain the prophetic or demanding aspect of our balancing place, especially for gay men: "The [gay male] community is potentially free from the psychological need to establish
their male identity by means of violence, . . . [re]-
conditioned by their ability to accept and celebrate
their sexuality" as the source of other passions (p.
59, emphasis added). Gay men are thus called to be
models of a new masculinity free of both violence and
domination, spiritually open and receptive instead, and
to be both symbols and embodiments of a secure male
identity without gender roles (cf., McNeill, 1983).

Dostourian (1978) anticipates many of these concerns in his own earlier writing. Focusing upon the
ways in which traditional gender-based roles of domination (masculine) and subordination (feminine) preclude
genuine uncoercible love, he contends that gay men and

lesbians already find the separation/polarization of sex roles "false and destructive" and therefore reject those roles and instead affirm their humanity apart from the sanctification of either "acceptable" sexual preference or gender roles, thus repudiating the "domination-subordination syndrome" (pp. 340, 341). Only overcoming or destroying the roles allows for equality, mutuality, and truly humane relations:

> The overriding fact is that all people in our society have deep problems in relating to one another. Our society does not provide a healthy environment [or models] for individuals to relate to one another in a loving, intimate, and responsible way. [Our prophetic gay liberation theology, therefore, needs] to uphold a concept of human sexuality based on love and responsibility, irrespective of sexual orientation or way of life. (p. 348)

What ultimately comes through Dostourian's (1978) work is a call for gay men and lesbians to be at the forefront of a process which moves sexuality from the possessiveness of domination/subordination and gender roles toward mutually "intimate friendship, care and concern for others" (p. 342, cf., Heyward, 1984). He thus describes and advocates a spectrum, rather than any hierarchy, by which to understand, envision, and embody relational forms and sexual expressions.

As with discovering in the work of St. Aelred an historical precedent within the Judaeo-Christian tradition for the reunion of gay eroticism and spirituality, we are equally fortunate to have an historical precedent or model for the third-gender, intermediate, balancing function of our gay being, albeit a paradigm outside western, Judaeo-Christian culture. The native American berdaches may in fact be our best example of homosexual persons who were able, through interaction with one another, their cultures, and their communities, to synthesize both sexuality and spirituality, both masculinity and femininity, for both personal and social benefit, insofar as they consistently embodied a synthesis of spiritually and sexually different presence in their lives (Clark, 1984, 1987a, cf., Roscoe, 1987). In his groundbreaking text Williams (1986), for example, describes the male berdache as a unique third gender intermediary between, and thus balancing, the opposites both of masculinity and femininity and of the psychic and the physical. Importantly, these individu-

als, who most frequently combined male and female at-
tire with cross-gender occupations and homosexuality,
were far from outcast by their pre-colonial native societies; they were instead a blessed and highly es-
teemed spiritual presence for their tribes, in accord
with native mythology and religion. Williams (1986)
describes native religions as believing that "the
spirit of one thing (including a human being) is not
superior to the spirit of any other"; such an egalitarian and ecological vision believes everything is spiritual (p. 21). Moreover, according to native religions,
every human possibility exists for a reason, by divine
intent, which provides a spiritual explanation for human difference, at once precluding exclusion and accepting human diversity--including the berdaches' role
and sexuality. Says Williams (1986),

> . . . Receiving instructions from a
> [spiritual] vision inhibits others from trying to
> change the berdache. . . . It also excuses the
> community from worrying about the cause of that
> person's difference, or the feeling that it is so-
> ciety's duty to try to change him.
> By the Indian view, someone who is different of-
> fers advantages to society precisely because she
> or he is freed from the restrictions of the usual.
> (pp. 30, 42)

Among those advantages were that "native Americans, of
course, saw no opposition between matters of the spirit
and of the flesh" (Williams, 1986, p. 88). The berdaches held together or balanced not only the spectrum
of sexual and gender forces, but also the opposites of
sacred (sky) and profane (earth), of clean and unclean,
of psyche/mind and body, and of control and respect for
nature (Clark, 1984, 1987a). Moreover, the berdaches
understood their sociocultural participation and the
benefits they provided their tribes as part and parcel
of their spirituality; as we would have our gay liberation theology, their theology and spirituality was
their praxis (cf., Roscoe, 1987).
    Williams (1986) is quick to point out, however,
that the paradigmatic figure of the berdache is more
androgynous, spiritual, and communally interconnected
than urbanized and secular gay men, in particular, have
tended to be heretofore. His work consequently admonishes gay men both to reclaim our spiritual aspects,
our mythico-spiritual third gender or androgynous spe-
cialness, and our capacities for balancing secularity

and spirituality, and to embody a spectrum of sexual expressions and modes of being. He is especially concerned that gay men should focus, as did native cultures, upon individual character and the uniqueness of our gay perspective or sensibility rather than upon mere sexual difference and sexual activity. Building upon a reappreciation and reunderstanding of native religions, with particular regard for the berdache as a paradigmatic figure, our activity of gay liberation theology can insist that resacramentalizing homosexuality as part of cosmically designed pluralism could enable us, as it did the berdaches, to remind our secular and homophobic culture of the value of accepting, integrating, and even ritually celebrating human diversity. Moreover, as contemporary gay men and lesbians, we also need to seek a reunion of the cosmic, sexual, and moral polarities; we can embody in our own lives that all things are interdependent, processive, fecund, and dynamic. Such skilled balancing, at our unique existential place on the margins of our cultural and religious traditions, may in fact be our special route to wholeness as gay people.

Fortunato (1987) has described the importance, specifically before the spectre of AIDS, of our overcoming the fragmentation of our sexuality from the wholeness of who we are by our accepting/integrating our sexuality-spirituality-selfhood as the "inner cohesiveness" and grounding for confronting and transcending our experiences both of homophobic oppression and AIDS-related suffering (p. 24). Not dissimilarly, Ruether (1983a) also says that being a liberation people, a portion of "redeemed humanity," further means,

> . . . not only recovering aspects of our full psychic potential that have been repressed by cultural gender stereotypes; it also means transforming the way these capacities have been made to function socially. We [gay people as well as women!] need to recover our capacity for relationality, for hearing, receiving, and being with and for others, but in a way that is no longer a tool of manipulation or of self-abnegation. (p. 113)

As we are able to cease accepting and internalizing the homophobic devaluation of ourselves as fragmented and merely sexual people, which causes us to lose our good gay selves, and are able to openly assert our gay being and gay pride instead (cf., Saiving,

1979), then will we be equally able to move into a horizontal and intimate relation with a God who is "immanent, acting in the world, suffering with it and redeeming it through human agency" (Collins, 1981, p. 347). As we are able to achieve such psycho-spiritual-sexual wholeness, an integrity of gayself at the margins, we are also freed to realize that "concern for self must be balanced with steady social action" (Boyd, 1984, p. 167) and we are empowered for the tasks of liberation: for combining prophetic outrage with our commitment to social justice as well as personal growth for all people, for doing justice in the face of contempt, and for "loving in the face of oppression" (Fortunato, 1987, p. 32, cf., Boyd, 1984). Ultimately, as we are able to come out and accept and embrace our gay/lesbian being and our gay/lesbian selves as sanctified and good, as we are able to penetrate duality and resacramentalize our sexuality, as we are able to claim our power and capacity for achieving and creating social justice, as we are able to embody balance in our lives intimately interdependent with a God who stands with us as compassion and empowerment for justice-seeking and liberation, through all these marvelous activities do we discover, create, nourish, and sustain our wholeness as gay people. Moreover, upon the strength and power of our wholeness at the margins do we discover not only the blessing and love of divine presence, but our very ability to (re)envision and to build our gay and lesbian community as truly that of a liberation people.

*　*　*

VIII. Revisioning Gay Community

(i) Reclaiming Gay/Lesbian Uniqueness and Vision

A number of writers within the gay and lesbian community have struggled to understand and to articulate how and why gay people as a group have frequently been both unable to bless and embrace our sexual difference as a standpoint for liberational activity, and thus also unable to claim and use our power fully, effectively, and consistently. Bronski (1987), for example, divides the community into two groups, "reformists," whose primary concern is gay acceptability by or assimilation into mainstream society through legislative reform, and "activists," who insist upon "flaunting" gay uniqueness and who envision more radical change (p. 14). Thompson (1987a) is particularly critical of merely reformist efforts. He believes that, at best, assimilation will yield only a "mediocre, conditional type of [limited] acceptance," purchased at the cost of denying or losing touch with our unique perspective(s) and spiritual depths as gay men and lesbians (p. 293). Moreover, he fears that such limited goals, in the absence of a more radical vision, will actually keep gay people in a reactive and therefore easily oppressed position, forever on the margins, rather than in a proactive and liberated position: "We define ourselves always in terms of reacting to events [acts of homophobic violence, acts of discrimination, AIDS], so seldom with creativity borne from a culture [or all-encompassing vision] of our own making" (p. 297). Caught on the horns of Bronski's (1987) dichotomy, Thompson's (1987) concerns commingle both cynicism and hope for the gay/lesbian community:

> Gay people can be as banal, myopic and prejudiced as anyone else. Homosexuality does not necessarily imply a difference from the norm [the assimilationist position]. . . . Only when we interpret and use our [gay/lesbian being] as a signal, a sign, a blessing will we understand it as the significant tool it can be--[propelling us] at least

one step beyond prevailing social role patterns
into an awkward self-awakening about [the value of
our] difference. (p. 299)

An analysis by means of dichotomizing the gay and
lesbian community, however, quickly breaks down. Bronski (1987) himself readily admits that "most gay people
fall between these two positions: They want legal re-
forms but also need the cultural affirmation for their
lives offered by gay liberation" (p. 14). Certainly
within our current sociopolitical climate, both are
necessary. Equally as certain, a minority which cuts
across and includes all other racial, religious, economic, gender, and political groupings cannot be easily
divided into only two mutually exclusive camps. Some
gay people do keep their heads apathetically in the
sand, whether in regard to politics, AIDS issues, or
sex/health concerns. Socially, professionally, and/or
materially comfortable, they may even react hostilely
to efforts to dislodge them from complacency. Other
gay people may indeed feel that being gay or lesbian is
merely a matter of sexual difference, but these gay men
and lesbians may be either apathetic or politically
active in pursuit of legal and social rights and protections for gay people. Still other gay men and lesbians may feel that being gay or lesbian is a more all-
encompassing standpoint; they may be involved in poli-
tical/civil rights issues as activists in cooperation
with the more assimilation-oriented, in gayspirit
questing apart from the nitty-gritty of politics, or in
some combination of both. Ours is simply a too richly
varied, multi-layered "community" to yield to easy analysis. What is clear, however, is that we have alternatives. We have the capacity to choose how we will
envision and create our lives and our community(ies) as
gay men and lesbians. In that very freedom, though,
lies our responsibility.
Taking the responsibility, the demand/command, of
our gay and lesbian being as an all-encompassing existential standpoint in all its seriousness necessarily
moves our theology-as-praxis away from any goal of
"mere" assimilation. Knowing from our anthropologically theological analyses that God is most empower-
ingly with us when we assume responsibility for our
lives and our liberation further entails acknowledging
the demand/command that we act accordingly. Our gay
liberation theology, therefore, must work both compassionately and prophetically to motivate all of us,
wherever we may fall within the rich texture of commu-

nity, to exchange complacency for activity. We must claim/celebrate and not deny/hide our difference or uniqueness; we must not be willing to purchase assimilation into the heterosexist structures of patriarchy uncritically or at any price: "Our lives are justified by every moment we live, not by some ultimate purpose laid on us. To sacrifice our lives to someone else's long term goals [is] the ultimate betrayal" (Kepner, 1987, p. 169, emphases added). We must instead realize that our difference, our marginalization, is the very locus not only of our personal and communal power, but of our encounter with divine co-empowerment as well: "The path of gay enspiritment . . . says that there is a reality to being gay [or lesbian] that is radically different from being straight (note: different, not better or worse). This reality is inside of us, and it is substantial and meaningful" (Kilhefner, 1987, p. 126).

Embracing that difference and imbuing it with meaningfulness can further enable us to move from defensive reaction to a more radical/thoroughgoing vision and proaction as a liberation community (cf., Edwards, 1984). Grounded in such an understanding, for example, Foucault could insist in an interview before his death (Gallagher and Wilson, 1987) that "not only do we have to defend ourselves, but we have to affirm ourselves; not only affirm ourselves as an identity but as a creative force" (p. 29). Our ability to create new and genuinely alternative forms--socially, culturally, politically, religiously--requires that we affirm our gay/lesbian difference, that we claim our power and celebrate our sexuality, and that we develop workable visions of ourselves as a people, as a liberation community. As Hay has insisted in another interview (Thompson, 1987b), gay people have a "special window, our own way of seeing, our own vision" which utterly rejects both the devaluation of "gay" and "lesbian" as merely sexual as well as any assimilation into heterosexist values (p. 196). Moreover, according to Goodman et al. (1983), "There is power in expecting . . . that we can be assertive. . . . As more of us realize we have power, enlist allies, and boldly stand up against all injustice, we will experience more fully the act of liberation" (p. 144). We can in fact create visions for ourselves and assertively bring them to fruition.

Our visionary process may best begin with how we as gay people envision or understand ourselves, our gay/lesbian being, as well as with how we understand ourselves vis-a-vis the non-gay and too often anti-gay world. Much like Foucault (Gallagher and Wilson, 1987), Heyward (1984) links the necessity of our defensiveness under a homophobic patriarchy with the broader ramifications of our position on the margins of heterosexist acceptability:

> Both women and gay/lesbian people have to struggle fiercely to keep themselves from being squeezed into the heterosexual box in which women must submit, and gay/lesbian people must repent.
>   . . . [Moreover], deprived of civil and religious trappings of [or social support for] romantic love, we [lesbians and gay men] may well be those who are most compelled to plumb the depths of what it really means to love. Our deprivation becomes an opportunity and a vocation.
>   . . . [Consequently], I believe we are compelled, and empowered, to risk whatever we must risk to create with God a climate in which all people can be who they are. It is a matter of doing justice, of standing up to be counted. (pp. 80, 84-85, 31)

Clearly then, in Heyward's (1984) writing just as earlier in Fackenheim's (1970), emerges a demand/command that we move from reactive defensiveness/oppression/ victimization to empowerment, not only for our own sake, but for others as well. We may thus envision our lives and our relationships as prophetic witnesses "not on behalf of homosexuality per se [or only], but rather on behalf of mutuality and friendship in all relations" (Heyward, 1984, p. 81). We may understand ourselves as embodiments of relationality, apart from sex-roles or other socially constructed roles, wherein real mutuality is nurtured, a mutuality which in turn fosters our urge toward just relations, justice, for all people. Consequently, an understanding of gay/lesbian being emerges throughout Heyward's (1984) work which not only rejects mere defensiveness or easy assimilation, but which also absolutely rejects a reductionist view of gayness as "just sex." Her particular vision always includes and demands a more radical, all-encompassing perspective:

> If we see that our lives as lesbians and gay men constitute a judgment not only on the rules about who sleeps with whom, but also on the sexual and economic fabric out of which human relations are cut, we are able to hear more exactly the word

that our lives speak. . . . The prophetic speech
of our own lives calls into question not only the
rules about where we put our genitals but also
about where we put our money, our energies, our
values, our actions. (p. 209)

Very importantly, this need to maintain in our vi-
sion(s) a perspective broader than our defended ghettos
permeates the beginning visionary work of a plethora of
gay and lesbian writers whose efforts fill out and com-
plement these efforts toward a gay liberation theology-
as-praxis (cf., Altman, 1987). With Heyward (1984),
for example, our vision begins in supportive community,
exorcising our internalized oppression, inferiority,
and self-hatred (cf., Clark, 1987a), and moves to encompass "a world of total justice, compassion, beauty,
equality, pleasure, and grace, where all people come
together to actualize our finest potentials" and where
all people are free from heterosexist (male) domination
(Walker, 1980, p. 43, cf., p. 88). Goodman et al.
(1983) have even gone so far as to itemize the kinds of
"fundamental institutional change" our vision might ultimately encompass (pp. 51ff): (1) meaningful, cooperative labor for all people and non-discrimination for
eligibility to all work and activity; (2) egalitarian
rather than hierarchical structures of governance and
cooperation with, rather than domination/exploitation
of, the earth and its resources; (3) the development of
and respect for the genuine pluralism of a "multi-cul-
tural, multi-ethnic society" which realizes and em-
bodies that "unity in diversity is essential for
strength" (pp. 51, 62); (4) non-elitist arts and cultural opportunities; (5) nonviolent conflict resolution; and, (6) friendship networks or voluntary surrogate families, rather than hierarchical nuclear families, and more opportunities therein for men to be nur-
turers. This latter concern reiterates an ongoing
theme or goal in our process of creating a gay liberation theology--the utter demise of gender roles. Uhrig
(1984), for example, insists that as gay men and lesbians, "we can offer a healing transformation of the
oppressive sex roles which have debilitated [all] American men and women for generations. . . . We can offer
symbols of hope," he adds, which are "badly needed by
men and women trapped by roles defined by others" (pp.
106-107).
Another concern of Goodman et al. (1983), which is
shared and expanded by various writers, is that of cooperation, even empathy, with the earth/cosmos. Not

only must our vision include recovering an attuneness to the spiritual empowerment of cosmos/nature/people as a dynamic unity (Evans, 1978); it must also include re-embracing our embodiedness, "lifting up the sacredness of creation," and proclaiming the reality and even a priori goodness of human mortality and limits (Fortunato, 1987, pp. 79-80). At the risk of becoming scapegoats for a death-fearing culture, lesbians, and gay men in particular, must work both abstractly to reunite life and death as a unity and concretely to focus people upon living this limited life fully rather than denying death, thereby encouraging all people "to cherish this time, this space, this creation, in all its glorious sensuousness," here and now (Fortunato, 1987, p. 82).

The other area in which our vision broadens beyond the ghetto is also that of another kind of cooperation, an "assertive cooperation between all groups oppressed by [patriarchal] industrialism" (Evans, 1978, p. 155). Rejecting the assimilation and cooptation of all oppressed peoples, both Evans (1978) and Edwards (1984) envision liaisons, coalitions, and mutual exchanges of support by gay men and lesbians with other marginalized groups--women, third world citizens, the poor, the unemployed--in order to effect fundamental (radical) change. Much like Heyward (1984), Edwards (1984) believes that our marginalized sexual loving is the ground for our empowerment to join our forces to those of all other liberation communities:

> The human condition in our time is such that fragments of freedom, bits and pieces of wholeness, and islands of well-being must open themselves to the total human outcry against violence and oppression and must resist every segmentation that makes our specific social concern oblivious or unrelated to others whose consciousness of freedom is not similarly shaped.
> . . . The future of gay/lesbian liberation lies not only in its ability unitedly to pursue justice for homosexual people but also in its ability to embrace in love the outcry for freedom among all people, whether near or far. It is, furthermore, responsiveness to this same outcry that gives to sexuality . . . its appropriate place. (pp. 128-129)

As the working vision of gay liberation theology broadens from its unique grounding in our particular sexual/

relational difference to embrace global concerns of ecological, economic, and sociopolitical justice for all the earth and all its inhabitants, our cooperation with others becomes absolutely necessary. Moreover, such a gay/lesbian vision is remarkably close to that of our female colleagues in their specific struggles for gender and sexual justice. Closely echoing the concerns of Goodman et al. (1983), for example, Ruether (1983a) best elaborates this, ideally shared/cooperative vision:

> . . . a society that affirms the values of demo-
> cratic participation, of the equal value of all
> persons . . . and their equal access to . . . edu-
> cational and work opportunities . . ., [a] society
> that dismantles [hetero]sexist and class hierar-
> chies . . ., [a] society built on organic [and
> voluntary] community . . ., [an] ecological soci-
> ety in which human and nonhuman . . . systems have
> been integrated into harmonious and mutually sup-
> portive, rather than antagonistic, relations.
> . . . We might encourage a plurality of
> household patterns, homosexual as well as hetero-
> sexual, voluntary as well as [kinship-related].
> (p. 233)

One other area or dimension which our burgeoning vision must also include and nourish is an ability to engage in tender and constructive self-criticism. No sound liberation theology can risk naively championing the oppressed-who-can-do-no-wrong; and yet, we must also avoid engaging in the kinds of homophobically self-hating infighting, back-biting, and classist one-upmanship which often plague and undercut gay community efforts. We must avoid setting some portions of our community against other portions, if we are going to nurture true cooperation closest to where we live and shape our lives (cf., Clark, 1987a, Ruether, 1972). Insisting, instead, upon the empowerment of our unity-in-diversity may in fact become the basis for our self-reflective, prophetic word to ourselves. Goodman et al. (1983) contend that, as a people, gay men and les-bians need to work on our own latent racism in our or-ganizations and bars; on our classism, elitism, or con-sumerism, particularly the frequent disregard of those materially comfortable gays for their brothers and sis-ters without "disposable incomes"; and, on our ageism, our over-valuation of youth and physical beauty, which often excludes older gay men and lesbians. Not dissi-

milarly, and again consistent with the anti-gender-role
thrust of our gay liberation theology, gay men in particular need to develop relational styles which do not
imitate patriarchal roles, which renounce male privilege, and which instead humanize sexual sharing with a
greater depth, intimacy, and tenderness, rather than
dehumanizing our partners as mere sexual objects (cf.,
Clark, 1987a). Goodman et al. (1983) contend that gay
men need to get (back) in touch with our capacities for
gentleness and mutually informed empathy and caring for
others, while also relinquishing our needs for either
domination or control. And Hay (1987) reiterates that
as gay men (and lesbians) we have an opportunity and a
responsibility to relate to one another, even sexually,
in mutually subjective, equal, co-sharing, and healing
ways, rather than solely as sexual objects, despite our
heterosexist enculturation to just such objectification
(cf., Thompson, 1987b). Thus our tender and compassionate self-criticism, our reflective listening to our
own prophetic voice, can further nurture our healthy
wholeness as a diverse yet united people.

Overall, as we are able to accept and to celebrate
ourselves, our sexuality, and our lives as gay men and
lesbians and thereby to claim our power as a liberation
community, we also discover a capacity to dream dreams
and to create visions of our liberation. As our vi-
sion(s) enables us to transcend our experiences of oppression within and without and to move beyond fear
and/or complacency, we may also find that we are capable both of healing the divisiveness among us and of
broadening our perspective beyond just gay-specific
concerns. We simultaneously become increasingly responsible for our own liberation and cooperatively responsible for those forms of fundamental or radical
change whose goals are the liberation of all marginalized persons. Ultimately, our tender self-criticism
can help to keep our vision clear and our purposes
sure. Moreover, what begins as a visionary process--
healing, nourishing, and empowering us--becomes increasingly practical. Indeed, a gay liberation theology-as-praxis must insist that only as our vision informs our actions do we really encounter and embody
horizontal divine co-empowerment, do we really approach
wholeness and maturity as a people. Thus we must prag-
matically use our vision and values to shape our gay
liberation community, to nurture our cooperation
therein across gender lines (and all other divisive
categorizations), and to stimulate our compassion--even
toward our oppressors themselves.

(ii) Nurturing Gay/Lesbian Community and Cooperation

Rubenstein (1966) describes three different kinds
of communities, all of which are relevant to our efforts to understand, create, and nourish gay community.
He distinguishes between our inherited kinship communities (such as those from which gay men and lesbians are
too frequently exiled), our thrown-into communities
(such as the gay/lesbian subculture and/or the gay/les-
bian ghettos to which we flee upon discovering our gay
or lesbian identity and, subsequently, upon being exiled from our inherited communities), and, finally, our
intentionally created communities (such as our gay/les-
bian surrogate families and friendship networks). Our
common sense understanding of "gay community" usually
vascillates confusingly between the latter two types of
community, a vascillation which raises a number of
questions for our theological reflection, whether we
are ultimately able to answer them notwithstanding
(Feinstein, personal communication): Is the informal
network of gay and lesbian businesses, organizations,
AIDS-support services organizations, and churches/syna-
gogues so loosely knit partially as a result of our being both frequently transient (exiled/relocated from
our families) and always essentially first-generation
(not self-propagating)? Does any form of interaction
with or reliance upon that gay-identified network, by a
homosexual person, constitute membership in "the community?" Is there a relational/sexual connection from
the openly gay-identified network to non-network participants (does the "gay community" include all homosexuals, even those deep in the closet)? What about
lovers/couples who "pull out" of the gay network or
rural gays living in isolation from gay places and networks and even other gay people? Is the openly gay/
lesbian subculture of ghettos, bars, and the business-
social-religious network best understood as only a sub-
set of "the community?" What does the "gay community"
ultimately mean?

As these questions suggest, gay men and lesbians,
as "a people," are surely the most diverse minority
among all humankind. The phenomenon of homosexuality
cuts across all economic, racial, religious, political,
and gender lines, thereby functioning to defy the usual
patriarchal categories. Unfortunately, however, the
resultant diversity among gay people frequently makes
creating intentional community very difficult. In addition, the widely ranging variations upon the spectrum
of openness/closetedness which gay men and lesbians em-

body, coupled with our general diversity, requires that our discourse about the gay community continue to refer simultaneously to the thrown-into community of all homosexuals, to the loosely knit ghettos and networks of openly gay-identified people and organizations, and to the intentional communities which overlap with these and which also include our loving relational patterns and surrogate families. Despite the ambiguity of discourse, however, an understanding of gay/lesbian community is possible, as we actively use our diversity and overcome our frequent divisiveness to transform our ghettos and networks, our accidental, circumstantial, and thrown-into communities, into the physical loci, but not the exclusive loci, for our intentional communities. Heyward (1984) has in fact elucidated that which can enable genuine community to emerge from our questioning and from our great diversity:

> I believe our commonality to be deeper and stronger than our differences. For while our differences derive from the separate cultural expectations in which [we] have been steeped, the commonality lesbians and gay men share is that all of us are yearning for meaningful relationship in a society in which we are absolutely forbidden to seek and to find such relationship with members of our own sex. (pp. 37-38)

Our common denominator, then, our point for bonding in community, is the combination of our sexual difference, of our gay/lesbian being as an all-encompassing existential standpoint, and of our various experiences of oppression and injustice in a homophobic society.

If despite some possible discursive confusion the concept of gay/lesbian community still makes sense, then our gay liberation theology as both vision and praxis needs to begin to examine that concept. Boyd (1984), for example, encourages our community to develop both self-reliance and sociopolitical organization, channeling individual empowerment to empower the whole community. At the same time he strongly advocates learning to integrate ourselves in such a way as to enable us to move back and forth from gay to non-gay worlds, both avoiding a feeling of "split personality" and dissolving those factors which separate gays and non-gays. Ruether (1983a) shares Boyd's (1984) concern that, like our vision itself, our sense of community should remain broad, open, and not imprisoning, when she contends that as any oppressed community gathers and strengthens itself, it needs a balance of in-group needs fulfillment and participation in larger social concerns as well. Our very process of coming together as a community not only bears the redemptive energies for healing ourselves and for nurturing us as a community; it also enables us to move beyond a confining ghettoization. Ruether (1983a) describes this redemptive process of gathering, healing/nurturing, and opening as necessarily a "communal, not just an individual experience. . . . Rebirth to authentic self-hood implies a community that assembles in the collective discovery of . . . [renewed] humanity and that provides the matrix of regeneration" (p. 193). Moreover, without our gathering as a community we would have no "matrix" either for discerning our own identity or for discovering, articulating, and enacting our liberation struggles:

> Consciousness is much more of a collective social product than modern individualism realizes. No one can affirm an idea against the dominant culture unless there is at least a subcultural group that gives people both the ideas and the social support for an alternative position. (Ruether, 1983a, p. 184)

Very importantly, as we come together in the dynamic of a liberation community which is necessary for our joint efforts against the forces of oppression, we must absolutely and carefully avoid the common error of other historical "exodus communities" which ultimately liberated only men and (re)subjugated both women and human sexuality (cf., Ruether, 1985, pp. 157-162). As we as gay people become an exodus or liberation community from both heterosexism and the patriarchal structures which undergird it, we must exclude neither men nor women. We must, at all costs learn to establish and sustain cooperation and respect across gender lines. Gay men and lesbians must be increasingly able to cooperate in the tasks of liberation. Gay men in particular must not only absolutely rid ourselves of any latent, enculturated sexism, in order both to cooperate more effectively with our lesbian sisters (cf., Clark, 1987c) and to respect/honor their occasional need for women-only spaces as well; we must also realize that the lesbian/feminist movement has much to teach us, that our liberation as gay people is inherently linked to the liberation of women (cf., McNeill, 1983). After all, the same hierarchy of opposites which rigidly prescribes gender roles equally rigidly proscribes all non-procreative sexuality.

Heyward (1984) best articulates our shared dilemma and our shared prophetic opportunity to stand together as gay men and lesbians against (hetero)sexism:

> The women's movement and the gay movement are fundamentally the same movement, and . . . this movement constitutes a serious threat to the religious and social order of our time. . . . Our interest in eliminating sexism and homophobia goes hand in hand with an interest in eliminating all forms of repression and discrimination.
>   . . . [Moreover], gay men, as well as lesbians, have a particular opportunity . . . to embrace [a radically] incarnational faith, because-- like all women--gay men have been cast in the role of "body lovers." (pp. 139, 198)

Heyward (1984) has also articulated a number of specific ways in which gay men and lesbians can work together cooperatively for the liberation of both women and gay people: We can stand together and enact in our lives and relationships a defiance of both gender role categorization and of all homophobic definitions of "normality," whether ecclesiastical or clinical. We can insist together upon the absolute goodness of all human sexuality "by the boldness, visibility, and articulateness of our lives as we yearn for" and create and nurture/sustain relationships (p. 41). Within those relationships we can refuse to act out gender roles "in order to diffuse . . . the uses of power and control to avoid intimacy and to master the unknown" (p. 41, cf., p. 195). And, most obvious of all, we can build and sustain gay/lesbian community across gender lines.

Importantly, as gay men and lesbians come together in community and join together to cooperate in the joint empowerment required for the tasks of liberation, we may just discover a special deepening of our capacity for compassion. Not only are we able to love passionately those gay individuals of our own gender who may have been or who might yet be sexual partners; we are also capable of passionate friendship and caring for members of the opposite gender, friendships wherein, for us, there is no sexual tension, no need for domination and subordination. Perhaps the best concrete example of such sacrificial loving in our community to date comes in the wake of AIDS. The lesbian community has been heroically involved in caring for their gay brothers who still constitute some two-thirds of all AIDS cases, as well as in AIDS-related fund-raising and political action. Gay men in turn must be equally available to our sisters' needs, on their terms, as they arise. Clearly then, our experiences of community and of gay/lesbian cooperation are already nurturing our compassion for one another, for our com-munity as a whole, and for all persons. Borne in our sexual difference and loving sexual relationships, our compassion for one another need not be restricted to our own gender or even to our own community. Our com-passion is deeper than that and may indeed enable us to sustain the broader liberational perspective which Boyd (1984), Ruether (1983a), and others have urged upon us.

(iii) Synthesizing Compassion and Prophetic Judgment

Fox (1983) has written that "a good test of the homosexual's spiritual liberation . . . will be that person's dedication to the liberation of other persons. . . . If compassion is not the result of gay and les-bian liberation, then that liberation has not been at all radical, at all spiritual" (p. 196). Over and over again our activity of developing a gay liberation theo-logy is reminded that we must deepen into/through/past our anger at oppression to that point at which our rage, our righteous and divinely nourished anger at in-justice and human cruelty, is tempered by our capacity for compassion (cf., Fortunato, 1983). Heyward (1984), in fact, repeatedly suggests that compassion and pro-phetic judgment go hand and hand; our prophetic role as gay men and lesbians in a homophobic culture is mean-ingless unless it speaks judgment compassionately:

> Our passion as lovers is what fuels both our rage at injustice--including that which is done to us--and our compassion, or our passion, which is on behalf of/in empathy with those who violate us and hurt us and even destroy us. Rage and compas-sion, far from being mutually exclusive, belong together.
> . . . [Moreover], a person who is truly com-passionate . . . is not timid in taking stands which . . . carry judgment about what is right and wrong, just and unjust. . . . A compassionate per-son . . . realizes the bond, the commonness, be-tween [him/her]self and those whose actions or at-titudes [he/she] challenges, criticizes, or con-demns. (pp. 87, 239)

Our very marginalization, our experience of oppression, comes to us because of our particular sexual loving of one another; how can our response to oppression be any less grounded in our vast capacity for loving? That we are fundamentally a people bound by our (sexual) loving who also share a common yet flawed humanity with other oppressed persons, as well as with our oppressors themselves, requires that our prophetic word of judgment, our quest for justice, be equally borne of our loving compassion as well as our righteous anger. As a marginalized people, we are in fact empowered to live as a people of compassion, of judgment, of witness, and of radical change (Heyward, 1984).

Our constitution as a people of loving compassion, bound in common humanity even with those who oppress us and others, may be the very key to our effectiveness as a liberation community. Of our common humanity, for example, Boyd (1984) says that "a significant contribution gay people can offer is the awareness that virtually everybody occupies some kind of closet. Everybody knows what it means to hide and experience loneliness, refusing or being unable to share and explain deep feelings and truths" (p. 168). Similarly, Heyward (1984) goes on to insist that we share the same world, the same problems and dilemmas, as well as the same human failures, as do all people; each person's "destiny is bound up with one's own" (p. 237):

> Our lives are linked fundamentally with/in the deep-seated structures of injustice that trouble us: sexism, racism, economic injustice. And so we speak judgment and . . . compassion--toward others, toward ourselves, and perhaps toward God as well. (p. 205)

In other words, our compassion links our own failures and injustices, any occasion of our exclusion of another person or group of persons, in empathy with our oppressors' exclusion of us. Our compassion at once judges us both and demands that we, as a gay/lesbian liberation community, work harder for an all-encompassing justice which would include ourselves and others. Our compassion thus enables us to be "more conscious of what justice is in our own lives and in the world; conscious of our own passion with and for each other" (Heyward, 1984, p. 92). As if anticipating this realization that our judgment and compassion, together, must be directed "to ourselves as well as 'them'" (Heyward, 1984, p. 206), Rubenstein (1966) has similarly said that "whatever improvement the human condition affords will come about only through . . . compassionate joining together. . . . Such human fellowship requires a sense of solidarity rather than . . . radical separation of one human being from another" (p. 185). For our prophetic role to be most effective, then, our gay liberation theology must encourage us both to heal any divisiveness within our own community, while strengthening our cooperation, and to forge a strong identity for ourselves as a separate people (cf., Hay, 1987), while also owning our common humanity with compassion for all people(s) as well. Our prophetic and compassionate judgment begins at home, in our own abilities to accept and nurture one another even when we disagree with and speak prophetically to ourselves.

Our prophetic word to ourselves, then, brings us back again to our identity as a people set apart from/ by the structures of an oppressive heterosexist patriarchy. Not only by refusing to be divided against ourselves, but also by refusing "mere assimilation" into an oppressive system, we can instead stand in consolidarity, in shared humanity, with other oppressed persons seeking liberation. In so doing, we also stand in consolidarity with a horizontal, empowering, companion God whose primary concern is "to overthrow [all] unjust relationships" via championing the poor, the oppressed, and the socially or religiously stigmatized and marginalized, including gay people; moreover, we join God in the processes of liberation only when we also recognize and assume this preference for the oppressed "by identifying [our]selves with the cause of [all] the oppressed" (Ruether, 1983a, p. 157). Similarly, Rubenstein (1966) has written,

> . . . Denial of opportunity is a dehumanizing process. Anyone who accepts less than full equality of opportunity within [his/her] own society consents to [his/her] own partial dehumanization. . . . One does not lose dignity because a power situation imposes social limitations which cannot be overcome. One most assuredly loses dignity when one consents to second-class status (p. 174),

. . . whether for oneself, for one's own minority group, or for any group of people. Consequently, we must absolutely eschew assimilation into and hence endorsement of any social, economic, religious, or other form(s) of hierarchical privilege.

Fortunato (1983) would argue that the psycho-social effects of marginalization upon gay/lesbian identity, sensibility, and mode of being-in-the-world ultimately maladjust us to the system which oppresses us. If that is in fact the case, then lesbians, and gay men in particular, should be more critically reflective toward simplistic upward mobility as well as firmly iconoclastic toward white, heterosexist (male) values, power, and status. We must, in fact, fight discrimination and the restriction of opportunity wherever they occur and demand openness and acceptance and justice for all people. By accepting and celebrating our own identity and difference, by insisting upon the (re)valuation of genuine diversity/pluralism and hence of all people, gay men and lesbians who are truly marginal to the structures of economic, social, religious, and political success, privilege, or status bear the opportunity and responsibility for being at the, at least symbolic, forefront of authentic liberation for all people. We can demand not just acceptance by or full participation in the present system, but a critically reflective revisioning and reformation of that whole system which excludes us and others, affirming that all people possess a full and equivalent humanity (cf., Ruether, 1983a, Rubenstein, 1966). Heyward (1984) elaborates:

> We who are lesbians [and] gay men . . . need to be on guard against being . . . engulfed by the powers that be, and convinced that the only way we can survive in the world is to accommodate ourselves . . . in conformity with the norms of the present order.
>   . . . What homosexuals [should] be about . . . is not simply the right to lead our own private lives, but rather an overhauling of the social structures of our time. (p. 91)

At once celebrating our particular difference and affirming the value of genuine pluralism, while also wrestling with our own failures and divisiveness and the temptations of easy assimilation, all of these activities together keep us in consolidarity or common humanity with our oppressors. The compassion with which we consequently address ourselves in this light must then in simple fairness also color and shape our prophetic response to others.

Developing a gay liberation theology ultimately requires that we nurture compassion even for our oppressors, and thus a broadened view of all humanity, as part of our liberational goals (cf., Clark, 1987a). Or, as Ruether (1983a) has insisted, affirming the humanity of the oppressed as "more fundamental" than their present condition under heterosexist patriarchy demands "a like affirmation of the humanity" of those who oppress, lest we simply seek to invert oppressive structures (p. 231). Our gay liberation theology must embrace compassion and conciliation not only toward non-gays, but toward those who are actively anti-gay as well, because the ultimate goal of any liberation theology is cooperation in human liberation, in the freeing and uplifting of the worth and dignity of all people. As Greenberg (1981) has reflected, "Suddenly it occurred to me that part of my liberation . . . is that I also am responsible for what goes on in the world. If this society fails, it is also my failure" (p. 176). We do not really have the comfort or the luxury of a dualistic "us vs. them" situation; our liberation as gay and lesbian people is dependent both upon the liberation, revaluation, and resanctification of all people and upon the establishment of justice for all people. Moreover, we cannot succeed in our own full and genuine liberation unless we reach out in compassion to liberate not only other oppressed people, but all humanity as well. Thus are Goodman et al. (1983) able to reiterate the truism that those structures which undergird/sustain our oppression have also entrapped those who oppress us: "We will not create a new society or end gay oppression by convincing ordinary citizens that we are harmless. Rather we must show them that society harms them in the same ways that it harms us" (p. 130).

Heyward's (1984) compassionate analysis of sexism may consequently prove analogously informative for us on this score: She has insisted that "individual men cannot be held personally responsible for sexism's demonic and bitter history. . . . [Individual men, however], are responsible for what they have done, and do, to [women, gay people], and to themselves" (p. 65). Realizing the systemic or "structural character" of sexism (p. 225), and of heterosexism and its attendant homophobia, in conjunction with recognizing our common humanity, enables us to speak prophetically with both compassion and forgiveness. Both sexism and heterosexism/homophobia are systemic, structural, and embedded in western consciousness, perception, and valuation. We cannot hold contemporaneous individuals personally responsible for this "systemic demon," although we may

certainly hold them responsible for actions which are
unreflectively borne of and which reinforce/sustain
systemic evil. Our compassionate tasks are to attack
and change the system(s) of oppression and to invite/
encourage others to join us in these efforts (on behalf
of all people), rather than to judge individuals. Our
passion for the liberation and wholeness of our own gay
and lesbian people will be empty and even potentially
destructive without compassion both for those within
our own group whose "commitments are different from
[our] own," for those simply outside our particular
community, and even for those who oppress us (cf., Heyward, 1984, p. 72).

Our liberational influence may in fact be most effective when we shape ourselves as a compassionate
people. Only as such a liberation people may our prophetic words and actions possibly have a corrective impact upon sociopolitical and religious institutionalized forms, even while we hold out and embody the hope
for eventual justice, openness, and inclusivity for all
people. From outside the system, from our existential
standpoint on the margins, we can evolve liberational
forms of compassionate being and relating which may
eventually influence those inside the system and even
the system itself (cf., Umansky, 1985). Moreover, the
opportunity and challenge to us to be a people of utter
compassion and healing and co-empowerment, for gay men
and lesbians and for non-gays alike, has arisen no more
undeniably than in the current health crisis of AIDS.
More than any other crisis within or without our particular community in recent times, AIDS has called forth
gay/lesbian responsiveness and compassion.

(iv) Responding to the AIDS Crisis

Compassion and responsiveness have indeed become
the primary attributes of a gay and lesbian people
whose praxis in confronting the AIDS crisis during the
1980s, even prior to any theological articulation, has
nevertheless resounded with theological depth. AIDS
has fused theology and praxis for us and given our particular, exiled loving an even more poignant and prophetic quality:

A truly extraordinary witness to the kind of full
human love that can exist between two gay persons
is being manifested daily by AIDS victims and
their lovers and friends. The exceptional fidel-
ity, self-sacrifice and affection, as well as the

-164-

pain, grief and sorrow and the deep spiritual response to the suffering and bereavement that is
being expressed, is a sign . . . of the presence
. . . of [prophetic and compassionate] love in
these relationships. (McNeill, 1987, p. 246)

Marginalized by institutionalized religion and repeatedly told by certain self-appointed religious
spokespersons that AIDS is a divine punishment upon homosexuality, gay people have defiantly asserted that
responsibility cannot be so easily shifted either upon
the divine nature or upon a cosmic scheme of dualistic
goods and evils. The victim of tragedy must not be
blamed! Consistently, a gay liberation theology articulated in the wake of AIDS has insisted instead that
response-ability must be reassumed at the human level.
The AIDS crisis thus demands not only that we articulate an adequate theological response/understanding of
God and tragedy, but also that we provide both the
physical and the spiritual companionship--the love--so
sorely needed by those who suffer and grieve because of
AIDS.
    One of the first implications, then, of gay liber-
ation theology's reconceptualization of God, not as a
judgmental cosmic tyrant, but as a compassionate and
co-suffering presence in victimization and tragedy, is
that guilt-laden self-deprecation is no longer necessary. Those people, particularly gay men, who have
been marginalized because of our sexual orientation or
our immune system's breakdown can instead regain our
"self-respect and sense of goodness without having to
feel that God has judged us or condemned us" (Kushner,
1981, p. 45, cf., Clark, 1986a, 1987a). Confronting
AIDS and our homophobic/AIDS-phobic detractors has en-
abled many gay men at least not to succumb to victim
blaming, but instead to assume an even deeper and
stronger degree of self-acceptance and self-validation
(cf., Shelp, Sunderland, and Mansell, 1986). Shelp,
Sunderland, and Mansell (1986) even go so far as to
argue that our experience of anti-gay oppression as
well as our successful transcendence of oppression in
claiming our gayness and in constituting ourselves as a
defiant, liberation-seeking people, together provide
gay men in particular with a resiliency for coping with
and responding to AIDS. Having dealt with being gay
enables us to deal with AIDS:

    Gay men, in particular, have had to wrestle with
    discoveries about who they are as sexual beings in

an unaccepting, condemning cultural and [reli-
gious] environment. The resiliency with which
they negotiated this discovery and subsequent personal declaration [coming out] may have been a
helpful preparation for negotiating the additional
discovery of having ARC [AIDS-related complex] or
AIDS. In addition, their capacity to withstand
cultural condemnation may have helped equip them
to withstand the indifferent and hostile reactions
to the disease [which they encounter]. Despite
these assaults on self-esteem, it seems remarkable
that within the gay AIDS and ARC populations [as
well as within the larger, at-risk gay male commu-
nity] almost no one regrets being homosexual.
These gay men maintain, almost without exception,
a pride about themselves. (p. 182, emphasis added)

Confronting and responding to AIDS in both theology and
praxis leads gay people and gay theology to insist, absolutely, that the harsh reality of AIDS does not invalidate the basic worth of gay (or lesbian) being as
one of the various forms of human life which God has
created and blessed. Nor does AIDS invalidate the basic goodness of sexuality or of (homo)sexually intimate
and mutual relationships. Indeed, while we can all responsibly lessen our AIDS-related health risks, neither
sickness nor health are matters of divine judgment or
some part of a cosmic scheme. AIDS simply happened
(cf., Clark, 1986a, 1987a). Therefore, rather than being defeated by AIDS, rather than succumbing to the
sex-rejecting AIDS-phobia which now bolsters homophobia, gay men and lesbians are defiantly asserting their
self-acceptance and revaluing all human sexuality with
renewed vigor and pride.
    The gay/lesbian community's confrontation with
AIDS has not only led to a stronger acceptance of our
selfhood and our very being; it is also leading us to a
prophetic acceptance of human limits, of human mortality. Fortunato (1987), for example, insists that by
acknowledging the irrational and random quality of AIDS
and by realizing that no divine intervention or rescue
can be forthcoming, we can penetrate our experience of
god-forsakenness, yielding to the reality of our pain
and our limitations and therein finding relief and the
subsequent strength for responsible actions of love and
compassion and mercy. Relinquishing false hopes and
moving through our pain and grief--accepting the realities of both AIDS and human mortality--leads us to an
empowerment for "tending to the needs of the afflicted"

(p. 111, cf., pp. 109-110). While Fortunato (1987) subsequently becomes entangled in an eschatological dilemma, torn between the mystery and uncertainty which point toward God and the persistent human need for something more, some final or ultimate validation of loss and pain, his earlier insistence upon confronting and penetrating the hard realities of both gay oppression (1983) and AIDS (1987) allows a thoroughgoing realism to remain in his overall work. Both our gay theology and our praxis can affirm God's reality as a horizontal companion and co-sufferer with and for us, without requiring any traditional notions about the "hereafter"; we can commend ourselves, those grieving among us, and those dying among us to trust God and to await God, while assuring our friends of their continuing value and meaning in this life.

We cannot in fact make promises about the "beyond" without threatening to invalidate our good gay lives here and now. Kushner (1981) reminds us that "the dead [and the dying] depend on us for their redemption and their immortality" (p. 138) and Heyward (1982) insists that although "the dead be dead, the power in our relation[s] to [these] person[s] is not dead. The power in the relation[s] is alive. It is not broken except in our denial of its present movement within and among us" (p. 52). In other words, as we gay men and lesbians help our dying friends to maintain self-esteem by realizing the tremendous value and meaning of their lives, and as we enable ourselves and others to retain the goodness of those lives (however tragically and painfully shortened) and their effects (over and above the effects of their deaths) in our own continued, future-ward living, thusly can we contribute to redeeming the tragedy of AIDS (cf., Clark, 1986a, 1987a). Moreover, in so doing we again join the co-creative God who effectively sustains the memory and value of every moment and every life for the ongoing creation and nurturance of life and being. Ruether (1983a) has articulated this synthesis of realistically accepting human limitation (mortality) and of retaining/sustaining the meaning and value of those whom we have lost. Her synthesis may provide an element of comfort for our theology and praxis in the wake of AIDS:

> Acceptance of death, then, is acceptance of the finitude of our individuated centers of being, but also our identification with the larger matrix [of Being] as our total self that contains us all.

. . . That great collective personhood is the
Holy Being in which our achievements and failures
are gathered up, assimilated into the fabric of
Being, and carried forward into new possibilities.
(pp. 257, 258)

The realism which gay people are bringing to our
confrontation with AIDS--our defiant revaluation of all
human sexuality and gay/lesbian being; our struggles
with sociopolitical givens and our tireless efforts to
wrest justice and mercy from the medical system, while
relinquishing hope for any swiftly rescuing deus ex machina in either realm; and, our refusal to relinquish
the value and meaning of our friends' lives either to
homophobic judgment in the present or to any illusory
eschatological future--has further entailed revaluing
anger and grief while learning the appropriateness of
forgiveness for transforming our righteous anger and
our undeniable grief into the energies of compassionate
response. Our renewed self-acceptance and our acceptance of both human and divine limits have led us to
recognize that our anger at life's unfairness and our
compassion for those who suffer, far from being opposed
to God, are in fact nurtured by the divine presence
(cf., Clark, 1986a, 1987a). Writes Fortunato (1987),
"I am persuaded that God swells with compassion at our
angriest moments [in our dealing with AIDS], aching
with us in our rage" (p. 115). Anticipating such an
AIDS-specific endorsement of guiltless and righteous
anger, Kushner (1981) has similarly insisted that "we
can feel that our indignation is God's anger at unfairness working through us" (p. 45, cf., pp. 108-109).
     It is OK to be angry! Kushner (1981), however,
enjoins those who suffer and grieve to be angry at the
situation. If there is no cause for AIDS, if AIDS
simply happened, the only real thing toward which we
can legitimately direct our anger is the situation itself, the reality of AIDS and/or the human cruelties it
has engendered. Although God is certainly strong
enough to accept and understand our anger, our anger
can alienate us from him/her and from other sources of
comfort. Anger toward God, or toward other gay/gay-
sensitive people, or toward ourselves is misdirected
(cf., Shelp, Sunderland, and Mansell, 1986). To keep
our anger or that of others from remaining destruc-
tively misdirected we must (re)learn the art of forgiveness to temper our anger. We must, for example,
forgive God for being limited, accept flawed reality,
and take responsibility for creating justice, compas-

sion, and mercy here and now. Forgiving God entails
realizing that while people need God, God also needs
humanity. God depends upon humanity for genuine, unco-
erced love that is freely given in spite of suffering,
injustice, and death. Forgiving God means loving God
not for his/her power or his/her rescuing, but for the
beauty and order which we do experience and as the
source of strength, hope, courage, compassionate presence, and supportive others (Kushner, 1981). Forgiving
God and the cosmos may be very difficult, but it is the
only wholistic means by which to continue to love God,
to love life and creation, and to love one another
(cf., Clark, 1986a, 1987a).

Forgiving God/cosmos is also the necessary prerequisite which then enables us to forgive ourselves and
others, to accept one another, and to celebrate existence in spite of AIDS. Forgiveness means not only
ceasing to blame God or God's absence for AIDS suffering, but, certainly for gay men, also ceasing to blame
ourselves, our sexual partners, and/or our long term
mates for a combination of factors and risks we can
know at best only vaguely and in hindsight. Our capacity for forgiveness may even bear prophetic, transfor-
mative power toward those people seemingly outside the
AIDS crisis, ultimately diffusing all blaming, including blaming the victim. Shelp, Sunderland, and Mansell
(1986), for example, have noted the particular irony
that,

> . . . people with AIDS tend not to blame God
> for [the HIV virus'] attack on their bodies. . . .
> People who contract AIDS by blood transfusion or
> . . . blood products tend to blame neither God nor
> gay men. Why is it [then] that . . . some seg-
> ments of the [healthy or minimally at risk] public
> are willing to attribute AIDS to God and link it
> to God's alleged condemnation of homosexuality?
> (p. 184, emphasis added)

As we thus exchange and enable others to exchange all
forms of blaming for forgiveness, our righteous anger
and our pain shared with God and with one another can
yield the empowerment we need to take up the real tasks
of appropriate response. Indeed, although we cannot
control the chaotic inbreaking of AIDS, we can take responsibility for enhancing the quality both of our own
lives and deaths and of the lives and deaths of others.
Although our choices may be limited to promoting sexual
responsibility henceforth ("safe sex"), to embodying

compassionate presence for those who are currently suffering, and to responding with theological maturity to
AIDS-death, within these options we still have numerous
opportunities for appropriate response (cf., Clark,
1986a, 1987a).

Like the reality and legitimacy/righteousness of
our anger, our grief and our sense of loss before AIDS
are also very real, and God is present in our grief
even as he/she has been present in the suffering and
dying of our friends. Based upon his understanding of
God's limits and of cosmic randomness (evil), Kushner
(1981) contends, for example, that while tragedy does
not have meaning or purpose, when it happens, we can
give it meaning: "We can redeem these tragedies from
senselessness by imposing meaning on them" (p. 136).
He urges the survivors of tragedy to relinquish the focus upon the past (why did "X" happen, or "Y" die?) in
exchange for a future orientation (where does a tragedy
lead us?) (p. 137). Since life and death are neutral,
a yin/yang oneness which is part of the greater oneness
of God/cosmos, we can use our experience of AIDS-death
to propel us back into life, into God's future, or we
can despair and lose faith (cf., Clark, 1986a, 1987a).
Ultimately, neither our anger (at the fact of AIDS) nor
our grief (over the losses from AIDS) should be repressed or ignored. Indeed, as we are able to be co-
suffering companions with and for one another as anger
and grief are spent, we contribute to the transformation of those energies into a future-directed empowerment. The energies of our anger and our grief can
actually become the motivation or empowerment for the
activism and the volunteerism so desperately needed to
pursue the political and financial, as well as medical
and sociological, resolutions for the AIDS crisis. As
such, anger and grief serve to empower the creation of
justice and mercy in the present and future. Similarly, although we cannot control who becomes ill or
why they do, we can be responsible for who we become as
a result of the AIDS crisis, both in our own lives and
in our caring roles with others. Working to develop
more responsible sexual behavior, deepened relationships, and increasingly cooperative community is a part
of this process, as is the building of cooperative liaisons between gays and non-gays for confronting the
crisis and for translating theological reflection into
compassionate praxis (cf., Clark, 1986a, 1987a).

The reality of AIDS, particularly in the gay male
community (still some 70% of U.S. cases), unrelentingly
fuses theology and praxis. It has compelled gay men

(and lesbians as well) toward a deeper self-acceptance and a more realistic acceptance of limitations, both human and divine. It has forced us to wrestle simultaneously with the theological issues of anger and grief and of blaming and forgiveness, as well as with the sociopolitical and medical issues of homophobia and AIDS-phobia which complicate the processes of resolution. Most of all, this crisis in our community has compelled us to act, even as we reflect on the issues which shape and are shaped by our actions. Again and again AIDS demands human responsibility for compassionate acts of caring. Consequently, Fortunato (1987) insists that "it is principally the task of those of us without AIDS to provide human sympathy and to be vehicles of God's love for those afflicted. And in the act of responding, I believe we too shall find comfort" (p. 116). He goes on to reiterate that in relinquishing victim-blaming (for healthy individuals), survivor-guilt (for gay men), and all our efforts to make AIDS seem either humanly or cosmically reasonable instead of randomly and chaotically inbreaking evil in itself (for everyone), then "it is precisely through our acts of loving--of tending the sick and dying, of comforting the bereaved, and of striving to find a cure--that we spiritually feed and heal one another" gay and non-gay, well and ill, all alike (pp. 117-118).

Anticipating Fortunato's (1987) admonition, Shelp, Sunderland, and Mansell (1986) have outlined a number of specific ways in which people might respond to the AIDS crisis. They view persons-with-AIDS (PWAs) and persons-with-AIDS-related-complex (PWARCs), as well as all gay people, in the prophetic role of the oppressed, powerless outcasts whom God champions and for whom God demands appropriate response. As such, these overlapping communities embody the courage and compassion needed by all people both to overcome and to heal irrational fears about AIDS, PWAs, PWARCs, and gay people as well; to relinquish the human urge to categorize and reject any group of people; and thus to heal the wounds of gay oppression and the broken relationships of homophobia. Shelp, Sunderland, and Mansell (1986) also urge healthy gay and non-gay individuals alike to be responsive to grief and empathetic with suffering, to provide an unhurried and undistracted presence for both those who suffer and those who grieve. Above all, they call for a commitment on the part of healthy individuals not to abandon PWAs and PWARCs, but to be instead a "sustaining presence" all the way through the processes of AIDS (pp. 168, 191).

The work of Fortunato (1987) and of Shelp, Sunderland, and Mansell (1986) gradually focuses our gay liberation theology-as-praxis upon the specific needs of PWAs, particularly their need for human companionship. Indeed, if God is reconceptualized as a limited, co-suffering companion, ultimately everyone, and especially we gay men (and lesbians) ourselves, are called to embody or to incarnate this divine companionship. Assuming human responsibility in the AIDS crisis, apart from any deus ex machina, means we absolutely must not avoid being with our friends and others who are suffering. Simple physical presence and genuine listening are two forms of appropriate response, as is physical comforting and embracing insofar as AIDS is not casually transmissable. Through our empathy at the unfairness of AIDS, we can also help those who suffer by both accepting and encouraging/blessing their righteous anger and by further allowing them their right to grieve. Together we can set aside blaming and guilt (including our "survivor guilt"). As we share anger and pain, we mediate the processes of forgiveness and reconciliation, both reestablishing trustworthiness in human relationships--with ourselves, with lovers and friends, with family--and finding meaning and celebrating the good in even a foreshortened life. We can also share our beliefs that God is not a harsh judge who vindictively or whimsically punishes people with illness; that instead God loves and upholds those who suffer and in fact inspires people to help other people; that God empowers and nurtures doctors, nurses, medical researchers, social workers, and therapists; that God is a source of strength, courage, and perseverance; that God and faith work through human agency to reaffirm the self-worth and self-esteem of the dying (cf., Kushner, 1981). All these shared acts of sympathy and empathy, of compassion and reassurance, help to maintain and reinforce the human dignity, the self-respect, and the self-esteem of the PWA, as well as to provide a sense of connectedness to the human community for that individual, despite the social ostracism which AIDS too often entails (cf., Clark, 1986a, 1987a).

As we move from reflection to action to our specific one-to-one interactions with PWAs and PWARCs, our theology and praxis indeed conflate (cf., Clark, 1987d). Our confrontation with AIDS, as a gay and lesbian community, has already begun to (re)shape us as a people of compassion and ministry, as described by McNeill (1987). In spite of the disproportionate, unreasonable unfairness of AIDS in our particular community, we are already beginning to live more fully and more committed in the present, discovering therein an energy for shaping community and for seeking and creating liberation, as well as for bearing up the pain and grief of AIDS with our good gay/lesbian loving (Fortunato, 1987). Shelp, Sunderland, and Mansell (1986) have even more specifically articulated ways in which our confronting and responding to AIDS is redemptively (re)shaping our lives. As gay men, in particular, have confronted the suffering and dying of our friends, we seem not only to be gaining a sense of perspective on life and human mortality; we are also becoming more genuine as individuals--at once more free from socio-religious judgments and more at home in our self-understandings--and, consequently, more capable of deep, meaningful, and sustained relationships and couplings. According to Shelp, Sunderland, and Mansell (1986), our realistic perspective on our mortality is making us more perceptive, more aware of details in our environment and more appreciative of both the diversity and similarity--the basic goodness--of all people. It is also enabling us to revalue time and to prioritize and engage in increasingly meaningful activity. Confronting our mortality while interacting regularly with suffering friends is also nurturing a greater introspection among gay men, as well as the qualities of honesty, courage, patience, understanding, and selfless compassion, including a heightened empathy for other minorities similarly struggling for justice.

The overall force of these developments among gay men, according to Shelp, Sunderland, and Mansell (1986), is that the gay male community is achieving a deeper, more genuine maturity, as well as an enhanced spirituality or spiritual perspective utterly apart from gay-excluding institutionalized religion. Unlike the experiences of many of our lesbian sisters, the gay male subculture in the decade immediately following liberation unwittingly fell prey to a heterosexist conditioning which resulted in a frequently dehumanizing, sexually competitive, and ultimately isolating ghetto experience for gay men which discouraged spiritual depth. The assault of AIDS upon our community has transformed the gay ghetto and the bar subculture into a significant location for AIDS-activism, -fundraising, and -volunteerism, and has transformed our relational styles into more caring and more humanizing patterns (cf., Clark, 1986b). While all gay men, of course, are not responding in these ways, while some lovers succumb to AIDS-phobia and desert their dying partners or while some gay men avoid the issue by plunging deeper into unsafe anonymous sex, the majority of the gay male and lesbian community is indeed becoming a prophetic people of responsive, loving compassion (cf., McNeill, 1987). Our process of developing a gay liberation theology must adamantly underscore the fact, however, that no matter how ultimately beneficial and redemptive the maturation and spiritual enhancement of our community are for us, these benefits in no way theologically justify the existence of AIDS. Again AIDS, like any other tragedy, simply happened. Our developmental processes are a part of our responsibility-assuming and meaning-creating response to that tragedy, as we join in co-partnership with a horizontal companion God to redeem and transform, but not deny, the tragedy of AIDS (cf., Kushner, 1981, Clark, 1986a, 1987a).

Overall our encounter as a gay and lesbian community with AIDS has made us painfully aware that for the haunting "why?" of suffering and death, there is no easily satisfying answer which so "makes sense of it all" as to cancel the pain, anguish, and sense of unfairness we feel in confronting this monumental tragedy. Our anger at this random inbreaking of chaos (evil) and our grief at the loss of lives are valid and real, as well as divinely experienced and understood. As a result of the spectre of AIDS ever present in the processes of developing a constructive gay liberation theology, our work absolutely refutes any theological formulations or religious pronouncements which seek to justify gay suffering by condemning homosexual orientation, which seek too easily to explain away the reality of any suffering, or which seek to stifle anger or grief. The reality of AIDS has led us instead to relinquish our inherited notions of God's all-powerfulness, either as the source of tragedy or as the rescuer from tragedy. Instead, as we come to accept the unitary balance of God and chaotic randomness, we discover in our experience of god-forsakenness God's real compassion and empowerment on behalf of the victims of both oppression and tragedy. This divine intimacy enables us to forgive God, the cosmos, ourselves, and one another, and hence further enables us to keep living, loving, and prudently risking. We find in our transformed faith not rescue, but the spiritual resources for assuming appropriate responsibility for our own lives and for caring for our suffering friends. We also learn to redeem those foreshortened lives by actively retaining them in our own lives and memories. Our refusal to succumb to despair, our facing the future, and our continuing to shape a gay community which is that of a proactive, liberation-seeking people, all in spite of the realities of suffering and tragedy, provide some measure of immortality in this world for the friends we have lost (cf., Clark, 1986a, 1987a). We are indeed called into "God's future" (cf., Kushner, 1981), as we continue the work both of caring for and remembering our friends, of building community and creating justice for gay people and for other minorities, and of shaping theological reflection and creating rituals to bless and nurture our good gay and lesbian lives.

(v) Developing New Rituals and Symbols

One other, final area which our revisioning of gay and lesbian community might also at least begin to explore is that of developing or recasting rituals and symbols in accordance with our understandings of gay liberation theology and gay/lesbian community. Fox (1983), for example, emphasizes the importance of celebration as a balance for the hard work of justice-seeking and -making. He insists that we must learn to celebrate both our being and our sexuality "in the midst of sadness [AIDS] and oppression [homophobia]" (p. 200). Feminist theology also reiterates the importance of developing appropriate rituals in the midst of our various struggles (cf., Christ, 1980). Indeed, the very preciousness of our lives under the shadow of AIDS and the urgency of our liberational efforts in the midst of increasing homophobia make our celebrations all the more valuable to us. Among our present sources for a liberation theology, Washburn (1979) has best articulated an understanding of ritual(s) for our purposes. She writes,

> . . . Religious questions and reflections about the meaning of what is holy or ultimate arise at times of crisis in the life of the individual and of the community. These crises may be historical or personal events, but because of them we are forced to respond.
> . . . [Moreover], particular life crises . . . are not just psychological phases to be negotiated but turning points that raise fundamentally religious questions. (pp. 246, 247)

She goes on to cite Rubenstein (1966) in suggesting that ritual(s) emerges from the needs of individuals within communities to give meaning to personal and social identity questions, particularly in relation to the past and the future as these converge in present life crises.

Insofar as the gay and lesbian community is not primarily a religious community and these efforts to develop a gay liberation theology have purposely avoided allegiance to any particular institutionalized religious community within the whole Judaeo-Christian spectrum, while nevertheless drawing upon that entire spectrum, our provisional work in this area might best begin by examining and accounting for/embracing/sanctifying the shared symbols or rituals which already exist and which carry mythic, if not actually religious, significance for gay people. The gay bar subculture, for example, clearly entails individually or idiosyncratically ritualized patterns of preparation and entry, as well as communally accepted rituals for behavior within the bars. Elaborate systems of symbols and behavior patterns already exist for signaling, meeting, and engaging previously unknown sexual partners. Certain patterns of sexual activity, as well, particularly within the leather community, are also highly ritualized. Moreover, the entire bar subculture and its rituals or games are played out under the mythic archetype of the heroic penetration of and reemergence from the primordial Underworld or Hades (Clark, 1987a, 1987b). Apart from the bar subculture, our engagement with AIDS has also created numerous rituals within the gay community, from the repeated formal patterns of AIDS-support volunteer training sessions, to the periodic services of healing (particularly in the Episcopalian community), to the annual or semi-annual memorial services for the friends and lovers whom we have lost to date. A third area in which we already have rituals and traditions developing is that of our relationships; within our couplings we need to become more aware of, and thus to bless and sanctify, the shared rituals which nourish our love and commitment to one another, whether the simple ritualistic patterns of how we shut down our homes to retire for sleep or how we wake up and begin new days, the somewhat more complex ways in which we customarily structure weekends and leisure time, or the elaborate repeated ways in which we celebrate holidays and anniversaries.

Aside from all these ways in which gay men and lesbians are already engaged in meaning-bearing (religious or mythic) rituals, the implicit demand in Washburn's (1979) writing, as well as in that of Christ

(1980) and Fox (1983), is that we not only recognize
and honor already existing rituals, but that we create
intentional rituals as well. Responding to "life
crises" thus entails creating gay rites of passage
(cf., Washburn, 1979, p. 247). Perhaps the most crucial of passages discussed herein is that of coming
out, and once again, the historical precedent of the
native American berdache has much to teach us. Many
native societies, for example, traditionally had elaborate communal ritual processes both for an individual's
selection for or acknowledgement of berdachehood and
for formally initiating or consecrating an individual
into his/her new role. The latter process frequently
included a symbolic, ritual bathing or "baptism" to
mark the individual's actual transformation. These
complex rites provided a public ritual for coming out
which also symbolized an individual's rebirth or the
exchange of one's previous identity for one's new identity as a berdache (Devereux, 1937, cf., Clark, 1984,
1987a). As we move from theology to praxis, a respiri-
tualized gay community might likewise develop rituals
which simultaneously ease the anxiety of self-dis-
covery, which sanctify coming out as a transitional or
rebirthing stage or passage, and which celebrate both
human destiny and human variety, all within the context
of an individual's newfound community (cf., Clark,
1984, 1987a).
     Other obvious rites of passage which we might also
wish to develop include: (1) rituals to hallow our relationships, even apart from traditional religious
faiths (the Universal Fellowship of Metropolitan Community Churches [MCC], a primarily gay denomination, already performs such ceremonies of blessing [cf., Uhrig,
1984] as do the Unitarians and some Episcopalians upon
request); (2) rituals for blessing our first homes together as couples; (3) rituals to celebrate longstand-
ing relationships or to dissolve ending relationships;
and, (4) rituals to celebrate our children's development (e.g., Bar/Bat Mitzvah celebrations in gay/lesbian
synagogues). Once we are committed as a community to
the development of intentionally gay-supportive rituals, we have only our imaginations to limit our possibilities.
     Closely akin to rituals are those symbols or those
holidays of symbolic importance which we may wish to
create or recast/reinterpret for our gay communal contexts. Gay men in particular have already, for example, claimed Halloween, New Year's Eve, and Mardi
Gras as especially gay celebrations, times for more

than the usual amount of "drag" and "camp" in community festivities. One of the most powerful examples, however, of an established religious holiday discussed in the sources for our efforts toward a gay liberation theology, a holiday which easily yields to reinterpretation, is Passover (cf., Cantor, 1979, Fackenheim, 1970). The Jewish holiday of Passover (Pesach) clearly symbolizes and remembers God's historical empowerment of one particular marginalized people to assume human responsibility and to enact human liberation. Its tremendous power as a symbol, however, transcends its particularity and points to God as a liberator, to the divine urge for justice, on behalf of any marginalized group. So understood, Passover celebrates not only God's liberating power in history, but God's liberating co-empowerment on behalf of all people still on the margins. It also symbolically signifies God as the grounding and source of empowerment for any people to actively seek their own liberation. Furthermore, by its customary celebration in a familial and/or communal context, Passover underscores our need as gay men and lesbians to celebrate and sanctify our couplings and our surrogate families.

Overall for Fackenheim (1970), celebrating Passover mixes remembrance with defiance, with the sheer endurability of the Jewish people; it also mixes hope and longing with defiance, yielding a renewed determination to persevere and to seek justice and to create/ enable God's presence, even in the midst of oppression and the experience of seeming god-forsakenness. Passover celebrates a God who sides with the powerless. The memory of Auschwitz, for Fackenheim (1970), and the experiences of homophobic oppression and AIDS devastation, for gay people, reiterate for us the fact that sometimes God, too, is not just with the powerless, but is actually one of them/us. That intimate presence as one of us in our pain--whether at Auschwitz, or in homophobic violence, or with AIDS--can fuel and nourish our defiance. God sanctifies the defiance of all those who suffer human injustice or nature's unfairness and premature suffering and death. That blessing of defiance creates hope and demands that we take responsibility for not just enduring, but for persevering both in our compassion for those persons suffering with or grieving over AIDS and in our quest for justice and for liberation, for all people.

Thusly does just one particular, traditional holiday open itself symbolically to embrace and celebrate and reiterate the concerns of our efforts in gay liberation theology. As individual gay men and lesbians, as gay couples, and as gay communities, we may similarly recast and celebrate other traditional holidays in gay-supportive ways. We shall certainly also continue to celebrate the holidays of our own particular making, such as our annual celebrations of gay/lesbian pride which remember and sanctify the contemporary birth of our liberation movement, in the 1969 Stonewall Inn/Christopher Street riots in New York, and which, through remembrance and celebration, empower us anew for our ongoing tasks of liberation. Such celebrations are, of course, only the beginnings of our efforts to ritually celebrate our good gay and lesbian lives.

* * *

Ultimately, of course, these preliminary reflections on rituals and symbols bring our process of shaping a gay liberation theology virtually full circle, insofar as creating rituals and recasting symbols is akin to reconceptualizing God and other theological images. At the same time, this whole dynamic process actually functions more like a spiral toward other goals of filling out the details of our vision(s) of gay/lesbian community, of developing real workable liaisons of lesbians and gay men, of enlisting allies of our community for future sociopolitical strategies, of discovering more effective ways to respond to AIDS and to our suffering friends and lovers, and of continuing to shape and (re)interpret rituals and symbols to nurture and celebrate our lives as gay men and lesbians. As a dynamic and never completed process, our activity of gay liberation theology also supersedes itself, as theological reflection is given over to action. A theology which is our liberational praxis provides the necessary grounding and then immediately commands us to be about the business of compassionate, liberation-seeking, justice-making action--on behalf of our own community and of all the peoples of the earth.

* * *

IX. Notes

I. Introduction

[1] Noteworthy exceptions to this otherwise dismal situation at the present time include the Reconstructionist branch of Judaism, the United Church of Christ, and the Unitarian-Universalists; unfortunately, the independent, congregationally autonomous nature of these three groups means that ordination alone does not guarantee gay clergy access to parish ministry (cf., Comstock, 1987).

[2] Gay Atheist League of America (G.A.L.A.), P.O. Box 7838, Atlanta, Georgia 30357.

[3] To date both "faerie" and "gay spirituality" have primarily concentrated upon the development of sources and means for nurturing the "inner life" of gay men and upon the elucidation of an oftimes mystically informed and "radically different" vision of "the future." So preoccupied, they at least appear detached from sociopolitical realities (Thompson et al., 1987, Clark, 1987b, 1987a, except pp. 55-75). While faerie is not opposed to gay civil rights politics as such, how gay spirituality might/can/should inform gay/lesbian cooperation and politically realistic activism remains unclear. An uneasy tension or a disjointed relationship of theory to praxis thus permeates a spectrum from disdain for "mere" or "assimilationist" legal rights activism (Thompson et al., 1987) to just short of a call for (violent) gay revolution (Mitchell and Asta, 1977, Evans, 1978). Moreover, faerie and gay spirituality have tended thus far to treat AIDS obliquely, mystically, or symbolically, rather than as a real sociopolitical, life-and-death issue. Thompson (1987c) even concedes, for example, that "to outsiders, the fairies often appear politically naive. . . . Yet, for the men who respond to its call, the fairie movement is rooted in the firm belief that the only liberation . . . worth having is one that . . . begins inside. Personal evolution is the true agent for change" (p. 269). While both personally and communally gay men and lesbians do in fact need to listen more to our depths and to nur-

ture our inner spiritual centeredness or grounding, a spiritual emphasis focused solely on the inner life may be unable or even unwilling to motivate actions; and we cannot afford to wait for our spiritual renewal to reach some desired level before we do in fact act. Our spiritual deepening must rather occur simultaneously with our activism. Moreover, our inner life and our shared vision must not become disconnected from our real and present experience(s) of gay/lesbian being, of homophobia, and of AIDS. Our spirituality must not be allowed to become too esoteric, or isolationist, or escapist; it should be the source of our empowerment rather than a reactionary retreat from the lethargy or even the failures of sociopolitical change. We must, in other words, deepen, enrich, and nurture our depths and our spirituality, while simultaneously finding therein the ground and empowerment for liberating praxis, for gay/lesbian legal, political, and social activism. Gay liberation theology, therefore, must pursue and articulate this fusion or synthesis of spirituality and praxis, promoting actions which are compassionately and wisely empowered and informed by spiritual depth rather than any inward retreat from participation in sociopolitical reality, here and now.

II. Method, Experience, and Gay Theology

[4] Similarly, gay theology is deeply indebted to and dependent upon the analyses of gender and sexism which feminist theology has so clearly articulated. Feminist theology is thus another necessary prerequisite, both historically and substantively, for gay theology; cf., Clark, 1987a, pp. 13-27 (Chapter III, "Shared Sexism and Spirituality").
[5] Crompton (1978) describes a (civil) "statutory policy of gay genocide" which spread concurrently with Christianity: Theodosius' edict of 390 CE demanded burning at the stake; Justinian's edict of 538 CE resulted in terrorism unleashed against homosexuals; and, an English parliamentary civil statue of 1533 CE declared "gay love a felony with hanging as its penalty" (pp. 69-70). He goes on to indicate that these laws remained in the criminal codes "in France till 1791, in England till 1861, and in Scotland as late as 1889" (p. 70). Moreover, in America the Massachusetts Bay Colony used the Old Testament formula verbatim: "America's first settlers condemned their gay sons to death, and in the case of a 1656 New Haven statute, their lesbian daughters" (p. 71). Although only three gay executions

are on record in the United States, not until 1786 did Pennsylvania begin the move to repeal the death penalty (pp. 71, 73).

⁶ For example studies of homosexuality in mythology and in native America, as well as for a study of the gay saint, Aelred, see Clark, 1987a, pp. 5-12, 28-54.

III. Patriarchy and Gay Oppression

⁷ While lesbians and gay men have become increasingly aware of the interrelationship of sexism and heterosexism and while gay theology is clearly dependent upon the articulate analyses of much of feminist theology, gay male efforts to cooperate with feminists remain tentative and provisional. Many gay men retain their enculturated sexism toward women, lesbians, and even toward one another (cf., Clark, 1987c), and some feminists are still uncomfortable with gay men and/or with homosexuality itself. For example, in her early work, Daly (1973) is clearly sympathetic toward gay men and links feminist and gay concerns:

> By its sex role stereotyping, phallic [patriarchal] morality has created the "problem" of homosexuality, which prevents us from seeing that two people of the same sex may relate authentically to each other. . . . It also uses the label as a scare term to intimidate those who even appear to deviate from the norms dictated by role psychology. . . . The label, then, is an instrument of social control. (pp. 125-126)

Yet, very shortly thereafter (Daly, 1978), she shifts to her current lesbian separatist position which combines women's and lesbians' concerns while sharply separating gay male and lesbian issues. She thus eschews the conciliatory function of gay theology as it hopes to reconcile the various differences in the gay/lesbian community, including gender. Another example is that of Ruether (cf., 1983a), whose various astute work is vital for all liberation theology and particularly for gay theology. Her apparent inability, however, to deal adequately with lesbians and homosexuality--to barely use the word "lesbian" (only four index references in Ruether, 1983a) and to mention homosexuality only once and gay men not all (1983a)--causes her to miss completely the human embodied location of male-feminist connections in her discussion of this issue (1983a). She thereby fails to acknowledge the potentially paradigmatic role of gay men as co-partners with all women in battling sexism. Moreover, her "all oppressed women" does not really address lesbians, whose experience she reduces to mere political choice (1983a, p. 228). She acknowledges lesbians as a subgroup of radical feminists, but appears unable to confront sexual orientation or gay/lesbian being in its own right. Her feminist and antisexist efforts thus appear weakened by her own heterosexism, by her own Catholic entrapment in a dualistic hierarchy of sexual behavior values. That the same systemic structures which sustain sexism also sustain homophobia, that common ground, unfortunately, is ignored by her. These various problems in feminist theology notwithstanding, gay theology and gay men and lesbians still remain deeply indebted to feminist theology, especially for its groundbreaking efforts in sex role and gender analysis.

IV. Reconceptualizing God

[8]Christ and Plaskow (1979) have further elaborated on the ways in which the pragmatic/liturgical emphasis in Judaism, in contrast to the dogmatic/theological focus of Christianity, has led Jewish feminists, in particular, to wrestle with God language, insofar as that language affects the role(s) of women in Judaism:

> Since Judaism is a religion of ritual, law, and study, rather than theology, creed, and doctrine, Jewish feminists have devoted their efforts not so much to defining and overcoming the patriarchal structures of Jewish thought as to criticizing specific attitudes toward women and to working for the full incorporation of women into Jewish religious life. . . . Even those Jewish thinkers who are most theoretical express a practical concern. (p. 134)

Not dissimilarly, Ozick (1983) even goes so far as to say that the "'nature of divinity' is a theological question, and Jews traditionally have no theology. Concerning the nature of God, we are enjoined to be agnostic, and not to speculate" (p. 122). Our efforts to synthesize the liberationist insights of both Judaism and Christianity, in order to develop an inclusive gay liberation theology, will necessarily focus not only upon images and language, but upon the conceptions of God which underlie/shape those images and/or to which those images point. Such reflections upon the "nature of divinity," however, are not without their pragmatic or praxis-oriented side, insofar as those reflections ultimately constitute a process which leads gay theology to focus less upon the "nature of God" and more upon the absolute importance of human responsibility.

[9]Christina's and Julian's early efforts toward an androgynous or bisexual spirituality (McLaughlin, 1979) are also contemporaneous with the twelfth century theology of St. Aelred of Rievaulx, who understood God as a loving friend and companion who could be revealed in same-sex relationships (Clark, 1987a, Russell, 1982). God as friend or companion actually transcends gender duality or simplistic gender balancing, insofar as this image ultimately applies to any human relational model, regardless of the gender of the partners. Moreover, this image also shifts our understanding of God from a vertical (hierarchical or oppressive) reliance upon a parent to a horizontal, co-equal partnership. God as companion both transcends gender duality and helps resolve theodicy, as discussed below.

[10]Process philosophy as herein presented is the present author's own rendition into everyday language of ideas and concepts whose origin is the writings of Alfred North Whitehead and his theological followers, with the intention of applying process philosophy to the practicalities of daily experience. While specific references are cited in the text, Cobb (1965, 1969), Hartshorne (1948), Sherburne (1966), and Whitehead (1926) constitute the full range of sources distilled herein and should be consulted for their original ideas and philosophical completeness. The author also gratefully acknowledges the prior publication of many of these ideas in slightly different forms and contexts (cf., Clark, 1986a, and 1987a, pp. 55-75).

VI. Dechristologizing Jesus

[11]Compare, for example, Hillel's negatively phrased "what is hateful unto thee, do not unto thy neighbor--this is the entire Torah; the rest is commentary" in the Talmud (Shabbat 31A, cf., Falk, 1985, p. 25) with Jesus' positively phrased "whatever you wish that men would do to you, do so to them; for this is the Law and the prophets" in the New Testament (Matthew 7.12, RSV, cf., Falk, 1985, p. 32).

[12]Falk's (1985) overall conclusions about both Jesus and Christian antisemitism are that Jesus,

. . . never wished to see his fellow Jews
change one iota of their traditional faith. He
himself remained an Orthodox Jew to his last moment. He only wished to see his people return to
the teaching of . . . Hillel, which stressed love,
humility, and the salvation of all mankind. His
attacks on the Pharisees were directed against the
School of Shammai, who were in control of Judaism
in his time.

. . . The Jewish people of today do not iden-
tify with the "scribes and Pharisees" whom he condemned. . . . Hence, there is no basis for Christian enmity toward the Jews of today because of
the actions of certain individuals who lived in
the first century. (p. 158)

Of potentially greater importance in Falk's (1985)
work, for a gay liberational understanding of Jesus, is
that in the efforts of Hillel (and perhaps Jesus) to
extend Judaism to the Gentiles based solely on their
adherence to the "Noahide commandments" ("the prohibitions against idolatry, blasphemy, killing, stealing,
sexual sins, . . . [cruelty to animals], and the obligation to establish courts of justice" [p. 83]), rather
than on their adherence to the entire 613 commandments
of the Torah (Shammai's position), the Levitical prohibitions against homosexual <u>acts</u> were <u>not</u> included;
those prohibitions were only added to the Noahide requirements for Gentile conversion in the third century
C.E. (p. 87).

VII. Resanctifying Gay Being

[13]Gay and lesbian Jews, particularly those gay men
and lesbians actively involved in the growing number of
gay/lesbian synagogues, have the special opportunity
and responsibility to exemplify this synthesis of God's
advocacy on our behalf and God's command for our active
pursuit of justice, to appropriate and conjoin both
Jewish and gay/lesbian survival throughout history, and
thus to embody this appropriation of liberational power
in history for present acts of liberation.

* * *

X. Literature Cited

Adams, S. (1980). The homosexual as hero in contemporary fiction. New York: Barnes & Noble.

Alpert, R. T. (1984). Sisterhood is ecumenical: Bridging the gap between Jewish and Christian feminists. Response, 14(2),3-16.

Altman, D. (1987). What price gay nationalism? In M. Thompson (Ed.), Gay spirit: Myth and meaning (pp. 16-19). New York: St. Martin's.

Austen, R. (1977). Playing the game: The homosexual novel in America. New York: Bobbs-Merrill.

Barrett, E. M. (1978). Gay people and moral theology. In L. Crew (Ed.), The gay academic (pp. 329-334). Palm Springs: Etc.

Bauman, B. (1983). Women-identified women in male-identified Judaism. In S. Heschel (Ed.), On being a Jewish feminist: A reader (pp. 88-95). New York: Schocken.

Bloch, A. (1983). Scenes from the life of a Jewish lesbian. In S. Heschel (Ed.), On being a Jewish feminist: A reader (pp. 171-176). New York: Schocken.

Bonhoeffer, D. (1953). Letters and papers from prison. E. Bethge (Ed.). New York: Macmillan.

Boswell, J. (1980). Christianity, social tolerance, and homosexuality. Chicago: Univ. Chicago.

Bowers v. Hardwick 478 U.S. __, 106 SC 2841, 92 L. Ed. __ (1986).

Boyd, M. (1984). Take off the masks. Philadelphia: New Society.

---. (1987). Telling a lie for Christ? In M. Thompson (Ed.), Gay spirit: Myth and meaning (pp. 78-87). New York: St. Martin's.

Bronski, M. (1984). Culture clash: The making of gay sensibility. Boston: South End.

---. (1987). Reform or revolution? The challenge of creating a gay sensibility. In M. Thompson (Ed.), Gay spirit: Myth and meaning (pp. 10-15). New York: St. Martin's.

Cantor, A. (1979). A Jewish woman's Haggadah. In C. P. Christ & J. Plaskow (Eds.), Womanspirit rising: A feminist reader in religion (pp. 185-192). San Francisco: Harper & Row.

Carpenter, E. (1910). On the connexion between homosexuality and divination. Revue d'Ethnographie et de Sociologie, 11-12,301-316.

---. (1919). Intermediate types among primitive folk (2d ed.). London: Allen & Unwin (photo reprint, 1975, New York: Arno).

Christ, C. P. (1979a). Spiritual quest and women's experience. In C. P. Christ & J. Plaskow (Eds.), Womanspirit rising: A feminist reader in religion (pp. 228-245). San Francisco: Harper & Row.

---. (1979b). Why women need the goddess: Phenomenological, psychological, and political reflections. In C. P. Christ & J. Plaskow (Eds.), Womanspirit rising: A feminist reader in religion (pp. 273-287). San Francisco: Harper & Row.

---. (1980). Diving deep and surfacing: Women writers on spiritual quest. Boston: eacon.

Christ, C. P. & Plaskow, J. (1979). Introduction(s). In C. P. Christ & J. Plaskow (Eds.), Womanspirit rising: A feminist reader in religion (pp. 1-24,63-67, 131-135,193-197). San Francisco: Harper & Row.

Clark, J. M. (1984). The native American berdache: A resource for gay spirituality. R.F.D., 11(1),22-30.

---. (1986a). AIDS, death, and God: Gay liberational theology and the problem of suffering. Journal of Pastoral Counseling, 21(1),40-54.

---. (1986b). Liberation and disillusionment: The development of gay male criticism and popular fiction a decade after Stonewall. Las Colinas, TX: Liberal.

---. (1987a). Gay being, divine presence: Essays in gay spirituality. Garland, TX: Tanglewüld.

---. (1987b). Gaymyth: Reflections on male homosexuality in mythology. R.F.D., 13(3),40-44.

---. (1987c). Pink triangles and gay images: (Re)claiming communal and personal history in retrospective gay fiction. Arlington, TX: Liberal Arts.

---. (1987d). Special considerations in pastoral care of gay persons-with-AIDS. Journal of Pastoral Counseling, 22(1),32-45.

Cobb, J. B. (1965). A Christian natural theology. Philadelphia: Westminster.

---. (1969). God and the world. Philadelphia: Westminster.

Collins, S. D. (1974). A different heaven and earth.
  Valley Forge: Judson.
---. (1979). Theology in the politics of Appalachian
  women. In C. P. Christ & J. Plaskow (Eds.), Woman-
  spirit rising: A feminist reader in religion (pp.
  149-158). San Francisco: Harper & Row.
---. (1981). Feminist theology at the crossroads.
  Christianity and Crisis, 41(20),342-347.
Comstock, G. D. (1987). Aliens in the promised land?
  Union Seminary Quarterly Review, 41(3-4),93-104.
Cosmos [pseud.]. (1984). Remembering forgotten dreams.
  R.F.D., 10(3),32.
Cotton, A. (1987). Backtracking. Amethyst, 1(1),44-45.
Crew, L. & Norton, R. (Eds.). (1974). Special homosex-
  ual imagination issue. College English, 36(11).
Crompton, L. (1978). Gay genocide from Leviticus to
  Hitler. In L. Crew (Ed.), The gay academic (pp.
  67-91). Palm Springs: Etc.
Curb, R. & Manahan, N. (Eds.). (1985). Lesbian nuns:
  Breaking silence. Tallahassee: Naiad.
Daly, M. (1973). Beyond God the father: Toward a phil-
  osophy of women's liberation. Boston: Beacon.
---. (1978). Gyn/ecology: The metaethics of radical
  feminism. Boston: Beacon.
---. (1979a). After the death of God the father:
  Women's liberation and the transformation of
  Christian consciousness. In C. P. Christ & J.
  Plaskow (Eds.), Womanspirit rising: A feminist
  reader in religion (pp. 53-62). San Francisco:
  Harper & Row.
---. (1979b). Why speak about God? In C. P. Christ & J.
  Plaskow (Eds.), Womanspirit rising: A feminist
  reader in religion (pp. 210-218). San Francisco:
  Harper & Row.
DeStefano, G. (1986). Gay under the collar: The hypo-
  crisy of the Catholic church. The Advocate, no.
  439, 43-48.
Devereux, G. (1937). Institutionalized homosexuality of
  the Mohave Indians. Human Biology, 9,498-527.
Doustourian, A. (1978). Gayness: A radical Christian
  approach. In L. Crew (Ed.), The gay academic (pp.
  335-349). Palm Springs: Etc.
Dunkel, J. & Hatfield, S. (1986). Countertransference
  issues in working with persons with AIDS. Social
  Work, 31(2),114-117.
Edwards, G. R. (1984). Gay/lesbian liberation: A biblical perspective. New York: Pilgrim.
Evans, A. (1978). Witchcraft and the gay countercul-
  ture. Boston: Fag Rag.

Ewing, W. B. (1976). Job: A vision of God. New York: Seabury.

Fackenheim, E. L. (1968). Quest for past and future: Essays in Jewish theology. Bloomington: Indiana Univ.

———. (1970). God's presence in history: Jewish affirmations and philosophical reflections. New York: Harper & Row.

Falk, H. (1985). Jesus the Pharisee: A new look at the Jewishness of Jesus. New York: Paulist.

Fiorenza, E. S. (1979). Feminist spirituality, Christian identity, and Catholic vision. In C. P. Christ & J. Plaskow (Eds.), Womanspirit rising: A feminist reader in religion (pp. 136-148). San Francisco: Harper & Row.

Fortunato, J. E. (1983). Embracing the exile: Healing journeys of gay Christians. New York: Seabury.

———. (1985). AIDS: The plague that lays waste at noon. The Witness, 68(9),6-9.

———. (1987). AIDS, The spiritual dilemma. San Francisco: Harper & Row.

Fox, M. (1983). The spiritual journey of the homosexual . . . and just about everyone else. In R. Nugent (Ed.), A challenge to love: Gay and lesbian Catholics in the church (pp. 189-204). New York: Crossroad.

Gallagher, B. & Wilson, A. (1987). Sex and the politics of identity: An interview with Michel Foucault. In M. Thompson (Ed.), Gay spirit: Myth and meaning (pp. 25-35). New York: St. Martin's.

Geller, L. (1983). Reactions to a woman rabbi. In S. Heschel (Ed.), On being a Jewish feminist: A reader (pp. 210-213). New York: Schocken.

Goodman, G., et al. (1983). No turning back: Lesbian and gay liberation for the '80s. Philadelphia: New Society.

Goodstein, D. (1985). Opening space [Editorial]. The Advocate, no. 414, 6.

Grahn, J. (1984). Another mother tongue: Gay words, gay worlds. Boston: Beacon.

———. (1985). Flaming without burning: The role of gay people in society. The Advocate, no. 415, 31,33.

Green, A. (1983). Bride, spouse, daughter: Images of the feminine in classical Jewish sources. In S. Heschel (Ed.), On being a Jewish feminist: A reader (pp. 248-260). New York: Schocken.

Greenberg, B. (1981). On women and Judaism: A view from tradition. Philadelphia: Jewish Publn. Soc. of America.

Gross, R. M. (1979). Female God language in a Jewish
    context. In C. P. Christ & J. Plaskow (Eds.),
    Womanspirit rising: A feminist reader in religion
    (pp. 167-173). San Francisco: Harper & Row.
---. (1983). Steps toward feminine imagery of deity in
    Jewish theology. In S. Heschel (Ed.), On being a
    Jewish feminist: A reader (pp. 234-247). New York:
    Schocken.
Hallier, A. (1969). The monastic theology of Aelred of
    Rievaulx. C. Heaney (Trans.). Shannon: Irish Univ.
Hartshorne, C. (1948). The divine relativity. New
    Haven: Yale Univ.
Hay, H. (1987). A separate people whose time has come.
    In M. Thompson (Ed.), Gay spirit: Myth and meaning
    (pp. 279-291). New York: St. Martin's.
Heyward, I. C. (1979). Coming out: Journey without
    maps. Christianity and Crisis, 34(10),153-156.
---. (1982). The redemption of God: A theology of mutu-
    al relation. Washington: Univ. Pr. America.
---. (1984). Our passion for justice: Images of power,
    sexuality, and liberation. New York: Pilgrim.
Hillman, J. (1979). The dream and the underworld. New
    York: Harper & Row.
Horner, T. (1978). Jonathan loved David: Homosexuality
    in biblical times. Philadelphia: Westminster.
Howell, L. (1985). Churches and AIDS: Responsibilities
    in mission. Christianity and Crisis, 45(20),483-
    484.
Janowitz, N. & Wenig, M. (1979). Sabbath prayers for
    women. In C. P. Christ & J. Plaskow (Eds.), Woman-
    spirit rising: A feminist reader in religion (pp.
    174-178). San Francisco: Harper & Row.
Jung, C. G. (1954). Psychological aspects of the mother
    archetype. In: Four Archetypes. R. F. C. Hull
    (Trans.). Princeton: Princeton Univ. (reprint edi-
    tion, 1970).
Katz, J. (1978). Gay American history. New York: Avon.
Kepner, J. (1987). I should have been listening: A mem-
    ory of Gerald Heard. In M. Thompson (Ed.), Gay
    spirit: Myth and meaning (pp. 165-175). New York:
    St. Martin's.
Kilhefner, D. (1987). Gay people at a critical cross-
    road: Assimilation or affirmation. In M. Thompson
    (Ed.), Gay spirit: Myth and meaning (pp. 121-130).
    New York: St. Martin's.
Kushner, H. (1981). When bad things happen to good
    people. New York: Schocken.
Macourt, M., et al. (1977). Towards a theology of gay
    liberation. London: SCM.

McLaughlin, E. L. (1979). The Christian past: Does it hold a future for women? In C. P. Christ & J. Plaskow (Eds.), Womanspirit rising: A feminist reader in religion (pp. 93-106). San Francisco: Harper & Row.

McNeill, J. J. (1976). The church and the homosexual. Kansas City: Sheed, Andrews, & McMeel.

---. (1983). Homosexuality, lesbianism, and the future: The creative role of the gay community in building a more humane society. In R. Nugent (Ed.), A challenge to love: Gay and lesbian Catholics in the church (pp. 52-64). New York: Crossroad.

---. (1987, March 11). Homosexuality: Challenging the church to grow. The Christian Century, pp. 242-246.

---. (1988). Taking a chance on God: Liberating theology for gays, lesbians, their lovers, families, and friends. Boston: Beacon.

Mehler, B. (1979). In neo-Nazi Germany. Christopher Street, 3(11),60-67.

Mitchell, L. & Asta, N. (1977). The faggots and their friends between revolutions. Ithaca: Calamus.

Moritz, W. (1987). Seven glimpses of Walt Whitman. In M. Thompson (Ed.), Gay spirit: Myth and meaning (pp. 131-151). New York: St. Martin's.

Morton, N. (1979). The dilemma of celebration. In C. P. Christ & J. Plaskow (Eds.), Womanspirit rising: A feminist reader in religion (pp. 159-166). San Francisco: Harper & Row.

---. (1985). The journey is home. Boston: Beacon.

Neusner, J. (1979). The tasks of theology in Judaism: A humanistic program. Journal of Religion, 59(1),71-86.

Nugent, R., et al. (1983). A challenge to love: Gay and lesbian Catholics in the Church. New York: Crossroad.

Ozick, C. (1983). Notes toward finding the right question. In S. Heschel (Ed.), On being a Jewish feminist: A reader (pp. 120-151). New York: Schocken.

Perlinski, J. (1984). Gay as spirit: To be, not to have. The Advocate, no. 408, 29-30.

Plant, R. (1986). The pink triangle: The Nazi war against homosexuals. New York: Henry Holt.

Plaskow, J. (1979). The coming of Lilith: Toward a feminist theology. In C. P. Christ & J. Plaskow (Eds.), Womanspirit rising: A feminist reader in religion (pp. 198-209). San Francisco: Harper & Row.

---. (1983a). Language, God, and liturgy: A feminist perspective. Response, 13(4),3-14.
---. (1983b). The right question is theological. In S. Heschel (Ed.), On being a Jewish feminist: A reader (pp. 223-233). New York: Schocken.
Roscoe, W. (1986). The Zuni man-woman. San Francisco, unpublished paper.
---. (1987). Living the tradition: Gay American Indians. In M. Thompson (Ed.), Gay spirit: Myth and meaning (pp. 69-77). New York: St. Martin's.
Rowland, C. (1986). The call for quarantine. The Advocate, no. 443, 42-46.
Rubenstein, R. L. (1966). After Auschwitz: Radical theology and contemporary Judaism. Indianapolis: Bobbs-Merrill.
Ruether, R. R. (1972). Liberation theology. New York: Paulist.
---. (1975). New woman, new earth: Sexist ideologies and human liberation. New York: Seabury.
---. (1978). The sexuality of Jesus: What the synoptics have to say. Christianity and Crisis, 38(8),134-137.
---. (1983a). Sexism and God-talk: Toward a feminist theology. Boston: Beacon.
---. (1983b). To change the world: Christology and cultural criticism. New York: Crossroad.
---. (1985). Womanguides: Readings toward a feminist theology. Boston: Beacon.
Russell, K. C. (1982). Aelred, the gay abbot of Rievaulx. Studia Mystica, 5(4), 51-64.
Saiving, V. (1979). The human situation: A feminine view. In C. P. Christ & J. Plaskow (Eds.), Womanspirit rising: A feminist reader in religion (pp. 25-42). San Francisco: Harper & Row.
Saslow, J. M. (1987). Hear, O Israel: We are Jews, we are gay. The Advocate, no. 465, 38-41,44-49,108-111.
Satloff, C. R. (1983). History, fiction, and the tradition: Creating a Jewish feminist poetic. In S. Heschel (Ed.), On being a Jewish feminist: A reader (pp. 186-206). New York: Schocken.
Shelp, E. E., Sunderland, R. H., & Mansell, P. W. A. (1986). AIDS: Personal Stories in pastoral perspective. New York: Pilgrim.
Sherburne, D. W. (1966). A key to Whitehead's process and reality. Bloomington: Indiana Univ.
Shurin, A. (1987). The truth come out. In M. Thompson (Ed.), Gay spirit: Myth and meaning (p. 259). New York: St. Martin's.

Siegel, P. (1979). Homophobia: Types, origins, remedies. Christianity and Crisis, 39(17),280-284.
South, K. T. (1985). Pastoral care to people with AIDS. Atlanta: AID/Atlanta.
Squire, A. (1981). Aelred of Rievaulx: A study. Kalamazoo, MI: Cistercian Publns.
Steakley, J. D. (1975). The homosexual emancipation movement in Germany. New York: Arno Pr.
Stiles, B. J. (1986). AIDS and the churches. Christianity and Crisis, 45(22),534-536.
Thompson, M. (1986). Diversity and future directions stressed at first-ever conference on gay spirituality. The Advocate, no. 446, 32-33.
---. (1987a). The evolution of a faerie: Notes toward a new definition of gay. In M. Thompson (Ed.), Gay spirit: Myth and meaning (pp. 292-302). New York: St. Martin's.
---. (1987b). Harry Hay: A voice from the past, a vision for the future. In M. Thompson (Ed.), Gay spirit: Myth and meaning (pp. 182-199). New York: St. Martin's.
---. (1987c). This gay tribe: A brief history of fairies. In M. Thompson (Ed.), Gay spirit: Myth and meaning (pp. 260-278). New York: St. Martin's.
Thompson, M., et al. (1987). Gay spirit: Myth and meaning. New York: St. Martin's.
Tillich, P. (1948). You are accepted. In The shaking of the foundations (pp. 153-163). New York: Scribner's.
Topper, C. J. (1986). Spirituality as a component in counseling lesbian-gays. Journal of Pastoral Counseling, 21(1),55-59.
Uhrig, L. J. (1984). The two of us: Affirming, celebrating, and symbolizing gay and lesbian relationships. Boston: Alyson.
Umansky, E. M. (1982). (Re)imaging the divine. Response, 13(1-2),110-119.
---. (1984). Creating a Jewish feminist theology: Possibilities and problems. Anima, 10(2),125-135.
---. (1985). Feminism and the revaluation of women's roles within American Jewish life. In Y. Y. Haddad & E. B. Findly (Eds.), Women, religion, and social change (pp. 477-494). New York: S.U.N.Y.
Walker, M. (1980). Visionary love: A spiritbook of gay mythology and transmutational faerie. San Francisco: Treeroots.
Washburn, P. (1979). Becoming woman: Menstruation as spiritual challenge. In C. P. Christ & J. Plaskow (Eds.), Womanspirit rising: A feminist reader in

religion (pp. 240-258). San Francisco: Harper &
Row.

Waskow, A. I. (1983). Feminist Judaism: Restoration of
the moon. In S. Heschel (Ed.), On being a Jewish
feminist: A reader (pp. 261-272). New York:
Schocken.

Whitehead, A. N. (1926). Religion in the making. New
York: Macmillan.

Williams, W. L. (1986). The spirit and the flesh: Sexual diversity in American Indian culture. Boston:
Beacon.

Wright, E. & Inesse, D. (1979). God is gay: An evolutionary spiritual work. San Francisco: Tayu.

Young, I. (Ed.). (1981). Introduction. In On the line:
New gay fiction (pp. 5-10). Trumansburg, NY:
Crossing.

✻   ✻   ✻

XI. Index

        heritage 79-86, 92, 122
        idolatrous homosexuality 85-86
        redemption 81-82
        responsibilities of 83-84
        supportive of gay civil rights 86
Job (Biblical character) 70-71
Judaism 32-33
kairos-time 25
Leviticus (prohibition against homosexuality) 12, 186
MCC (see Universal Fellowship of Metropolitan Community
        Churches)
Nazis and gays 25, 26
National March on Washington (October 1987) 95
nuns, lesbians 2
priests, gay 2
PWAs (people-with-AIDS) 49-50, 67-68, 132, 171
        non-gay/non-lesbian 68, 171
        self-esteem 172-173
        survivor guilt 172
religion, institutionalized 37
Religious Right (fundamentalism) 67
Ruether, Rosemary Radford 92-94, 104, 183-184
salvation (as cosmic myth) 105
Satan (Biblical character) 70
safe-sex 169-170
sex 46
        as sinful (in tradition) 34, 46
        importance of 61
        negativity of (ideology) 132-133
        separated from love 35
        theology of 61-62
sex roles 31, 34, 142-143
        values related to 33, 62
sexual love 137-140
sin 45, 46, 90
suffering 76-78
Stonewall Inn Riots 23-24, 179
theology and sexuality 61
Universal Fellowship of Metropolitan Community Churches
        (MCC) 2, 11, 177
women, as scapegoats for men 46
Women's Movement (in USA) 29, 158

                    *   *   *